Paine and Cobbett
The Transatlantic Connection

McGill-Queen's Studies in the History of Ideas

PAINE AND COBBETT
The Transatlantic Connection

David A. Wilson

McGill-Queen's University Press
Kingston and Montreal

© McGill-Queen's University Press 1988
ISBN 0-7735-1013-3
Legal deposit 1st quarter 1988
Bibliothèque nationale du Québec

∞

Printed in Canada on acid free paper

This book has been published with the help of a grant from the Canadian
Federation for the Humanities, using funds provided by the Social Sciences and
Humanities Research Council of Canada.

Canadian Cataloguing in Publication Data

Wilson, David A., 1950-
Paine and Cobbett : the trans-atlantic connection
(McGill-Queen's studies in the history of ideas ; 12)
Includes index.
Bibliography: p.
ISBN 0-7735-1013-3
1. Paine, Thomas, 1737–1809. 2. Cobbett, William, 1763–1835.
3. Political scientists—United States—Biography.
4. Politicians—Great Britain—Biography.
5. Political science—United States—History—18th century.
6. Political science—Great Britain—History—18th century.
I. Title. II. Series.
JC178.V2W44 1988   320.5′1′0922   C87-090226-1

To Mum, Dad, Pat, and Andrew

Tom Paine, propped up by Satan, returns to haunt William Cobbett. Note the Crown and Bible on Cobbett's chamberpot. The "Old Life" and "New Life" of Paine refer to the work of the Tory Cobbett in editing and embellishing a scurrilous biography of Paine during the 1790s, and to the adulatory biography of Paine which the Radical Cobbett planned to write in 1819.

Contents

Preface

Tom Paine and William Cobbett were at the heart of the revolutionary changes that swept over the Atlantic world during the late eighteenth and early nineteenth centuries. Both men came from the ranks of the "common people" in England, both found their identity as political writers in America, and both eventually became central figures in the English popular Radical movement. The differences between them were equally striking. Paine entered politics in America as the author of *Common Sense*, the most forceful and explicit argument for independence and republicanism ever to appear in the Thirteen Colonies. Cobbett began his career as a political writer eighteen years later than Paine and emerged not as a Radical but as a High Tory who attempted to revive pro-British sentiment in the new republic. He did not become a Radical until some years after his return to England in 1800, when he was converted in part by Paine's earlier writings. Yet, despite these differences, the broad patterns of Paine's and Cobbett's careers display remarkable similarities and interconnections that have never received the attention they deserve.[1]

This book places the parallel careers of Paine and Cobbett in their Anglo-American context. It not only discusses the relationship between their ideas but also examines how their early experiences affected their success in America, and the way in which their perceptions of America were woven into their subsequent political writings in England. Special attention is paid to four major themes in Paine's and

---

1 For some brief but stimulating comparisons of Paine's and Cobbett's careers, see Hazlitt, "Character of Cobbett," pp. 50–59, and Thompson, *Making of the English Working Class*, pp. 820–37.

Cobbett's thought: the transformation of minority British Radical ideas into a democratic, republican, and revolutionary ideology in America; the eighteenth-century revolution in rhetoric which established new standards for the style and structure of persuasive discourse; the impact of the American and French revolutions on British popular Radicalism; and the American attempt to turn the United States into a new and powerful Empire of Liberty.

Any new work on Paine and Cobbett can only benefit from the immense literature on their careers. Of the two men, Paine has attracted more attention from historians; well over two hundred books, dissertations, and articles on Paine have appeared this century.[2] One school of thought, influenced by the work of Harry Hayden Clark, has examined Paine's writings in the light of eighteenth-century scientific deism, and perceives him as "essentially an ideologue or theorist" who applied popularized Newtonian notions of natural order to questions of politics and religion.[3] Other scholars, recognizing that Paine's writing style was central to his popularity, have concentrated on his rhetorical method.[4] In a significant change of emphasis, Eric Foner's *Tom Paine and Revolutionary America* has made an "early attempt" to locate Paine's republicanism in its social context.[5] And the recent work of Alfred Aldridge has attempted to analyse "the intellectual content of Paine's writings between 1775 and 1787."[6]

In clarifying where my own work stands in relation to earlier interpretations of Paine's thought and language, I would stress three points. First, my attempt to place Paine's political formation within the process of Anglo-American ideological interchange has led me in different

2 The American historiography of Paine between 1900 and 1970 has been documented by J. D. Wilson, "Thomas Paine in the Twentieth Century." Since 1970, six more books on Paine have been published: Williamson, *Thomas Paine*; Edwards, *Rebel!*; Hawke, *Paine*; Foner, *Tom Paine and Revolutionary America*; J. D. Wilson and Ricketson, *Thomas Paine*; and Aldridge, *Thomas Paine's American Ideology*.

3 H. Clark, "Toward a Reinterpretation of Thomas Paine," and *Thomas Paine: Representative Selections*. Studies influenced by Clark's approach include Metzgar, "Thomas Paine," and R. F. Smith, "Thomas Paine and the American Political Tradition."

4 This theme was developed by Clark himself in "Thomas Paine's Theories of Rhetoric." Other studies of Paine's literary style include Mercer, "Rhetorical Method of Thomas Paine"; Ginsberg, "Rhetoric of Revolution"; Betka, "Ideology and Rhetoric of Thomas Paine," and Boulton, *Language of Politics*, pp. 134–50.

5 Foner, *Tom Paine*, p. xiii.

6 Aldridge, *Thomas Paine's American Ideology*, p. 10.

directions from those pursued by Clark and Aldridge.[7] Clark's emphasis on scientific deism as the key explanatory factor in Paine's intellectual development not only projected views that Paine articulated later in life back onto his earlier writings and underplayed the pressure of events on his ideas, but also crowded out consideration of the influence of Anglo-American Radical traditions on Paine's work. Aldridge, in contrast, was concerned to identify the ideological origins of Paine's thought but looked for them in the wrong place. Whereas Aldridge embarked on a long and largely fruitless voyage to discover whether Paine was influenced by Locke, Rousseau, and Montesquieu, rejected the possibility that seventeenth-century republican writers may have affected Paine's viewpoint, and ignored the contribution of Real Whig notions to Paine's thought, I maintain that Paine's democratic republicanism grew out of the very traditions that Aldridge dismissed or overlooked.[8]

Second, my analysis of Paine's use of language links his writing style to eighteenth-century theories of logic and rhetoric engendered by the scientific revolution. Although earlier scholars have examined Paine's "rhetoric of revolution," I have drawn on Wilbur Howell's *Eighteenth-Century British Logic and Rhetoric* to argue that Paine's style is best understood as part of a wider "revolution in rhetoric."[9] In taking this position, I cannot accept Eric Foner's contention that Paine was "unique" in that he "forged a new political language" and "created a literary style designed to bring his message to the widest possible audience."[10] Paine did indeed aim at a wide audience. But to argue

7 In this respect my analysis of Paine has been influenced by the work of historians like Bailyn, *Ideological Origins of the American Revolution*; and Wood, *Creation of the American Republic*.

8 Aldridge, *Thomas Paine's American Ideology*, pp. 95–157.

9 This avenue of exploration was first suggested by Howell in his review of Boulton, *Language of Politics*, pp. 521–23. See also Howell, "Declaration of Independence," pp. 464–84. The one attempt to apply Howell's work to Paine's writings, Betka, "Ideology and Rhetoric," misinterprets Howell's analysis of the new logic and rhetoric, and is thus of little value to students of Paine's use of language.

10 Foner, *Tom Paine*, p. xvi. It is true that Foner acknowledges in passing that Paine "was not the first writer of the eighteenth century consciously to address himself to a wide readership" (p. 84), but he ignores the broader implications of his own observation. Rather than probing the similarities between Paine and earlier exponents of the plain style, and viewing such writers against the background of changes in rhetorical theory, Foner prefers to see Paine as the pioneer of a democratic literary

that his style was unique is to ignore the influence of the new rhetoric on him. Once this influence is recognized, it is difficult to view Paine's approach to language as essentially the product of his political position. In any case, Paine acquired the basic characteristics of his style well before he became a democratic republican writer in America.

The third area of difference is largely one of emphasis. Foner and Aldridge were primarily concerned with Paine's place in the American Revolution. From this perspective, Foner has provided a superb analysis of Paine's republicanism, although his attempt to link Paine to a distinct "artisan constituency" in Philadelphia is less successful.[11] Aldridge has written a detailed account of Paine's arguments and attitudes in America, and has assessed the strengths and weaknesses of his views on such matters as the origins of government, the relationship between society and government, and the role of providence in political developments. Rather than focusing on Paine's American career, I have stressed the relationship between his English and American experiences and have analysed Paine's political writings within an Anglo-American framework.

A similar perspective lies behind my approach to Cobbett's work. Until recently, most books on Cobbett concentrated on his career as a Radical journalist in early nineteenth-century England; his Tory origins in late eighteenth-century America have generally been neglected or treated as an aberration. In G. D. H. Cole's view, for example, Cobbett's American experiences "were from the political standpoint wander-years," and when Cobbett finally joined the English Radical movement the "prodigal son had come back to his own people."[12] Other biographical and analytical studies of Cobbett skated lightly over his American career, implicitly indicating its lack of importance.[13] Yet America played a central role in shaping Cobbett's distinctive ideology; his Radicalism in England was organically connected to his Toryism in America.

To some extent, this excessive preoccupation with Cobbett's English

----

style, and portrays Paine's approach to writing as being more innovative than it actually was.

11 For a perceptive critique of Foner's attempt to correlate Paine's ideology with the attitudes and aspirations of Philadelphia's artisans, see G. Wills's review of Foner, *Tom Paine*, pp. 21–23.

12 Cole, *Life of William Cobbett*, pp. 69, 129.

13 See, for example, Sambrook, *William Cobbett*; Osborne, *William Cobbett*; Duff, "William Cobbett's Agrarian Vision"; and R. Williams, *Cobbett*.

writings has been redressed by the two latest biographies of Cobbett. Both George Spater's *William Cobbett: The Poor Man's Friend* and Daniel Green's *Great Cobbett: The Noblest Agitator* pay careful attention to his American career.[14] Spater's book, in particular, has unearthed much valuable new material about its subject and is rapidly establishing itself as the authority in its field. In Spater's view, Cobbett was a personal romantic but a political realist, a man who may have portrayed his frequently troubled family life in terms of idyllic domestic bliss, but who retained a hard, practical grip on contemporary political developments.[15] Accordingly, Spater downplayed Cobbett's glorification of the past, and stressed his political Radicalism in England rather than his social nostalgia. "Those who claim that Cobbett was looking for the restoration of a golden age," asserted Spater, "are talking nonsense. . . . Cobbett never had the slightest notion that the poor should be made rich."[16]

In contrast to this viewpoint, I argue that not only Cobbett's personal life but also his political outlook was fuelled by a dynamic tension between the ideal and the real, and that his ambivalent relationship to Paine and the United States is crucial to understanding his complex and often contradictory career. I also take issue with Spater's contention that Cobbett was not striving to restore an English Golden Age. Although it is undoubtedly true, as Spater pointed out, that Cobbett did not desire social equality, he nonetheless wanted his country to return to the mythical past of honest patriotism, honour, and decency that supposedly preceded the corrosive influence of the public finance system and the spread of commercial values.[17] With this in mind, I differ in my approach from Spater and from Cobbett's other histo-

14 Spater, *William Cobbett*, pp. 39–109, and Green, *Great Cobbett*, pp. 119–77. For other treatments of Cobbett's American career, see the essentially descriptive M. Clark, "Peter Porcupine in America," and the perceptive analysis of List, "The Role of William Cobbett in Philadelphia's Party Press."

15 Among other things, Spater discovered that, while Cobbett in *Advice to Young Men* was portraying an idyllic picture of his family life, in reality his wife had attempted to commit suicide and his family was turning against him. The contrast between his self-image and his actual behaviour could not have been more striking.

16 Spater, *William Cobbett*, p. 201.

17 The problem here is that Spater confused a golden age with social equality. Cobbett's attempt to make nineteenth-century England conform with his ideal image of traditional English values envisaged an equality of respect but not of circumstances. It is clear that his social nostalgia struck a responsive chord among many of his English readers; in this sense, Cobbett's very lack of realism goes far to explain his popular appeal.

rians by focusing on the connection between his American and English careers, the influence of Paine's ideas on him, and the place of America in the blend of politically Radical and socially conservative attitudes which emerged in Cobbett's early nineteenth-century writings.

When discussing Paine's and Cobbett's careers, it is important to recognize and confront certain conceptual difficulties. One cannot always take at face value each man's statements about his past. Paine wrote little about his first thirty-seven years in England, and what he did write was frequently tailored to fit his self-image or literary *persona*. He portrayed himself as a man who only began writing with the outbreak of the American Revolution, and as a self-made political thinker who never troubled himself with other people's ideas. "I scarcely ever quote," he once commented; "the reason is, I always think."[18] Yet Paine did publish material before the American Revolution, and was highly sensitive to contemporary currents of thought; indeed, he cited well over a hundred authors in his writing. Paine may actually have come to believe his own self-image; the historian, however, should not.[19]

For his part, Cobbett was quite prepared to distort his past if it would help him win an argument. When he began his career as a Tory writer in America, for example, he cheerfully pretended to be an American to win support for his views. "I have frequented Christ Church [in Philadelphia] for near about thirty years," he told his readers in 1795; in fact, he had lived in Philadelphia for not much more than thirty weeks.[20] Or again when he was a Tory he indignantly denied having written in his youth a "democratical" pamphlet entitled *The Soldier's Friend*, but after his conversion to political Radicalism he claimed authorship of the work.[21] Given Cobbett's tendency to rewrite

18 Paine, *Forester's Letters*, 2: 78. Unless otherwise stated, all references to Paine are taken from Philip S. Foner, *The Complete Writings of Thomas Paine*, 2 vols (New York: The Citadel Press, 1945).

19 Paine's *Case of the Officers of Excise* was published in 1772, two years before he left England. On Paine's citation of other authors, see H. Clark, "Thomas Paine's Theories of Rhetoric," pp. 314–15, and Robbins, "The Lifelong Education of Thomas Paine," pp. 135–42. For some glimpses of Paine's literary self-image, see Paine to a Committee of the Continental Congress, October 1783, 2: 1229; *Rights of Man, Part 2*, 1: 406; *Age of Reason, Part 1*, 1: 496, and Paine to John Inskeep, February 1806, 2: 1480.

20 Cobbett, *A Bone to Gnaw*, pp. 19–20.

21 Cobbett completely dissociated himself from the pamphlet in *PR*, 20 August 1803. In *PR*, 5 October 1805, he again denied authorship but was less critical of the

his own history according to his present concerns, it is important to approach his work with considerable scepticism.

This pragmatic element in Paine's and Cobbett's writings should alert us to the danger of treating both men as coherent philosophical thinkers. Paine and Cobbett were persuasive political writers embroiled in a series of fierce political debates; writing in specific situations with specific purposes in mind, they were more interested in winning arguments than in winning prizes for intellectual consistency. Paine often sacrificed logical coherence to immediate polemical advantage, and Cobbett contradicted himself so many times that a minor industry grew up using his early Tory arguments to counter his later Radical ones.[22] Yet there were also broad consistencies within each man's approach. As Eric Foner pointed out, the chief components of Paine's republicanism were political egalitarianism, hostility to monarchy and aristocracy, an awareness of American potential, and faith in economic growth.[23] And through Cobbett's shifting position on details, one can detect some general themes: the idealization and glorification of traditional English liberty and justice, hostility to the misuse and abuse of power, and a deep sense of human dignity. Just as it is wrong to elevate tactical statements by Paine and Cobbett into part of a philosophical system, it is also misleading to ignore the central assumptions and attitudes behind their arguments.

In assessing the relationship between principle and pragmatism in Paine's and Cobbett's thought, and in examining the forces that helped shape their political views, the question of "influence" must be considered. At one pole, there is the notion that ideas are transferred directly from one individual to another; from this perspective, evidence for such influence is often found by establishing close textual

---

pamphlet's sentiments. However, in *PR*, 23 June 1832, and *PR*, 28 December 1833, Cobbett stated that *The Soldier's Friend* was the first work that he wrote for the press. The content, style, and timing of the pamphlet, together with Cobbett's later statements, indicate that he actually was the author.

22 A good example of Paine's pragmatism can be found in his first pamphlet, the *Case of the Officers of Excise*, where he argued in one breath that excise officers had no chance of getting alternative employment, and in the next that low wages drove officers to find work as accountants or teachers. See *Case*, 2: 7, 12. Anonymous works quoting Cobbett the Tory to attack Cobbett the Radical include *The Cameleon*; *Elements of Reform*; "Cobbett against Cobbett" in *The Times*, 14 November 1816; *The Beauties of Cobbett*; *The Book of Wonders*, and *Cobbett's Penny Trash*.

23 Foner, *Tom Paine*, pp. 71–106.

similarities between different writers, and the borrower is usually seen as a passive receptacle of earlier arguments. At the other extreme, the search for specific influences is dismissed as futile and misleading, and a writer is viewed as picking up ideas which are floating around "in the air." My own approach combines elements of both these positions. Writers like Paine and Cobbett were strongly influenced by the ideological atmosphere in which they moved, and they responded creatively to the ideas around them. The nature of this response and the degree of creativity depended on their particular experiences and personal capabilities. Specific influences could and did operate on specific works; direct borrowing coexisted with indirect influence. Thus in my discussion of *Common Sense* I maintain that Paine's arguments were not only affected by Real Whig and republican traditions in general but also by particular works belonging to those traditions. And both Paine and Cobbett transformed eighteenth-century opposition thought into new ideologies as they were hurled into trajectories they could not always understand but felt compelled to explain. Paine and Cobbett were many things, but they were not the passive receptacles of other people's ideas.

Finally, any study of Paine and Cobbett has to decide what to leave out. Interpreting their political writings from a transatlantic perspective, I make no claims that this book is comprehensive in scope or definitive in conclusions. Many important questions, such as the impact of Paine's *Rights of Man* on American politics, the nature of Cobbett's critique of the English financial system, and the place of Paine and Cobbett in the British working-class movement, deserve full-scale studies in themselves rather than the relatively brief treatment they receive here. Major works like Paine's *Age of Reason* and Cobbett's *Rural Rides* are given less attention than obscure and uninfluential pamphlets such as Paine's *Case of the Officers of Excise* and Cobbett's *The Soldier's Friend*. But since these comparatively unknown pamphlets throw valuable light on Paine's and Cobbett's attitudes shortly before their success in America, such an emphasis is considered justified here.

After a brief prologue establishing the importance of Paine's and Cobbett's careers and discussing the links between them, the book falls into two parts. Part One, which deals with Paine, is divided into three chapters. Chapter I examines Paine's social experiences in England, and explores the ideological, scientific, and literary influences on his intellectual formation before he left for America in 1774. Chapter II analyses his impact on the Thirteen Colonies from the perspective of his English background; it focuses on his changing definitions of England and America in 1775, his transformation of eighteenth-century British Radical arguments into a new form of democratic republicanism, and the rhetorical style and structure of *Common Sense*. Chapter III discusses the way in which Paine's participation in the American Revolution affected the tone, content, and appeal of the *Rights of Man* in Britain.

Part Two examines the parallel Anglo-American pattern of Cobbett's career. Chapter IV shows how Cobbett's early experiences in England and New Brunswick turned him into a young Paineite republican, and Chapter V attempts to explain his subsequent emergence as a Tory pamphleteer and journalist in the United States. My discussion of Cobbett's American career emphasizes his attitude towards democracy, democrats, and Tom Paine, his use of language, and his attempt to strengthen Britain's position in the struggle between rival British, French, Spanish, and American imperialisms for hegemony in the New World. In Chapter VI, I discuss Cobbett's experiences back in England after 1800, his disillusionment with the English political system which he had glorified in the United States, his conversion to a species of Tory Radicalism, his changing perception of Paine's writings, and his increasingly ambivalent attitude to the American Empire of Liberty.

The epilogue summarizes the differences and similarities in Paine's and Cobbett's careers, examines their strategies for change, and discusses their ambiguous legacies to the nineteenth and twentieth centuries. By this time, one central point should be clear: America played a pivotal role in the development of both Paine's and Cobbett's thought.

Acknowledgments

Like an eighteenth-century journeyman "on the tramp," I have written this book in a variety of locations and have received much help, hospitality, and friendship on the way. At the University of York, England, Professor Gwyn A. Williams stimulated my interest in Anglo-American Radicalism and suggested many of the themes explored in this work. He is a remarkable man, a kind of modern-day Tom Paine, and I am fortunate to have worked with him. At Queen's University, Kingston, Professors George A. Rawlyk, Donald H. Akenson, and Robert W. Malcolmson have been a constant source of support and encouragement. George Rawlyk, who supervised the doctoral dissertation on which this book is based, set exacting standards of scholarship, shared his knowledge of United States history, kicked, cajoled, and coerced me out of my pre-industrial work habits, and then gave me plenty of rope on the generous assumption that I would not hang myself. I hope he was right. Donald Akenson was, as always, imaginative, iconoclastic, challenging, and controversial. His assistance is very much appreciated. Robert Malcolmson is one of the most articulate and incisive people I have ever met, and his clear-minded approach to eighteenth-century England has influenced me perhaps more than he realizes. Professor Robert Calhoon of the University of North Carolina and Professor Alfred Young of Northern Illinois University read an earlier version of this work, and made a number of astute observations and valuable suggestions which I have incorporated into the final product. Thanks also go to the people who read all or part of the book at various stages of its development: Stephen Patterson and Ann Condon of the University of New Brunswick; David G. Bell, gentleman scholar, also of New Brunswick; Richard

Davis of the University of Tasmania; Irene Whelan of Queen's University, Belfast, and Klaus Hansen of Queen's University, Kingston. Mary McDougall Maude skilfully copy-edited the book and ensured that I wrote in twentieth-century paragraphs.

During the research and writing of this book, I made many good friends. In England, Richard Rigby was especially helpful. In Northern Ireland, special thanks go to Ronald Buchanan and the inmates of the Institute of Irish Studies. In Canton, New York, Ruth Meyerowitz, Hugh Gunnison, and John and Ginnie Schneider made my time there enjoyable. In New Brunswick, Bill Buxton, Jaromir Cekota, and David Smith saved me from a severe bout of Frederictonitis. In Ontario, I would like to thank Dan Borowec and Marie Anderson for the music and laughter; the Garrett Group of Joseph Jones, Bruce Walton, and Terry Campbell for their bohemian brilliance; Mary "life-is-tough-and-then-you-die" McGillivray, now at St Francis Xavier University; Emer Killean, *bon vivant extraordinaire*, now in Montreal; and the people to whom this book is dedicated.

This book has been published with the help of a grant from the Canadian Federation for the Humanities, using funds provided by the Social Sciences and Humanities Research Council of Canada. I would like to thank them for making it possible.

Finally, a special word of appreciation, as promised, for Karen Kelly and Jackie Doherty, who deciphered the semi-legible scrawl that passes for my handwriting, and typed the manuscript with unfailing good humour.

Abbreviations

BL	British Library
HO	Public Record Office, Home Office Papers
Paine	*The Complete Writings of Thomas Paine*, edited by Philip S. Foner
PC	*The Political Censor, or Monthly Review of the Most Interesting Political Occurrences, Relative to the United States of America*, by Peter Porcupine [William Cobbett], 1796-97
PG	*Porcupine's Gazette*, 1797-1800
PJ	*Pennsylvania Journal*, 1775-76
PL	*Pennsylvania Ledger*, 1775-76
PM	*Pennsylvania Magazine*, 1775
PP	British Library, Place Papers
PR	*Cobbett's Weekly Political Register*
PW	*Porcupine's Works; Containing Various Writings and Selections, Exhibiting a Faithful Picture of the United States of America*
SWA	*Sussex Weekly Advertiser, or Lewes Journal*

PAINE AND COBBETT

Prologue

AT DAYBREAK on a September morning in 1819, William Cobbett, one of the most influential and controversial figures in English working-class politics, arrived at the corner of a rugged, barren field near the town of New Rochelle. Cobbett and his small entourage had travelled twenty-two miles from New York that night. They began at once to dig away at a neglected, isolated grave, for they had come to gather up the bones of Tom Paine, and take them home to England.[1]

Cobbett's immediate purpose was to honour the memory of Paine, and thus regenerate the cause of reform in England. "Those bones," he told an American friend, "will effect the reformation of England in Church and State." He planned to give Paine the kind of funeral worthy of a reformer, in which "twenty waggon loads of flowers can be brought to strew the road before the hearse." There were even rumours afoot that Cobbett intended to carry the bones at the head of a revolutionary army, bound for Westminster. "Never will England be what it ought to be," he asserted, "until the marble of Pitt's monument is converted into a monument to the memory of Paine."[2]

At a deeper, more personal level, Cobbett also saw his action as an act of atonement for past political sins. For Cobbett had not always been a Radical. Over twenty years earlier, as an English Tory living in Philadelphia, Cobbett had been one of Paine's principal opponents. 'How Tom gets a living now, or what brothel he inhabits, I know

---

1 *PR*, 1 May 1819, 18 September 1819, 13 November 1819. See also Bressler, "Peter Porcupine," pp. 176–85.

2 Cobbett to J. W. Francis, quoted in *Life and Letters*, ed. Melville, 2: 116; *PR*, 27 January 1820, 18 September 1819.

not. . . ," Cobbett had written in 1796. "Whether his carcass is at last
to be suffered to rot on the earth, or to be dried in the air, is of very
little consequence. Whenever and wherever he breathes his last, he
will excite neither sorrow nor compassion; no friendly hand will close
his eyes, not a groan will be uttered, not a tear will be shed. Like *Judas*
he will be remembered by posterity; men will learn to express all that
is base, malignant, treacherous, unnatural and blasphemous, by the
single monosyllable, *Paine*." And even in 1819, well after his conversion to political Radicalism, Cobbett was still careful to point out that
"we do not look upon ourselves as adopting *all* Paine's opinions upon
all subjects. He was a *great man*, an *Englishman*, a *friend of freedom*, and
the *first and greatest enemy of the Borough and Paper System*. This is enough
for us."[3]

Cobbett was right to remind his readers that he did not share all
of Paine's views. Paine was a republican, while Cobbett idealized and
glorified the British constitution. Paine wanted to sweep away the
accumulated "rubbish of errors" of the past; Cobbett wanted to roll
back history and return to a mythical Golden Age. Paine was an
internationalist who believed that the world was his country; Cobbett
was first and foremost an Englishman who thought and felt in national
terms. And as William Hazlitt observed, Paine constantly referred to
first principles, while Cobbett excelled in detailed polemics and the
personalization of politics.[4] Had they ever met, the two men would
probably not have liked one another; arrogance would have clashed
with arrogance. Cobbett found Paine's deist views offensive.[5] Cobbett
believed in sobriety; Paine liked his brandy.[6] Cobbett could not stand

---

3 Cobbett, *An Antidote for Tom Paine's Theological and Political Poison*, p. 49; *PR*, 13
November 1819. In speaking of Cobbett's conversion to Radicalism, roughly between
1804 and 1806, two things must be kept in mind. First, Cobbett viewed political Radicalism as a means to achieve socially conservative ends. And second, the word "Radical"
did not permeate political vocabulary until after the Napoleonic Wars. Cobbett in 1820
objected to being described as a "Radical"; within two years he had changed his mind
and accepted the term. See *PR*, 29 April 1820 and 1 June 1822.

4 Hazlitt, "Character of Cobbett," p. 52; Thompson, *Making of the English Working
Class*, p. 829.

5 As a Tory, Cobbett argued that Paine's religious views could not be separated
from Paine's political opinions. After Cobbett became a Radical, however, he adopted
precisely such a distinction. Compare *PW*, 11: 3–6, with *PR*, 7 November 1810, 11 May
1819, 15 January 1820.

6 Robert Aitken, publisher of the *Pennsylvania Magazine*, commented that Paine
needed at least three glasses of brandy before he could begin to write fluently. See

laziness; Paine worked in fits and starts. And both men found it extremely difficult to keep long political friendships.[7]

Nevertheless, it was appropriate that Cobbett should wish to honour the memory of Paine. When he exhumed Paine's bones, Cobbett was not in the United States by choice. He had left England in 1817, to escape the crack-down by Lord Sidmouth, the home secretary, on post-Napoleonic War political discontent, just as Prime Minister William Pitt's earlier repressive policies had driven hundreds of British democrats to seek sanctuary in the United States between 1792 and 1800. In his Tory phase, Cobbett had dismissed such men as "trans-Atlantic traitors," and sneered at the idea of the United States as an asylum of liberty.[8] Now, around 1819, things were different. Himself a political exile, Cobbett not only viewed the United States as a "place of refuge," but praised Paine for contributing "more than any other man to . . . make for us a place of safety" in that country.[9]

It was not really surprising that Cobbett recognized and magnified Paine's political accomplishments. After his conversion to Radicalism, Cobbett had increasingly come to identify with certain aspects of Paine's life. He stressed that Paine, like himself, came from the "lower orders" in England.[10] He saw himself as operating within and extending Paine's critique of England's national debt, taxation, and corruption.[11] When he was threatened with prosecution for his popular democratic writings in 1816 and 1817, Cobbett's immediate response was to compare his position with that of Paine after the publication of the *Rights of Man* in 1791 and 1792.[12] And when Radicals like Thomas Wooler

---

Aldridge, *Man of Reason*, p. 30. Cobbett rarely touched anything stronger than a small beer, and regarded drinking as a "beastly vice." See, for example, Cobbett, *A Year's Residence in the United States of America*, p. 202.

7 Cobbett, as a Radical, eventually fell out with fellow reformers like Francis Burdett and Henry Hunt; in Hazlitt's view, Cobbett liked to have "all the ring for himself" (Hazlitt, "Character of Cobbett," p. 54). It should be noted, however, that after his conversion to Radicalism, Cobbett remained friends with John Reeves, the man who spearheaded the loyalist movement against popular Radicals in 1792–93. Paine died a lonely man, ignored by most of his former political allies.

8 Cobbett, *A Little Plain English*, p. 70; *PG*, 26 September 1797; *PW*, 11: 95; Cobbett, *Prospectus of a new Daily Paper*; *PR*, 6 June 1802.

9 *PR*, 15 January 1820.

10 *PR*, 23 November 1816, 1 May 1819, 21 December 1822.

11 *PR*, 18 December 1819, 21 December 1822.

12 *PR*, 15 June 1816, 9 November 1816, 16 August 1817, 4 September 1819.

accused Cobbett of cowardice for fleeing England in 1817, he reminded his readers that Paine had left the country in similar circumstances in 1792.[13] Clearly, Cobbett recognized the similarities as well as the differences between Paine's career and his own.

And so Cobbett came to that remote field in New Rochelle in 1819. In the years between 1774, when Paine arrived in America, and 1819, when Cobbett took his remains back to England, the political and economic shape of the Atlantic world had been revolutionized. The British and Spanish empires had disintegrated, the French Revolution had sent shock waves throughout Europe and the Americas, and Britain had begun its take-off into industrialism. From the traditional mercantilist and pre-mercantilist transatlantic trade triangles based on the bullion trade, slavery, and plantation economies, the Atlantic became dominated by British economic imperialism, resting on the new technology and buttressed by the British navy.[14] In the course of these political and economic changes, Paine and Cobbett thrust themselves from the ranks of the common people to the centre of the political stage in Britain and America. Paine felt that he was living in "an age of revolutions, in which every thing may be looked for," while Cobbett described himself as "one of those, whom the spirit-stirring circumstances of these awful times have drawn forth from their native obscurity."[15]

Their impact on transatlantic politics was phenomenal and, in Paine's case, unprecedented. *Common Sense* went into thirty-six editions and sold over 100,000 copies in a total American population in 1774 of only 2.5 million. Paine boasted that it produced in America "the greatest sale that any performance ever had since the use of letters."[16] Fifteen years later, the *Rights of Man*, Paine's classic defence of the

13 *PR*, 4 October 1817. Cobbett also referred to the examples of Algernon Sidney and Voltaire.

14 The literature on this subject is of course enormous. Some studies which have influenced my own thinking are Davis, *Rise of the Atlantic Economies*; Hobsbawm, *Age of Revolution*, and *Industry and Empire*; Henretta, *Evolution of American Society*, esp. pp. 41–81; Lynch, *Spanish American Revolutions*; Ferns, *Britain and Argentina*, esp. pp. 1–15; Palmer, *Age of the Democratic Revolution*; G.A. Williams, "The Atlantic Revolution."

15 Paine, *Rights of Man, Part I*, 1:344; Cobbett, Preface to *PR*, vol. 8, July–December, 1805.

16 Paine estimated 120,000 sales in *Forester's Letters*, 2: 67; by 1779 he revised the figure to 150,000. See Paine to Henry Laurens, 14 January 1779, 2: 1163. Aldridge, "Influence of Thomas Paine," pp. 371–72, and A. King, "Thomas Paine in America," support Paine's guess of 120,000 sales by April 1776.

French Revolution against the criticisms of Edmund Burke, became "a foundation-text of the English working-class movement."[17] His writings reverberated through the Atlantic world; supporters of Spanish-American independence read Paine, and even Loyalist Upper Canada was not totally immune from his ideas.[18]

Cobbett's success was less spectacular but equally impressive. Despite, or more probably because of, his Tory views, Cobbett became an immensely popular pamphleteer and journalist in the United States between 1794 and 1800.[19] Back in England, sales of *Cobbett's Weekly Political Register* (1802-1835) increased from 300 to 4,000 a week in its first two years, and probably reached 40,000 a week during the political agitation of 1816 and 1817.[20] As early as 1807, his political enemies were forced to admit that Cobbett "has more influence, we believe, than all the journalists put together; and that influence is still maintained, in a good degree, by the force of his personal character."[21]

Paine's and Cobbett's sense of self-importance more than matched their very real accomplishments. "I am proud to say that with a perseverance undismayed by difficulties, a disinterestedness that compelled respect," Paine once wrote, "I have not only contributed to raise a new empire in the world, founded on a new system of government, but I have arrived at an eminence in political literature, the most difficult of all lines to succeed and excel in, which aristocracy, with all its aids, has not been able to reach or to rival."[22] Cobbett's egotism was even greater. "Mine is the most curious history that ever

17 Thompson, *Making of the English Working Class*, p. 99. Most historians agree that the *Rights of Man* sold 200,000 copies in Britain in 1792; it should be pointed out, however, that this figure is very much a rough guess.

18 Aldridge, "Thomas Paine in Latin America," pp. 139–47; see also Ontario, Department of Archives, *Sixteenth Report*, p. 73, where it was related that a man who claimed land was "not a Christian, denying Christ, and preferring the works of Tom Paine to the Holy Bible." I would like to thank Dennis Cannon for supplying me with this reference.

19 Gaines, "William Cobbett's Account Book," pp. 299–312.

20 Cobbett claimed these figures in *PR*, 31 December 1803, 30 November 1816, 2 August 1817. Even allowing for his habitual exaggeration, the reports of dozens of contemporaries tend to support his estimates. See Aspinall, *Politics and the Press*, pp. 30–32. Even Francis Place, who was not one of Cobbett's admirers, wrote that in 1816, "the sale was extraordinary, he is supposed to have sold upwards of 60,000 of some numbers" (*PP*, Add. Ms. 27809, f. 17).

21 *The Cameleon*, p. 7.

22 Paine, *Rights of Man*, Part 2, 1: 405–6.

recorded the life and actions of man," he wrote towards the end of his life. "I have all along, been right. I have foreseen and foretold every thing: at twelve or fourteen different epocha, all my predictions have been verified, and all my principles proved to have been true."[23]

This kind of arrogance alienated many of their acquaintances. Yet without it, Paine and Cobbett could not have sustained their powerful drive against the political and social evils they saw around them. Their arrogance was central to their ability and to their appeal; it helped them challenge existing patterns of deference and sheltered them against the wrath of the "political nation."[24] And, in a sense, Paine and Cobbett were right. When considered in the light of their humble beginnings, their achievements were indeed truly remarkable.

These achievements, it must be remembered, were built on an American foundation. It was America which transformed these unknown Englishmen into internationally renowned political writers; Paine as a democratic republican in the 1770s, and Cobbett as a High Tory in the 1790s. And it is clear that America played an important part in the development of their political thought and their subsequent impact as popular Radicals in England. To understand Paine's and Cobbett's careers, it is necessary to examine the forces which helped shape their responses to the American Empire of Liberty and to explore the way in which these responses affected their position as Founding Fathers of popular Radicalism in England.

23 *PR*, 12 January 1828.

24 This theme could be developed at greater length. One sees the same kind of arrogance, for example, in Daniel O'Connell's attempt to rally the Irish peasantry in the early nineteenth century, or in the attitude of militant black leaders in the United States during the 1960s. Compare Ben Franklin's comment that "I give it [vanity] fair quarter wherever I meet with it, being persuaded that it is often productive of good to the possessor and to others within his sphere of action" (*Benjamin Franklin: The Autobiography and Other Writings*, ed. Lemisch, p. 17). See also G. A. Williams, "Tom Paine," p. 238.

PART ONE

Paine

the *Brito-American* link-boy of rebellion

Elliot, *The Republican Refuted*

I

Intellectual Formation 1737–74

I

"IT IS to my advantage," Paine recalled in 1792, "that I have served an apprenticeship to life."[1] Yet at the time, it cannot have seemed particularly advantageous. Paine's first thirty-seven years in England were characterized by a gnawing sense of failure and frustration. He was intelligent, but as one of the "inferior set of people" he was shut out of the oligarchical world of English politics. He was on the fringe of leading scientific and literary circles in London but could never quite get the recognition he felt he deserved. He was not among the poorest, but was unable to escape the threat, and sometimes the reality, of poverty. By 1774, when he left England for America, Paine's fortunes had sunk to their lowest ebb. He had run up crippling debts in a tobacco business, his second marriage had fallen apart, and he had been sacked from the excise service for neglecting his duties. Only after he had become a writer in America was Paine able to impose some meaning on his early years.

Paine's direct experience of English society deeply affected his later views. He began his working life as an apprentice corset maker at his

---

1 Paine, *Rights of Man, Part 2* (Conway), 2: 462. Philip Foner has inadvertently omitted this statement from his edition of Paine's writings. Unless otherwise stated, all subsequent references to Paine are taken from Foner, *Complete Writings*. For some treatments of Paine's life see George Chalmers [Oldys] *Life of Thomas Pain*; Cheetham, *Life of Thomas Paine*; Rickman, *Life of Thomas Paine*; Sherwin, *Memoirs of the Life of Thomas Paine*; Conway, *Life of Thomas Paine*; Aldridge, *Man of Reason*; Williamson, *Thomas Paine*; Hawke, *Paine*. Chalmers's spelling, it should be added, was not a mistake. To spell Paine "Pain" in 1791 was an ideological declaration against his principles.

father's shop in Thetford, Norfolk. His artisan roots would later be used against him by political enemies who ridiculed his lowly origins and who felt that he had no business meddling in politics. Such an attitude to the artisan was, of course, commonplace among the propertied and "respectable" classes during the eighteenth century, and doubtless it fed Paine's resentment of the structure and values of English society.[2]

Yet Paine himself found his work dull and monotonous; he did not want to be an hereditary corset maker. Looking for something better, he turned to the excise service, only to become disillusioned with the "Continuance of Work, the Strictness of the Duty, and the Poverty of the Salary."[3] And the only alternative to these and other occupations that he found equally unfulfilling was the grim one of no work at all. When Paine was unemployed in London during the winter of 1765-66, he was, according to one hostile biographer, "absolutely without food, without raiment, and without shelter."[4] Even if this was an exaggeration, Paine's position must have been precarious. He was well qualified to write about the "vast mass of mankind" which was "degradedly thrown into the background of the human picture."[5] For a time, Paine had been part of that mass.

Paine's personal experience of economic insecurity and his grass-

2 In Edmund Burke's view, for example, "the occupation of a hairdresser, or of a working tallow-chandler, cannot be a matter of honour to any person—to say nothing of other more servile employments." See his *Reflections on the Revolution in France*, p. 138.

3 Paine, *The Case of the Officers of Excise*, 2: 11–12. (Unlike Foner, I have retained the original orthography.) Even the radical Mary Wollstonecraft, in an unguarded moment, referred to a "paltry exciseman's place." See *Vindication of the Rights of Men*, p. 41. Excisemen were frequently assaulted in the course of their work. One of Paine's colleagues in Hailsham was "terribly mauled" in a struggle with two smugglers, and the incident is reported in *SWA*, 26 March 1770. For a discussion of smuggling in Sussex during the mid-eighteenth century, see Winslow, "Sussex Smugglers," pp. 119–66.

4 Chalmers, *Life of Thomas Pain*, pp. 23–24.

5 Paine, *Rights of Man, Part 1*, 1: 267. Paine may well have been alluding to his own experiences in the winter of 1765–66 when he wrote later that "many a youth comes up to London full of expectations, and little or no money, and unless he gets employment he is already half undone. . . . Hunger is not among the postponable wants, and a day, even a few hours, in such a condition, is often the crisis of a life of ruin" (*Rights of Man, Part 2*, 1: 430). For a discussion of conditions in the capital, see Rudé, *Hanoverian London*.

roots knowledge of English society gave him a keen eye for injustices and hardships which were invisible to the relatively comfortable members of the ruling class. "It would seem, by the exterior appearance of such countries [in Europe] that all was happiness," Paine argued in the *Rights of Man*, "but there lies hidden from the eye of common observation, a mass of wretchedness that has scarcely any other chance than to expire in poverty or infamy."[6] Paine knew what it was like to be poor in England. He had witnessed "age going to the work-house, and youth to the gallows."[7] Paine knew what it was like to be on the road looking for work. He understood the needs and fears of artisans "on tramp," and argued that money was needed "to defray the funeral expenses of persons, who, travelling for work, may die at a distance from their friends."[8] And as an excise officer, Paine had also seen "the numerous and various distresses which the weight of taxes even at that time of day occasioned."[9] Paine's sensitivity to the problems facing artisans and labourers, a sensitivity born out of his own apprenticeship to life, was central to his later popular appeal in England.

At times it is possible to pin down specific events which influenced Paine's later radicalism. In the *Rights of Man*, he attacked England's poor laws—"those instruments of civil torture"—and condemned the system by which sick or dying people would be removed from the parish where they lived to the parish of their birth to avoid the expense of looking after them. After sketching out his proposals for social reform, Paine included among its benefits the prospect that "the dying poor will not be dragged from place to place to breathe their last, as a reprisal of parish upon parish."[10] Nineteen years earlier, while living in Lewes, Paine had encountered a particularly distressing example of this practice. A letter to the local newspaper in October 1773 reported that a sick man had been removed from a parish in Yorkshire to St Michael's parish in Lewes. Neglected and carried in an open cart in cold weather for almost a month, the man was emaciated and vermin-ridden when he arrived at Lewes. Within a few days he was

6 Paine, *Rights of Man*, Part 2, 1: 404–5.
7 Ibid., p. 404.
8 Ibid., p. 429.
9 Paine, "To the Sheriff of the County of Sussex," 30 June 1792, 2: 464. Paine was quick to point out that he had never vigorously enforced the excise regulations—which may help to explain why he was twice dismissed from the service.
10 Paine, *Rights of Man*, Part 2, 1: 431.

dead. The incident clearly demonstrates the kind of institutionalized oppression that Paine had witnessed in England, and against which he fought so strongly in the *Rights of Man*.[11]

In the light of Paine's early experiences in England, the tone as well as the content of his writings becomes more intelligible. Replying to *Common Sense*, the Loyalist Charles Inglis felt that Paine was "every where transported with rage—a rage that knows no limits, and hurries him along, like an impetuous torrent."[12] Although Inglis overstated his case, it is true that an undercurrent of anger ran through Paine's major works, and that this anger had its source in the poverty, misery, and frustration Paine had seen and felt in England. Inglis attributed Paine's anger partly to "a distempered brain" and partly to "a disaffection which only slumbered before."[13] Paine's sanity need not be doubted, but the notion that he had a kind of slumbering disaffection to monarchy before he left England needs pursuing. To get into Paine's mind during his early life in England, we must examine not only the social forces that influenced him directly, but also the ideas to which he was exposed.

II

Paine's Quaker background helped form some of his later political and social attitudes. Even during his attack on revealed religion in the *Age of Reason*, Paine acknowledged that the Quakers gave him "an exceedingly good moral education, and a tolerable stock of useful learning," and spoke highly of their philanthropy.[14] His humanitarianism, his attachment to simplicity in politics, and his hostility to aristocratic "luxury" all had roots in his Quaker upbringing. Yet too much can be made of this. While Paine admired Quaker ideals, he

11 "Humanus" to *SWA*, 9 October 1773; in *SWA*, 11 October 1773. The circumstantial evidence that Paine knew of the incident is overwhelming. He was a close friend of William Lee, the publisher of the *SWA*, and his wife advertised in the paper; thus it is likely that he was a regular reader of the *SWA*. We know that Paine was in Lewes in October 1773, since he attended the Law Day meeting on 25 October (See V. Smith, ed., *Town Book of Lewes*), and Paine's house was in the centre of St Michael's parish. Indeed, it is tempting to suppose that "Humanus" was Paine himself.

12 Inglis, *True Interest of America*, p. 34.

13 Ibid., pp. 21, 37.

14 Paine, *Age of Reason, Part 1*, 1: 496, 498. Paine's first serious biographer, Moncure D. Conway, placed considerable emphasis on Paine's Quakerism (Conway, *Life of Thomas Paine*, 1: 10–12).

refused to be imprisoned by them. He might, for example, agree in principle with Quaker notions of pacifism, but he felt that in practice such notions would only encourage power in its attacks on liberty.[15] Because the Quaker religion had a "direct tendency to make a man the quiet and inoffensive subject of any, and every government which is set over him," he argued, it offered no effective resistance to tyrannical rule.[16] And in any case, Quakerism was neither the only nor the most important intellectual influence impinging on Paine.

During the mid-eighteenth century, new channels of political and scientific knowledge were opening up for the broad group of artisans, manufacturers, and professional men that was growing into an important "bulge beneath the apex" of England's social structure. The increased number of newspapers made people more aware of political affairs. In 1702 London launched its first daily paper; by 1760 there were thirty-five such papers in the provinces. Circulating libraries introduced an increasing number of people to books, pamphlets, and encyclopedias. Itinerant lecturers toured the country, giving talks on "useful knowledge" and Newtonianism, and stimulating a spirit of critical inquiry which was not necessarily confined to scientific matters. Towards the end of the century, every major town in England had its own library, newspaper, and debating society. Within this intellectual culture, which fitted awkwardly into the hierarchical pyramid of English society, a significant minority of thinkers became drawn to radical political ideas, and discussed Real Whig and Bolingbroke Tory traditions of opposition.[17]

According to the Real Whigs, a dangerous gap had opened between British constitutional theory and actual political practice. Real Whigs accepted the widely held view that Britain possessed a "balanced" constitution in which the king, Lords, and Commons acted as brakes on one another's ambitions and held in check the competing claims of monarchy, aristocracy, and democracy. But in reality, they argued, the crown and chief ministers were subverting the system by using patronage to corrupt and undermine the independence of the Commons. To realign practice with theory, they wanted to strengthen the

15 Paine, "Thoughts on Defensive War," *PM*, July 1775, 2: 53.
16 Paine, "Epistle to Quakers," 2: 58.
17 Appleby, "Social Origins of American Revolutionary Ideology," p. 949; Plumb, "The Public, Literature, and the Arts," p. 31, and *In the Light of History*, pp. 15–19; Gibbs, "Itinerant Lecturers," pp. 111–17.

Commons through such means as a more rigorous separation of powers, the rotation of offices, the redistribution of seats, annual parliaments, and an extended franchise. By the early 1770s, some Real Whigs were moving towards universal manhood suffrage to protect "passive" liberty from "aggressive" power.[18]

At the other end of the ideological spectrum, men in the Bolingbroke Tory or Country Party tradition complained that corruption was eroding traditional social and political values, that the "moneyed interests" were feeding off the national debt and threatening the constitution, and that Parliament had elevated factional interests above the common good. In contrast to the Real Whig belief that liberty depended on the exertions of the "people," the Bolingbroke Tories pinned their faith on a Patriot King or Patriot Minister who would, it was hoped, regenerate British politics, society, and morality from above. But although their solutions were radically different, Real Whigs and Bolingbroke Tories were united in their opposition to current British political practice. Largely because of this area of agreement, men like James Burgh could travel rapidly from one end of the opposition spectrum to the other, both Real Whig and Bolingbroke Tory ideas could influence American revolutionary ideology, and even Britain's popular Radicals of the 1790s could quote Bolingbroke in one breath and argue for universal manhood suffrage in the next.[19]

Mixing with intelligent artisans and professional men, reading widely and participating in his local debating society, Paine must have become familiar with such political notions. Indeed, in Lewes, where he lived between 1768 and 1774, it would have been difficult to ignore them. The town had a long and vigorous tradition of religious and political dissent; it had been a Cromwellian stronghold during the Civil War and still had a reputation for radicalism in the eighteenth century.[20] Reflecting wider trends in England, Lewes had its own "social and intellectual" club, which met weekly at the White Hart Inn, and its own newspaper, the *Sussex Weekly Advertiser, or Lewes Journal*. During Paine's years in the town, the *Advertiser* reprinted Junius's attacks on the government, complained that under George III the "Tory tormenters" had "wriggled themselves into power," published articles

18 Robbins, *Eighteenth-Century Commonwealthman*.

19 Kramnick, *Bolingbroke and His Circle*; Bailyn, *Ideological Origins*; Hay, "Making of a Radical," pp. 90–117; Liddle, " 'A Patriot King, or None,' " pp. 951–70.

20 Connell, *Lewes*; Foner, *Tom Paine*, pp. 12–13.

supporting the American Whigs, and praised John Wilkes as a "great patriot"; when Wilkes passed through Lewes in 1770, he was given a hero's welcome.[21] The paper also provided a local forum for eighteenth-century Enlightenment ideas. One series of articles, written by "A Forester," upheld the values of "plain truth" and "common sense," and insisted that reason must prevail over passion. In true Enlightenment fashion, "A Forester" had an essentially benevolent view of nature, emphasized the importance of conscience as a guide to conduct, and believed that "Liberty of the mind" was necessary to overcome traditional superstitions. Criticizing honours, titles, and distinctions based on birth, he asserted that " 'ONE OF THE NOBILITY,' and 'ONE OF NO-ABILITY,' have now become little less than synonimous terms."[22]

Paine moved easily in the political and intellectual culture of Lewes. He was active in local politics, attending over half his parish public vestry meetings and all the Law Day meetings during his years in the town.[23] He later recalled that in Lewes "there was not a man more firm and open in supporting the principles of liberty than myself," and one of his contemporary biographers (himself from the town) wrote that Paine "was at this time a Whig." At the White Hart club, he won a considerable reputation for his debating skills and his obstinacy in argument; his friends crowned him the "General of the Headstrong War." It is not hard to imagine him talking about American news, the opinions of Junius, and the latest "Forester's" articles while drinking brandy and eating oysters at the White Hart.[24]

Outside Lewes, Paine's connections in London contributed to his political education. He became friendly with George Lewis Scott, a commissioner of the Board of Excise, a leading mathematician, and

21 *SWA*, 20 March 1769, 5 June 1769, 12 June 1769, 27 August 1770. Junius's letters were reprinted about once a month between 1769 and 1772.

22 *SWA*, 7 September 1772, 14 September 1772, 28 September 1772, 5 October 1772, 16 November 1772, 30 November 1772, 7 December 1772, 4 January 1773. It is worth noting that Paine in the *Rights of Man, Part 1*, 1: 310, denounced "what are called nobles or nobility, or rather no-ability, in all countries." Another point of interest is that Paine himself used the pseudonym "The Forester" when countering criticisms of *Common Sense*.

23 East Sussex Record Office, St Michael's Parish Vestry Minute Book, and Lewes Non-Conformist Registers; V. Smith, ed. *Town Book of Lewes*; Connell, *Story of an Old Meeting House*. For Paine's later comments about the cheapness and effectiveness of local government, see the *Rights of Man, Part 2*, 1: 399–400, 421.

24 Paine, "To the Sheriff of the County of Sussex," 30 June 1792, 2: 466; Rickman, *Life of Thomas Paine*, pp. 37–38.

a former sub-preceptor of George III. From Scott, who was suspected
of harbouring Jacobite sympathies, Paine learned the "true character"
of the king and his ministers. Scott also introduced him to other
scientific and political thinkers, including Benjamin Franklin; it was
Franklin's letter of recommendation that helped Paine find his feet
in the New World. Beyond this, it is impossible to recreate the world
of political debate which Paine inhabited in London. But it is quite
conceivable that his friends and acquaintances prompted him to read
the work of radical thinkers like John Hall, John Milton, Joseph Priestley, and James Burgh. Not surprisingly, given his background in Lewes
and London, Paine dismissed mainstream British politics as nothing
more than "Jockeyship."[25]

While the evidence suggests that Paine was aware of and sympathetic to radical political ideas, it cannot be assumed that he was already an internationalist democratic republican before he crossed the
Atlantic. In fact, there are several indications in his writings that Paine
shared common English notions of patriotism in his youth. He fought
for his country as a privateer during the Seven Years' War, and one
of his earliest English works was a song celebrating the exploits of
General James Wolfe at Quebec in 1759. In 1778, in the course of a
discussion about English assumptions of national superiority, Paine
admitted that "there was a time when I felt the same prejudices, and
reasoned from the same errors; but experience, sad and painful experience, has taught me better." On another occasion, he wrote that
living in a country the size of America could enlarge and liberate the
mind; it was only after he left England that he described himself as
a "universal citizen" who had "banished the contracted ideas I was,
like other people, brought up in." It is also dangerous to project
Paine's republicanism back onto his earlier years. His own comments
in *Common Sense* and the *American Crisis* state that he did not move
towards republicanism until April 1775, five months after he arrived
in Philadelphia, and there are no examples of republican sentiments

25 On Scott, see *Dictionary of National Biography*, 17: 961; for Paine's comments
about Scott, see Paine to Henry Laurens, 14 January 1779, 2: 1162. Franklin's letter
of recommendation is cited in Hawke, *Paine*, p. 20. Evidence that Paine was familiar
with the work of Hall, Milton, and Priestley is discussed below, pp. 43–48; Paine
mentioned Burgh's *Political Disquisitions* in *Common Sense*, 1: 38n. For Paine's remark
about "Jockeyship," see *Age of Reason, Part 1*, 1: 496.

in his writing before that date. In short, America turned him into an internationalist and a republican.[26]

Although the picture which emerges is necessarily impressionistic, some broad outlines can be discerned. Paine's artisan background, his experience of poverty, and his unfulfilling career as an excise officer gave him a deep feeling of dissatisfaction, which could easily be translated into some form of political Radicalism. At the same time, Paine's support for the "principles of liberty" did not yet embrace democratic republicanism or internationalism, and in any case remained largely theoretical. In the context of England in the 1760s and early 1770s, the opportunities for fundamental political change appeared remote; the "political nation" seemed secure and comfortable, and Real Whigs and Bolingbroke Tories alike were banging their collective heads against a brick wall.

Under these circumstances, Paine adopted a cynical attitude towards "official" politics and focused much of his intellectual energy on the study of modern science. His scientific pursuits played a central role in his intellectual formation; it is impossible to understand fully Paine's cast of mind and style of writing without reference to his scientific background. In particular, he was strongly influenced by the new theories of logic and rhetoric associated with the scientific rev-

26 Barry, "Thomas Paine, Privateersman," pp. 451–61; Paine, "Death of General Wolfe," *PM*, March 1775, 2: 1083–84; Paine, *American Crisis VII*, 1: 143; *American Crisis VIII*, 1: 164; *Letter to the Abbé Raynal*, 2: 256; Paine to the Marquis of Lansdowne, 21 September 1787, 2: 1265. For Paine's comments about his initial attitude to an independent American republic, see *Common Sense*, 1: 25 ("No man was a warmer wisher for reconciliation than myself, before the fatal nineteenth of April, 1775") and *American Crisis VII*, 1: 143 ("I had no thoughts of independence or of arms" before the Battle of Lexington on 19 April 1775). In *American Crisis III*, 1: 84, he wrote that "a general promotion of sentiment" occurred after Lexington, and that "those who had drank deeply into Whiggish principles, that is, the right and necessity not only of opposing, but wholly setting aside the power of the crown as soon as it became practically dangerous (for in theory it was always so), stepped into the first stage of independence"; this comment can be applied to his own political development. Elsewhere, in *American Crisis II*, 1: 72, Paine remarked that "I have . . . an aversion to monarchy, as being too debasing to the dignity of man; but I never troubled others with my notions till very lately." This fits with Inglis's statement about Paine's slumbering disaffection in England and with Rickman's observation that Paine was a Whig in Lewes. In America, in the process of a "general promotion of sentiment," Paine's latent aversion to monarchy became manifest and evolved into an articulated form of revolutionary democratic republicanism.

olution. Since this important aspect of Paine's education has been
generally neglected, it is worth considering at some length.

III

The scientific revolution, with its emphasis on observation and experiment, transformed traditional concepts of logic and rhetoric.[27] As
the new inductive scientific methodology dislodged deductive pro-
cedures of inquiry, it also rejected the theories of rhetoric associated
with deductive logic. The old rhetoric had been divided into two main
camps. There was the British elocutionary movement, which emphasized style and delivery to such an extent that it equated rhetoric solely
with voice and gesture. And there was the neo-Ciceronian school,
which insisted that speakers and writers draw their arguments from
the set topics of invention (such as causes, effects, adjuncts, comparisons, and the like), which generally recommended the classical six-
part oratorical arrangement of arguments, and which elevated the
grand style, with its panoply of tropes and elaborate figures of speech,
into a superior form of writing.[28] Under the pressure of the new
science, both these schools of thought were challenged by modern
theories of rhetoric emanating from London's Royal Society, dis-
senting academies in the provinces, and the remarkably progressive
Scottish universities. Exponents of the new rhetoric attacked the British elocutionary movement for separating style from substance and
allowing persuasive discourse to degenerate into empty and insincere
declamation. They also criticized the neo-Ciceronians for forcing arguments into anachronistic structures and for equating effective rhetoric with lofty and grandiloquent prose. In line with modern scientific
standards, the new rhetoric stressed the importance of drawing arguments directly from the facts of the case rather than consulting the
topics of invention, preferred a simple and flexible organizational

27 This discussion of the new logic and rhetoric is based on Howell, *Eighteenth-
Century British Logic and Rhetoric*. See also R. F. Jones, "Science and English Prose Style,"
pp. 977–1009.

28 See Howell, *Logic and Rhetoric*, pp. 145–256, on the elocutionary movement, and
pp. 75–142, on the eighteenth-century Ciceronians. He describes the traditional approach to the topics of invention (pp. 97–101); the old rhetoric's attachment to the six-
part oratorical structure, in which discourses were arranged into an introduction, nar-
ration, proposition, confirmation, refutation and conclusion (pp. 103–4, 129, 696–97);
and the neo-Ciceronian emphasis on the grand style, (pp. 105–17, 446–47).

structure over Ciceronian models, and adopted the plain style as the best means of communication.[29]

This amounted to a revolution in style. Far from associating the grand style with true eloquence, new rhetoricians regarded high-blown language as an impediment to the communication of knowledge. They argued that a style which relied heavily on tropes and figures revealed more about the author's vanity than the validity of his case. They maintained that conscious ornamentation and embellishment were usually employed to conceal weak arguments behind the glare of superficially impressive language. And they objected that the grand style involved an appeal to the passions, which relegated reason to a subordinate role and thus divorced persuasion from understanding.[30]

In contrast, the new rhetoric advocated standards of simplicity. As Thomas Sprat wrote of the Royal Society, its founders decided

to reject all the amplifications, digressions, and swellings of style; to return back to the primitive purity, and shortness, when men deliver'd so many *things*, almost in an equal number of *words*. They have exacted from all their members, a close, naked, natural way of speaking; positive expressions; clear senses; a native easiness: bringing all things as near the Mathematical plainness, as they can: and preferring the language of Artizans, Countrymen, and Merchants, before that, of Wits, or Scholars.[31]

Sprat's linking of "*things*" and "*words*" reflected the principle that verbal statements must correspond with the facts, just as his overall position echoes John Wilkins's view that "the greatest learning is to be seen in the greatest plainnesse."[32] And the plain style was addressed primarily to the reason, on the grounds that genuine conviction could only be achieved through the communication of true understanding.

29 For Howell's views on the weaknesses of the elocutionary movement, see *Logic and Rhetoric*, pp. 145–46, 243. He describes the attack launched by people like John Locke, Isaac Watts, François Fénelon, Adam Smith, and Hugh Blair on the topics of invention (pp. 293–96, 340–41, 512–13, 554, 573–75, 662–63); and the dismissal by Fénelon, Smith, and George Campbell of the classical six-part structure (pp. 513–14, 571–73, 602). New rhetoricians who rejected the grand style included Robert Boyle, Fénelon, Smith, and Campbell (pp. 465–81, 515–18, 545–46, 610–11).

30 See, for example, the comments of John Wilkins, Joseph Priestley, Hugh Blair, and John Witherspoon in Howell, *Logic and Rhetoric*, pp. 456–57, 643–45, 653–54, 676–80.

31 Sprat, *History of the Royal Society*, p. 113.

32 Quoted in Howell, *Logic and Rhetoric*, p. 456.

This did not mean, however, that new rhetoricians completely ruled out figures of speech or ignored the feelings. Rather, they rejected a system of rhetoric which substituted stylistic show for solid arguments, and they believed that feelings could only establish the goodness of an idea after reason had grasped its truthfulness. The important thing was to find the right balance between judgment and passion, so that feelings were anchored by reason.[33]

Along with the plain style went new methods of rhetorical arrangement. Jettisoning the classical six-part structure (about which neo-Ciceronians had themselves been divided), the new rhetoricians maintained that the arrangement of an argument should be conditioned by its subject matter. A particularly influential work in this respect was William Duncan's *Elements of Logick*, which was regarded as one of the best introductions to mathematics and philosophy in eighteenth-century Britain, and which went into nine editions in London between 1748 and 1800. When dealing with natural knowledge, Duncan argued, one should employ the "analytic method" of moving from particular observations to general propositions, so that one's arguments were firmly rooted in experienced realities. But when it came to the "abstract Ideas of the Mind," which by implication included matters of morality and religion, he advocated the "synthetic method" of reasoning from the general to the particular. According to Duncan, the synthetic method produced absolute certainty when it subjected self-evident first principles to a syllogistic examination that followed mathematical models of demonstration. A proposition was self-evident when a bare attention to its ideas enabled one intuitively to recognize its truth; the mathematical model of demonstration meant defining one's terms, laying down axioms and postulates, and reasoning step by step to "advance to Theorems." Thus Duncan's theory of method embraced both analytic and synthetic argumentative structures, depending on the nature of the question under discussion.[34]

33 On the relationship between reason and feelings, and on the place of tropes and figures in the new rhetoric, see the views of Locke, Fénelon, Campbell, Blair, and Witherspoon in Howell, *Logic and Rhetoric*, pp. 496–97, 510–11, 515–18, 580–604, 652–55, 678.

34 Duncan's theory of method is discussed in Howell, *Logic and Rhetoric*, pp. 350–61. As Howell points out in his "Declaration of Independence and Eighteenth-Century Logic," pp. 467–70, men like Campbell, Priestley, and Blair incorporated the analytic and synthetic methods of logic into their theory of rhetoric at the expense of the six-part oratorical structure.

The revolution in rhetoric can be linked to Paine's manner of think-ing and writing in two ways. First, he moved in circles where the new ideas were being discussed and developed. And second, there are close parallels between the central principles of the new rhetoric and Paine's own approach to the style and structure of arguments.

Paine's scientific leanings—he was particularly interested in math-ematics and astronomy—brought him into contact with some of the leading natural philosophers and itinerant lecturers of the day. In London, he attended the lectures of Benjamin Martin, a self-educated popularizer of Newtonian physics and a pioneer of itinerant lecturing whose interests embraced mathematics, music, astronomy, and rhet-oric.[35] Paine also met and was impressed with James Ferguson, an instrument maker, portrait painter, and astronomer who started life as a shepherd's boy in Scotland and wound up as a fellow of the Royal Society.[36] Rubbing shoulders with scientists in and around the Royal Society, Paine knew Dr John Bevis, a widely respected Newtonian scientist, and other proponents of "useful" knowledge.[37] From such people, Paine could and did learn a great deal.

Benjamin Martin, in particular, stressed the importance of the new logic and rhetoric. According to Martin, the fundamental rule of the "Modern Philosophy" was that "Propositions and Conclusions, de-duced from actual Experiments, must be esteemed true and accurate, notwithstanding any *Hypotheses* or received *Suppositions,* to the con-trary, and must be insisted on 'till some other Phoenomena, either rend them more accurate, or liable to Exception." Not surprisingly, he attacked theories which rested on "absurd and extravagant Hy-potheses" instead of rigorous scientific analysis. Yet he did not com-pletely rule out the use of hypotheses as tools of scientific inquiry,

35 Paine, *Age of Reason, Part 1,* 1: 496; Millburn, *Benjamin Martin.* In his crusade against superstition and ignorance, Martin sometimes encountered unexpected diffi-culties. "There are many places where I have been," he wrote in 1746, "so barbarously ignorant, that they have taken me for a magician; yea, some have threaten'd my life, for raising storms and hurricanes" (Millburn, *Benjamin Martin,* p. 41).

36 *Dictionary of National Biography,* 6: 1210. Shortly after arriving in Philadelphia, Paine wrote of the "ingenious and worthy Mr. Ferguson," and based the design of a "new threshing instrument" on Ferguson's model. See Paine, "Description of a New Threshing Instrument," *PM,* February 1775.

37 Paine, *Age of Reason, Part 1,* 1: 496. On Bevis, see *Dictionary of National Biography,* 2: 451–52. Among Paine's other scientific acquaintances, George Lewis Scott not only had a considerable reputation as a mathematician but also had edited a "universal dictionary of arts and sciences" (Scott, ed., *A Supplement to Mr. Chambers's Cyclopaedia*).

provided they met certain conditions. He laid down eight such conditions, including the requirements that hypotheses be "agreeable to just Reasoning," "consentaneous to Experience," and "free from all Suspicion of Prejudice, Affection, or Prepossession, in their Author." In contrast to the old logic, which stressed deductive methods of investigation and which downplayed induction as an irregular form of syllogism, Martin insisted upon inductive inquiry while allocating a subordinate and carefully prescribed role to deductive reasoning.[38]

Martin's system of logic had important implications for the communication of knowledge. His position that arguments must be based on demonstrable facts meant that one's language must reflect the realities with which it dealt. His emphasis on "Reason and Experience" to dispel "Prejudices and Errors" assumed that conviction and persuasion depended upon understanding rather than passion. His own work followed a clear and orderly structure. In *The Philosophical Grammar*, Martin began by carefully defining his terms, and then established certain self-evident "*Principles,* or *Axioms*" on which the new science was based, before describing the contribution of Newtonian physics to natural philosophy. Moreover, Martin stressed the importance of a "plain and easy" approach to writing. He joined in the modern attack on the grand style for relying on "Rhetorical Expressions"—by which he meant ornamentations and embellishments—to make the reader "swallow down for Truth" arguments that were actually closer to romance than philosophy. "The greatest Excellency of a Demonstration," he maintained, "is Conciseness and Perspicuity."[39]

James Ferguson took a similar position, attempting in his lectures "to avoid all superfluity, and to render every thing as plain and intelligible as I thought the subject would admit of."[40] Other influences on Paine must remain a matter of speculation. His study of mathematics may have led him to Duncan's *Elements of Logick*, and his interest in the Royal Society probably induced him to read Sprat's *History of the Royal Society*, with its emphasis on the plain style. But Paine was clearly part of a scientific and intellectual culture in which the new theories of logic and rhetoric were circulating. It is no coincidence that one of the literary figures Paine most admired at this time, Oliver

38 Martin, *Philosophical Grammar*, pp. 12–21.

39 Ibid., pp. 12, 18, 74; Martin, *Philosophia Britannica*, 1: n.p. See also Martin, *Institutions of Language*, p. 111.

40 Ferguson, *Lectures on Select Subjects*, 1: xiv.

Goldsmith, rejected the "sublime style" and strove for clarity of expression. "Convincing eloquence," wrote Goldsmith, "is infinitely more serviceable to its possessor than the most florid harangue or the most pathetic tones that can be imagined; and the man who is thoroughly convinced himself, who understands his subject, and the language he speaks in, will be more apt to silence opposition, than he who studies the force of his periods, and fills our ears with sound, while our minds are destitute of conviction."[41] It would be hard to find a better statement of the case for the plain style.

When we look at Paine's actual writings, it immediately becomes apparent that he responded consciously and creatively to the revolution in rhetoric. This is not to argue that he followed rigorously the recommendations of any particular rhetorician, or that he consulted handbooks on rhetoric wherever he went. Paine did not operate in that way; his approach was characterized by a kind of freewheeling eclecticism. But if he was less than a sophisticated philosopher, he was more than a superficial polemicist. And his numerous comments about the nature of effective writing, together with his own literary practice, indicate that he had assimilated the main elements of the modern outlook.

Whenever Paine used the word "rhetoric," he associated it with the high-blown language favoured by the British elocutionists or the neo-Ciceronians. This is understandable; "rhetoric" had become so closely connected with extravagant word-play that many progressive intellectuals preferred to drop the word altogether, and spoke instead of the "plain style."[42] Significantly, Paine's references to the old rhetoric were uniformly hostile; he argued that it was divorced from concrete realities and thus consisted of words without meaning. One of his earliest poems, probably written in Lewes, satirized disputatious "logic, rhetoric, and wit" where the appearance of erudition was pressed into the service of absurd and selfish ends.[43] Elsewhere, he maintained that practical experience was worth more than anything which "the

---

41 Goldsmith, *Collected Works*, 1: 463–64, 478.

42 Thus Martin used the word "rhetoric" to denote grandiloquent prose; the Royal Society insisted that in scientific reports "the matter of fact shall be barely stated, without any prefaces, apologies, or rhetorical flourishes"; Boyle associated "Matters Rhetorical" with stylistic ornamentation. See Howell, *Logic and Rhetoric*, pp. 446, 479–81. In contrast, people like Smith, Campbell, Priestley, and Blair maintained that the plain style not only deserved the name of rhetoric but was in fact the most effective form of rhetoric.

43 Paine, "Farmer Short's Dog Porter," *PM*, July 1775, 2: 1084–88.

most finished rhetoric can describe or the keenest imagination conceive."[44] And in the *Rights of Man*, he criticized Edmund Burke for relying on rhetorical "invention" instead of the facts of the case.[45] Throughout his career, Paine consistently rejected traditional rhetoric and its "invented deformities or needless embellishments."[46]

In its place, he advocated "plainness of conversation" and attempted to write "in language as plain as the alphabet."[47] Paine repeatedly referred to the importance of a clear and direct style, and for the most part his writing lived up to this ideal.[48] He insisted that "facts are more powerful than arguments," asserted the primacy of "practical" over "speculative" knowledge, and stressed the importance of attaching precise factual meanings to one's terms.[49] Unless this was done, Paine argued, the reader would be left with "words which impress nothing but the ear, and are calculated only for the sound."[50]

Paine's position on the relationship between reason and feelings in persuasive writing was also fully in accord with the principles of the new rhetoric. He placed considerable emphasis on the feelings and conscience of his audience, attempted to evoke "sympathetic sorrow" when describing other people's sufferings, and sharply criticized writers whose work lacked compassion.[51] He believed that appeals to the

44 Paine, *American Crisis VIII*, 1: 159.

45 Paine, *Rights of Man, Part 2*, 1: 360. See also *Rights of Man, Part 1*, 1: 318, where Paine dismissed rhetoric based on "memory and invention," and *American Crisis VII*, 1: 150, where he stated that "as my conclusions [about the impracticability of England conquering America] were drawn not artfully, but naturally, they have all proved to be true." Arguments had to rest on a thorough knowledge of the situation under discussion rather than relying on "artful" reasoning from the topics of invention.

46 Paine, *Six Letters to Rhode Island*, 2: 339. See also *Case of the Officers of Excise*, 2: 8, and *Letter to the Abbé Raynal*, 2: 246.

47 Paine, *Six Letters to Rhode Island*, 2: 357; *To the Public on Mr. Deane's Affair*, 2: 111.

48 See, for example, *American Crisis I*, 1: 56; *American Crisis VII*, 1: 150; *Public Good*, 2: 304; *Four Questions, Writings of Thomas Paine* (Conway), 2: 238. There are exceptions; in 1775, writing for the *Pennsylvania Magazine*, Paine occasionally lapsed into the grand style. See "Reflections on the Life and Death of Lord Clive," *PM*, March 1775, 2: 26.

49 Paine, *Letter to the Abbé Raynal*, 2: 230, 245. See also *Case of the Officers of Excise*, 2: 7; "Thoughts on Defensive War," *PM*, July 1775, 2: 54; *Dissertations on Government*, 2: 391; *Rights of Man, Part 1*, 1: 278, 287; *Rights of Man, Part 2*, 1: 360.

50 Paine, *American Crisis X*, 1: 191. For similar comments about words of sound without meaning, see *Common Sense*, 1: 8; *Rights of Man, Part 1*, 1: 255, *Rights of Man, Part 2*, 1: 372.

51 Paine's approach to "feelings" and "conscience" has not been given the attention

"passions of men" could not be ignored, and declared that "whenever the object is to convince or persuade, the influence of these passions should be turned to account."[52] But he also stressed that the "plain doctrine of reason" was central to his work, and constantly employed the criteria of "reason and reflection" to overcome "the prejudices which men have from education and habit."[53] From his perspective, "reason" and "feelings" were complementary; he often linked the words together and found no difficulty in asking the reader to "suffer his reason and his feelings to determine for themselves."[54]

Nevertheless, like the exponents of the new rhetoric, Paine insisted that reason must control the emotions. Thus his first article in America contained the view that wit, "like the passions, has a natural wildness that requires governing. Left to itself, it soon overflows its banks, mixes with common filth, and brings disrepute in the fountain."[55] It was not until 1782, however, that he fully elaborated his ideas on the subject. In his *Letter to the Abbé Raynal*, Paine argued that a writer must "combine warm passions with a cool temper, and the full expansion of the imagination with the natural and necessary gravity of judgment, so as to be rightly balanced within themselves, and to make a reader feel, fancy, and understand justly at the same time." Without "a certain degree of animation" and a "sufficient scope given to the imagination," he wrote, "the judgment will feel little or no excitement to office, and its determinations will be cold, sluggish, and imperfect." But if the passions were raised too high, Paine continued, "judgment will be jostled from its seat, and the whole matter, however important in itself, will diminish into a pantomime of the mind, in which we create images that promote no other purpose than amusement."[56] The point,

---

it deserves. He believed that benevolent affections distinguished human beings from common animals, and that kindly feelings were essential elements of the social compact. See "African Slavery in America," *PJ*, 8 March 1775, 2: 16–17; *Common Sense*, 1: 2–3, 23, 30; *Forester's Letters*, 2: 72; *American Crisis V*, 1: 106; *American Crisis VI*, 1: 131; *Prospects on the Rubicon*, 2: 624; *Rights of Man, Part 1*, 1: 260.

52 Paine, *Four Questions, Writings* (Conway), 2: 242.

53 Paine, *Forester's Letters*, 2: 61; *Rights of Man, Part 2*, 1: 352.

54 Paine, *Common Sense*, 1: 17; *Letter to the Abbé Raynal*, 2: 243.

55 Paine, "Utility of this Work Evinced," *PM*, January 1775, 2: 1112.

56 Paine, *Letter to the Abbé Raynal*, 2: 214. He often wrote disparagingly about "imagination," and recalled in the *Age of Reason, Part 1*, 1: 496, that in his youth he had "some turn, and I believe some talent for poetry; but this I rather repressed than encouraged, as leading too much into the field of imagination."

then, was to harness the passions and feelings in the service of reason
and judgment—a point which had already been made by modern
rhetoricians.

Similarly, Paine's views on rhetorical arrangement reflected the new
approach. Insisting upon an orderly argumentative structure, he attacked one adversary for having an "unprincipled method of writing
and reasoning," and dismissed much of Raynal's work on the American Revolution as a "wilderness without paths."[57] The particular method
of organizing any given argument, he maintained, depended on the
nature of the subject and the need for clarity. "To fit the powers of
thinking and the turn of language to the subject, so as to fully bring
out a clear conclusion that shall hit the point in question and nothing
else," he stated, "is the true criterion of writing."[58] When the subject
concerned fundamental matters of political theory, Paine adopted the
synthetic method of reasoning from first principles and presented his
readers with "a string of maxims and reflections, drawn from the
nature of things."[59] When he dealt with more specific issues, he opted
for the analytic method of moving from the particular to the general
and grounded himself on "known and visible facts."[60] In admitting
both syllogistic reasoning from "some polar truth or principle" and
inductive reasoning "from minutiae to magnitude," Paine's approach
to method had much in common with that recommended by William
Duncan.[61]

The connections between Paine's rhetorical standards and those of
the scientific world in which he moved are too close to be coincidental.
In his hostile attitude to traditional notions of rhetoric, his emphasis
on plain speech, his insistence that language must correspond with

57 Paine, *Forester's Letters*, 2: 69; *Letter to the Abbé Raynal*, 2: 246. See also *Candid
and Critical Remarks*, 2: 273, and *Rights of Man, Part 1*, 1: 272.

58 Paine, *Letter to the Abbé Raynal*, 2: 246.

59 Paine, *Forester's Letters*, 2: 69. See also *Common Sense*, 1: 6–7, and *Rights of Man,
Part 1*, 1: 272.

60 Paine, *American Crisis V*, 1: 116.

61 Paine, *Rights of Man, Part 1*, 1: 282, 318. It must be stressed that a direct link
between Duncan and Paine cannot be established. It is clear, however, that Duncan's
work was well known in London's scientific circles, that it influenced a new generation
of rhetoricians during the mid-eighteenth century, that Paine mixed in these scientific
circles, and that Paine's rhetoric fitted in with the new approach. It does not really
matter whether Paine did or did not read Duncan; the point is that Paine's rhetorical
method was based on assumptions developed and disseminated by Duncan's work.

the facts of the case, his concern for a balanced relationship between reason and feelings, and his preference for an orderly and flexible organizational structure, Paine shared the assumptions of the new rhetoric. And all these assumptions can be found in the one pamphlet which Paine wrote before he left England, *The Case of the Officers of Excise*. Because this pamphlet provides important insights into Paine's rhetoric and some of his social attitudes on the eve of his American career, its form and content deserve close attention.[62]

IV

The *Case* was written in 1772 as part of the excise officers' campaign to obtain a salary increase from Parliament. It was Paine's first venture into pamphleteering, and it won him a small but significant reputation as a writer. "I have received so many letters of thanks and approbation for the performance," he remarked, "that were I not rather singularly modest, I should insensibly become a little vain."[63] He sent a copy to Oliver Goldsmith, in the hope that Goldsmith would be sufficiently impressed to meet him over a bottle of wine. Although in retrospect it may seem a relatively obscure pamphlet, the *Case* was a carefully written, effectively argued work which gave Paine considerable pride. It not only provided the first outlet for his literary talent, but also anticipated the style and structure of his later, more famous writings.

Following new rhetorical theory, the *Case's* orderly structure was defined by the needs of the argument. After a general introduction setting out the purpose of the pamphlet, Paine examined the "state of the salary of the officers of excise" to show that the officers endured long hours, hard work, and isolation from their families, and were reduced to "wretched" conditions by low wages, occupational expenses, taxation, and inflation. This section analysed the conditions facing excise officers and argued that on humanitarian grounds alone they deserved a salary increase. Having established this position, Paine

---

62 Surprisingly, students of Paine's language have generally neglected the rhetorical techniques of *Case*. H. Clark in "Thomas Paine's Theories of Rhetoric" ignored the pamphlet and assumed that Paine acquired the plain style after he became a republican in America. Foner, *Tom Paine*, p. 15, noted in passing that Paine had "talent as a writer" before leaving England, but made no attempt to analyse the style and structure of *Case*.

63 Paine to Oliver Goldsmith, 21 December 1772, 2: 1129.

then shifted gear and discussed "the corruption of principles, and . . . the numerous evils arising to the revenue, from the too great poverty of the officers of excise."

In this part of the pamphlet, he appealed primarily to enlightened self-interest and reasoned from the basic premise that "Nature, in spite of Law or Religion, makes it a ruling Principle not to starve." "Nature," he continued, "never produced a Man who would starve in a well stored Larder, because the Provisions were not his own." Since he had already demonstrated that excise officers could not support themselves or their families on their present salaries, and since their occupation presented plenty of opportunities to defraud the government, it followed that dishonesty in the excise service was "the immediate Consequence of Poverty." And given that low salaries produced "CORRUPTION, COLLUSION, NEGLECT and ILL QUALIFICATIONS," he concluded that an "Augmentation of Salary, sufficient to enable them to live honestly and competently, would produce more good Effect than all the Laws of the Land can enforce."[64] The excise officers would benefit from increased pay, and the government would benefit from increased revenue as corruption was rooted out.

The arrangement of the argument, then, employed the analytic method of reasoning from the particular to the general to show that excise officers lived in poverty, and adopted the synthetic method of reasoning from self-evident premises to demonstrate that corruption was the product of poverty. The two approaches, in Paine's view, were fully compatible; he established the facts of the case, and then invoked a "ruling Principle" of nature to explain the consequences of those facts and to recommend new policies which would harmonize with first principles and improve everyone's position. It was a rhetorical strategy which he would use to great effect in his subsequent political and religious works.

Within this framework, Paine wrote in a clear, direct, and concise style. He did not bother citing respected authorities, making learned allusions or appealing to precedents, and criticized those forms of rhetoric that failed to ground themselves on practical experience and the "irresistible Necessities of Nature." "There is a powerful Rhetorick in Necessity," he wrote, "which exceeds even a *Dunning* or a *Wedderburne*. No Argument can satisfy the feelings of Hunger, or abate the Edge of Appetite." Wedderburne was a principal figure in the eigh-

64 Paine, *Case*, 2: 3–15.

teenth-century British elocutionary movement, and it is not surprising that Paine should distance himself from that rhetorical tradition. "A thousand Refinements· of Argument may be brought to prove, that the Practice of Honesty will be still the same, in the most trying and necessitous circumstances," he continued. "He who never was an hunger'd may argue finely on the Subjection of his Appetite; and he who never was distressed, may harangue as beautifully on the Power of Principle. But Poverty, like Grief, has an incurable Deafness, which never hears; the Oration loses all its Edge. . . ." And his dismissal of such oratory was combined with the position that "where Facts are Sufficient, Arguments are useless." Like a good eighteenth-century scientist, Paine insisted upon the supremacy of the "facts."[65]

The *Case* displayed other characteristics of Paine's approach to writing. The use of antithesis which gave such a memorable quality to his work first appeared in the pamphlet. He could observe that "the Tenderness of Conscience is too often overmatched by the Sharpness of Want," or that "Eloquence may strike the Ear, but the Language of Poverty strikes the Heart." And the *Case* also attempted to engage both the feelings and the reason of his readers. "Were the Reasons for augmenting the Salary grounded only on the Charitableness of so doing," he wrote, "they would have great Weight with the Compassionate." At the same time, Paine stressed the importance of reason and reflection as he developed his argument that a salary increase would make the revenue service more efficient. In this sense, the "Case of the Officers" was also the "Case of the Revenue."[66]

As well as illustrating Paine's rhetorical technique, the *Case* contained glimpses of his underlying social attitudes. Beneath the surface of this "humble Application" to Parliament lay feelings of sympathy with the poor, hostility to the "temptations of Ambition" and the "Luxury of Appetite," and the sense that the wealthy could not fully understand the conditions and consequences of poverty. "The Rich, in Ease and Affluence, may think I have drawn an unnatural Portrait," he wrote; "but could they descend to the cold Regions of Want, the Circle of Polar Poverty, they would find their Opinions changing with the Climate." Moreover, Paine maintained, through the mechanism of inflation the wealth of some was inextricably linked to the poverty of others. "To the Wealthy and Humane," he commented, "it is a

65 Ibid., 7, 8, 9, 11.
66 Ibid., 7, 8, 14.

Matter worthy of Concern that their Affluence should become the Misfortune of others. Were the Money in the Kingdom to be increased double, the Salary would in Value be reduced one half. Every Step upwards, is a Step downwards with them."[67] His identification with the poor, his dislike of excessive wealth and his opposition to inflation would remain central features of his outlook.

Paine's first pamphlet revealed a hint of radical sympathies, and indicates that he had absorbed the central tenets of the new rhetoric before he began his career as a revolutionary writer in America. Both his latent radicalism and his writing style must be located in the culture in which Paine moved. In England, he lived in a world of social, intellectual, and scientific associations meeting in local taverns, where intelligent artisans and professional men on the margins of society discussed publications on "useful knowledge," listened to itinerant lecturers speaking on Newtonian science, and argued about alternative political systems. Within this culture there existed a myriad of views, and there was certainly no automatic connection between one's political position and one's approach to rhetoric. To write in the plain style was not necessarily to be a Radical, and to be a Radical was not necessarily to write in the plain style.[68]

From this perspective, three central points about Paine emerge. First, Paine did not "create" a new literary style; instead, he participated in the growing movement towards plain speech that was part of his intellectual and cultural environment and not exclusively associated with any particular political viewpoint. Second, in Paine's case the "medium" preceded the "message." Although he had a "disaffection which only slumbered" in England, his outlook did not evolve into democratic republicanism until he arrived in America, and it is thus misleading to view his style as the literary by-product of his politics. And third, the culture in which he moved was a minority one in England, but at the heart of life in America. Paine quickly settled into Philadelphia's scientific and intellectual milieu, rapidly responded

67 Ibid., 3, 5, 8–9, 11.

68 One can speak of a democratic culture in which the new rhetoric (along with the new science) flourished, but one cannot assume that the new rhetoric was synonymous with a new democratic political ideology. Some new rhetoricians, such as Priestley and Witherspoon, were indeed political radicals; others, like Campbell and Blair, were not. As we shall see, William Cobbett wrote in the plain style during his career as a High Tory in America. And some members of the English democratic societies in the 1790s couched their ideas in melodramatic and extravagant language.

to the political radicalization around him, and articulated that response in a style which Americans had adopted as their own. When that happened, the medium and the message fused, with revolutionary consequences. The result was *Common Sense*, the most widely read and influential pamphlet America had ever seen.

II

The Making of
Common Sense, *1775–76*

I

PAINE arrived in Philadelphia on 30 November, 1774, half dead from typhus. He brought with him a letter of recommendation from Benjamin Franklin, and as he fought back to health he quickly made contact with the city's intelligentsia. Within weeks he was an editorial assistant on the newly established *Pennsylvania Magazine*, and he began to write regularly on scientific and humanitarian issues. He found the intellectual atmosphere of Philadelphia thoroughly congenial. With its scientific, literary, and debating clubs, its seven newspapers in a population of only 30,000, and its American Philosophical Society, Philadelphia was at the heart of the New World Enlightenment. The city was small enough for a man of talent to catch the eye, but large enough to be a centre of colonial culture. Paine, who had dominated the White Hart club in Lewes, now found himself in an environment where such clubs were in the mainstream of political, social, and cultural life.

After the poverty of London, Paine must have found Philadelphia a remarkably prosperous town. Although poverty was becoming a serious problem there during the 1770s, and although the gap between the richest and poorest was steadily widening, there was nothing quite like the Old World "contrast of affluence and wretchedness constantly meeting and offending the eye . . . like dead and living bodies, chained together," about which Paine would later write.[1] Dominating a rich agricultural hinterland and locked into a lucrative trans-

---

1 Paine, *Agrarian Justice*, 1: 617.

atlantic trade system, Philadelphia was one of the wealthiest cities in the Anglo-American world. Given the relative prosperity, egalitarianism, and stimulating intellectual climate of Philadelphia, it is hardly surprising that Paine's first writings in the *Pennsylvania Magazine* were permeated with a sense of American virtue and potential.

Philadelphia was the right place; 1775 was the right time. As Britain and America moved further apart, many of the city's merchants and artisans became politicized, challenged Pennsylvania's Quaker and Proprietary élites, and demanded vigorous anti-British measures as well as more egalitarian domestic policies.[2] The Anglo-American conflict interlocked with local political struggles, precipitating the radicalization of those Real Whig ideas Paine had encountered back in England. At the beginning of the year, most colonists were hostile to Lord North's ministry and disillusioned with the House of Commons, yet were generally "loyal" to the king. Twelve months later, they increasingly felt that the ministry, Parliament, and king were conspiring together against colonial liberties; some were even beginning to consider independence. "Scarcely had I put my foot into the Country," Paine recalled in 1783, "but it was set on fire about my ears."[3]

Throughout his transition from obscure former exciseman to the leading revolutionary writer in America, Paine's changing images of England and America played a central role. Paine increasingly identified with the New World; the man who was starting his own life over again soon believed that America itself had the power to "begin the world over again."[4] His first writings in America displayed the exuberance of released frustration; his failures in the Old World strengthened his sense of belonging in the New. "Degeneracy here is almost a useless word," he wrote barely six weeks after his arrival. "Those who are conversant with Europe would be tempted to believe that even the air of the Atlantic disagrees with the constitution of foreign vices."[5] He contrasted American "virtue" with English "profligacy and

2 On the impact of the Revolution in Philadelphia, see Foner, *Tom Paine*, pp. 56–69; Ryerson, *Revolution Is Now Begun*; Nash, *Urban Crucible*.

3 Paine to a Committee of the Continental Congress, October 1783, 2: 1227. One of the best discussions of political and ideological developments in 1775 can be found in Maier, *From Resistance to Revolution*, pp. 228–70.

4 Paine, *Common Sense*, 1: 45.

5 Paine, "Utility of this Work Evinced," *PM*, January 1775, 2: 1110. This kind of attitude would later stimulate some of Cobbett's characteristic satire. Cynics, he mockingly wrote in 1795, "do not, or rather will not, recollect, what the miraculous air of

dissipation," compared America's "large advances to manhood" with England's "dissolution of manners," and wrote with buoyant optimism about America's capacity for improvement. *"The degree of improvement which America has already arrived at is unparalleled and astonishing,"* he wrote, "but 'tis miniature to what she will one day boast of, if heaven continue her happiness."[6]

In Paine's view, commercial growth and the operation of scientific knowledge on America's vast natural resources were the engines of progress. Generally speaking, scientific advance gave many people a strong sense that nature could be harnessed for the general good and that humankind would at last be able to control its own destiny. With the diffusion of useful knowledge and the conquest of nature, it was felt, poverty and injustice would evaporate. Right from the start of his American career, Paine caught this spirit. Arguing that America's "reigning character is the love of science," he praised the American Philosophical Society for continuing the Royal Society's emphasis on "analysis and experiment," and rejoiced that the spread of "useful knowledge" would make America the most enlightened, prosperous, and progressive land in the world. At the *Pennsylvania Magazine*, he hoped that "all questions might be suppressed, but such as may be applicable to some useful purpose in life," and began writing on such topics as the generation of electricity, new types of threshing machines, and new methods of building frame houses. He was using the practical scientific knowledge he had acquired in England to promote the "public good" in America and to participate in the realization of America's potential.[7]

Initially, Paine's perception of American virtue and progress did not assume political dimensions. His first foray into politics came in

---

America is capable of. I have heard whole cargoes of imported Irish say (and swear too), that, when they came a few leagues off the coast, they began to feel a sort of regenerative spirit working within them, something like that which is supposed to work in the good honest methodist, when he imagines himself called from the lapstone to go and honour the pulpit" (Cobbett, *A Kick for a Bite*, p. 28).

6 Paine, "Utility of this Work Evinced," 2: 1109–10; "Useful and Entertaining Hints," *PM*, February 1775, 2: 1022.

7 Paine, "Useful and Entertaining Hints," 2: 1024; "To the Public," *PM*, January 1775; "A Mathematical Question Proposed," *PM*, February 1775; "Description of a New Electrical Machine," *PM*, January 1775; "Description of a New Threshing Instrument," *PM*, February 1775; "New Method of Building Frame Houses in England," *PM*, April 1775.

March 1775 in an article on slavery.[8] Viewing slavery as the one blot on America's character, Paine argued that it was hypocritical for Americans to "complain so loudly of attempts to enslave them, while they hold so many hundred thousands in slavery."[9] At one point, he even implied that British policies towards America represented divine retribution for the sin of slavery. Some observers believed that Paine was obliquely attacking the Patriot cause; it is more likely, however, that he wanted the colonists to realize the implications of their demand for liberty and extend it to all people regardless of race.[10] In other respects, Paine's anti-slavery article reveals much about his emerging outlook. His desire to turn emancipated slaves into useful small property owners provides an early glimpse of his social values.[11] And other characteristics of the article, such as its plain style, its moral indignation, and its attempt to undercut the scriptural justification of oppressive practices like slavery, would reappear in his later work.[12]

8 Paine, "African Slavery in America," *PJ*, 8 March 1775, 2: 16–19. Although almost all his historians attribute to Paine the political "Dialogue between General Wolfe and General Gage in a Wood near Boston," *PJ*, 4 January 1775, I have found no evidence to indicate that Paine was in fact the author. Since he had only been in the country for four weeks when the article was published, and since he was suffering "dreadfully" from typhus, it is highly unlikely that he wrote it.

9 Paine, "African Slavery," 2: 18. Cobbett in the 1790s also highlighted American inconsistency on this issue—although for Cobbett the point was to attack American democrats and not to emancipate slaves. See below, p. 123.

10 John Witherspoon's view in 1777 that when Paine "first came over he was on the other side, and had written pieces against the American cause" (quoted in Aldridge, *Man of Reason*, p. 52) may well owe something to Paine's article on slavery. On the other hand, Paine's position fits perfectly into Bailyn's thesis that opposition to slavery was part of the "spill-over" of the transformation of Real Whig thought during the American Revolution. As Bailyn put it, "the identification between the cause of the colonies and the cause of the Negroes bound in chattel slavery—an identification built into the very language of politics—became inescapable" (Bailyn, *Ideological Origins*, p. 235).

11 If Aldridge is correct in attributing to Paine an article by "Amicus" in *PM*, June 1775, another aspect of Paine's social outlook emerges. "Amicus" wanted to establish a fund to support young people starting off in life and to provide for the old; the same notion appears in the *Rights of Man* and *Agrarian Justice*. Aldridge concludes that Paine did not push his plan any further in Philadelphia because the "climate of opinion in colonial America" was "unreceptive to projects of social assistance" (Aldridge, *Thomas Paine's American Ideology*, p. 30). It is more likely, however, that in the relatively egalitarian society of Philadelphia, Paine did not feel the same need to pursue the project that he came to advocate so forcefully in Europe.

12 Paine, "African Slavery," 2: 18–19.

By April and May, Paine became drawn deeper into politics. As news of Lexington and Concord spread through the colonies, as reports of Britain's new Coercive Acts reached America, and as delegates for the Second Continental Congress converged on Philadelphia, Paine rapidly became radicalized.[13] In his "Reflections on Titles" (May 1775), an article which expressed classic Real Whig sentiments about the "absurdity" and "pomposity" of undeserved titles, Paine aligned himself clearly with the Continental Congress.[14] From that point, he moved on the leading edge of colonial Radicalism; his earlier images of America and Britain became politicized. His first political poem, "Liberty Tree" (July 1775) portrayed America as a land of egalitarianism, brotherhood, and freedom which was trying to protect itself from an aggressive and self-interested Britain. Like many other colonists, Paine equated British "tyranny" not merely with the ministry but with "King, Lords, and Commons"; by implicating the king, the ideological groundwork for independence was being laid.[15]

Paine's "Thoughts on Defensive War" (July 1775) similarly caught the radical colonial mood. Repeating the arguments of Jacob Duché's sermon to the first battalion of Philadelphia, Paine maintained that the Coercive Acts and the Quebec Act represented a twin attack on American political and spiritual liberty.[16] Faced with what he saw as a generalized conspiracy against American freedom, and confronted by a British government which, he later wrote, "looked on conquest as certain and infallible," Paine fully supported the declaration of Congress that Americans must be prepared to fight for their freedom. He used the same argument in *Common Sense*.[17]

As Paine became politicized, his writing style settled into its char-

13 For some general reactions to Lexington and Concord, see *PJ*, 26 April 1775 and 10 May 1775; for Paine's later comments about the impact of these battles on his own viewpoint, see *American Crisis VII*, 1: 143–44.

14 Paine, "Reflections on Titles," *PM*, May 1775, 2: 33–34.

15 Paine, "Liberty Tree," *PM*, July 1775, 2: 1091–92; Maier, *From Resistance to Revolution*, pp. 237–41, 288–94.

16 The Coercive Acts were passed by Parliament in response to the Boston Tea Party. Among other things, they closed the port of Boston and sharply curtailed the role of the House of Representatives in the government of Massachusetts. The Quebec Act established an authoritarian system of government in Canada, recognized the position of the Catholic Church there, and extended the boundaries of the province into the continental west. See Neatby, *Quebec: The Revolutionary Age*, pp. 125–41.

17 Paine, "Thoughts on Defensive War," *PM*, July 1775, 2: 53–55; Duché, *Duty of Standing Fast*; Paine, *American Crisis VII*, 1: 144, and *Common Sense*, 1: 17.

acteristic form. During his first months in America, he had experimented with the grand style and had written several light-hearted poems.[18] After Lexington and Concord, all this was dropped; he began writing about political issues in plain speech. Consider the language of his article on titles:

The *Honourable* plunderer of his country, or the *Right Honourable* murderer of mankind, create such a contrast of ideas as exhibit a monster rather than a man. Virtue is inflamed at the violation and sober reason calls it nonsense. . . . Titles overawe the superstitious vulgar, and forbid them to inquire into the character of the possessor; Nay, more, they are . . . bewitched to admire in the great, the vices they would honestly condemn in themselves. This sacrifice of common sense is the certain badge which distinguishes slavery from freedom.[19]

The effective use of oxymoron, the appeal to "sober reason," and above all the "demonic drive to demystify" would remain powerful elements of Paine's writing.[20] The aggressive tone also became typical; Paine would no longer make "humble" applications to his "betters" in England.[21] In his "Thoughts on Defensive War," Paine pulled no punches: Britain was nothing more than a "ruffian," a "plunderer," and an "invader," a kind of political highwayman holding up America. And for the first time, Paine attempted to cut through the "parent-child" image which was still widely used to describe the Anglo-American relationship. "The portrait of a parent red with the blood of her children," he argued, "is a picture fit only for the galleries of the infernals."[22] The metaphorical justification for continued colonial status was being turned against itself.

During the summer of 1775, Paine was heading in a revolutionary

18 Paine, "Reflections on the Life and Death of Lord Clive," 2: 23–27, and "Cupid and Hymen," *PM*, April 1775, 2: 1115–18, are good examples of his writing in the grand style.

19 Paine, "Reflections on Titles," 2: 33. The same attitude appeared in the *Rights of Man, Part 1*, 1: 286–87.

20 On Paine's "demystification," see G. A. Williams, "Tom Paine," pp. 237–38.

21 Compare Paine's letter for reinstatement in the excise service after his first dismissal in which he used the words "humble" and "humbly" six times in 175 words, and the *Case of the Officers of Excise*, which was part of a "humble application to Parliament." Paine to the Board of Excise, 3 July 1766, 2: 1128; Paine, *Case of the Officers of Excise*, 2: 3.

22 Paine, 'Thoughts on Defensive War," 2: 53.

direction; by the autumn, he came out unequivocally for independence. In his view, independence meant more than political emancipation from Britain; it was the political affirmation of American virtue, and was inseparable from humanitarian goals such as the abolition of slavery.[23] With independence, Paine believed, America could establish a new political and moral order. He wrote a few months later that the country "hath a blank sheet to write upon," and in 1783 described himself as "being ranked among the founders of a New Empire raised on the principles of liberty and liberality."[24] The powerful democratic vision which underlay *Common Sense* had its roots not only in Paine's English background but also in the perception of American potential that he developed in 1775.

Bernard Bailyn has written that Paine wanted to "tear the world apart."[25] But an examination of Paine's early American writings indicates that this is only half the story. He was certainly opposed to an Old World society which he perceived as being irrational and unjust, but he was equally committed to a New World of progress and liberty. Paine's positive image of the New World was brought into sharper focus by his experience of the Old, just as his negative image of the Old World was sharpened by his experience of the New. "You ask if I am not a little severe in my strictures upon England," he would later write. "I confess I have no partiality for what is called or understood by, the National Character of England. Had you been in America you would have seen it in a different point of view to what presents itself to you here."[26] Paine believed that America could shake off the corrupting influence of England's national character. The very forces that made Paine want to tear the Old World apart also made him want to turn the New World into the land of liberty.

From this perspective, the power of *Common Sense* becomes more intelligible. To understand that pamphlet fully, it is essential to grasp

---

23 Paine, "A Serious Thought," *PJ*, 18 October 1775, 2: 20. Aldridge plausibly argues that in November 1775 Paine wrote two articles under the pseudonym "A Lover of Order" and "A Continental Farmer," which confirm his place on the cutting edge of colonial Radicalism. As one contemporary noted, "A Lover of Order" displayed a "latent inclination to independency" (Aldridge, *Thomas Paine's American Ideology*, pp. 33–35).

24 Paine, *Forester's Letters*, 2: 82; Paine to a Committee of the Continental Congress, 2: 1228.

25 Bailyn, "Common Sense," p. 20.

26 Paine to anonymous, 1789, 2: 1297.

the intensification and politicization of Paine's mutually reinforcing, mutually exclusive definitions of British corruption and American liberty during 1775. In this process of definition, Paine evolved many of the elements that made *Common Sense* so successful. His sense of American destiny, virtue, and liberty, his perception of British conspiracy and corruption, his hostility to monarchy, his call to arms, his support for independence, his humanitarianism, and his powerful language of demystification—all were central to the impact of *Common Sense*. And all had been expressed by Paine in 1775. In effect, *Common Sense* represented the culmination of Paine's increasingly conflicting definitions of England and America.

II

Common Sense was a transatlantic pamphlet. Reflecting Paine's deep antipathy to the British system of government, and expressing the unbounded optimism of his first year in Philadelphia, its ideology drew on minority British republican and Real Whig traditions which were being transmitted to the New World and transformed into arguments for revolution and independence. The radical ideas Paine had discussed in England were at the centre of political consciousness in America.[27] A marginal figure in Britain, where Real Whig thought was a minority outlook, Paine became an important figure in America, where it was a majority outlook.

Well before Paine arrived in the New World, Real Whig notions had become commonplace in the colonies. Lacking a powerful church and state establishment, but with a broader electorate and a greater degree of independent landholding than Britain, America proved fertile ground for Real Whig thought. The colonists' assimilation of such ideas predisposed them to view Britain's post-1763 attempt to tighten control over its North American empire as part of a broader ministerial conspiracy against liberty. As Americans responded to this perceived threat, the pressure of events forced many of them to alter Real Whig assumptions about the relationship between the government and the governed.[28]

This "radical conceptualization" of Real Whig thought produced

27 On the place of Real Whig thought in the Thirteen Colonies, see Bailyn, *Ideological Origins*.
28 Bailyn, *Ideological Origins*, pp. 22–54, 94–159.

new definitions of representation, consent, constitutionalism, and rights.
While Real Whigs traditionally viewed the "people" as a check on
governmental power, American Radicals came to regard the people
as the actual basis of that power; the active and continuous consent
of the governed, they argued, was the only true foundation of government. While Real Whigs were concerned with restoring the "proper"
balance between monarchy, aristocracy, and democracy in the British
constitution, more and more Americans distinguished between the
principles of the constitution and the practice of the British Parliament.

Arguing that the parliamentary claim to raise taxes in America
violated the fundamental constitutional principle of "no taxation without representation," many colonists asserted that the constitution stood
above, and was separate from, the powers of Parliament. From this
position it was a short step to the view that a written constitution was
necessary to safeguard liberty. The desire to establish first principles
also produced a new approach to the relationship between human
rights and the law. Instead of assuming that the law should define
human rights, it was argued that human rights should define the law.
And through this process of change, there emerged what Bailyn has
called "the realization, the comprehension and fulfillment, of the inheritance of liberty and of what was taken to be America's destiny in
the context of world history."[29]

Paine was at the heart of this ideological transformation; indeed,
in some respects he personified it. At point after point, Paine's political
views in America were based on Real Whig assumptions. Just as Real
Whigs distrusted power and feared corruption, Paine argued that in
Britain the crown was gathering excessive power into its hands through
its use of patronage. Just as Real Whigs viewed Britain's imperial
policy in conspiratorial terms, Paine believed that there was "a secret
and fixed determination in the British Cabinet to annex America to
the crown of England as a conquered country." And just as the colonists pushed Real Whig thought in more radical directions, Paine
moved with them and sometimes beyond them. He moved with them
in his belief that the consent of the people was the basis of legitimate
power, and in his distinction between fundamental first principles and
the actual practice of government. He moved beyond many of them
when he began to turn radicalized Real Whig ideology into a new
vision of democratic republicanism, which insisted upon a "large and

29 Ibid., pp. 19, 160–229.

equal" representation and which rejected the whole concept of balanced government, whether in Britain or in America. In the process, he established himself as the most articulate advocate of American destiny. Paine's writings both reflected and reinforced America's ideological revolution; *Common Sense* transcended traditional Real Whig thought in the Thirteen Colonies.[30]

Within this general relationship between Anglo-American Radicalism and Paine's thought, it is entirely possible that individual Real Whig and republican thinkers influenced *Common Sense*. Paine himself always denied such influences, insisting that he "neither read books nor studied other people's opinions" and that he developed his ideas "without any help from anybody."[31] Yet he was remarkably receptive to the changing current of ideas in 1775, exchanged views with leading colonial Radicals like Benjamin Rush and David Rittenhouse, and probably drew on materials supplied by Franklin in the writing of *Common Sense*.[32] There is no doubt that Paine thought for himself, but he did so in the context of an Anglo-American crisis in which Real Whig and republican writings appeared increasingly relevant. Against this background, the connection between *Common Sense* and the arguments of Joseph Priestley, John Hall, and John Milton is worth exploring.

Paine's indebtedness to Priestley was first suggested by Felix Gilbert, who maintained that *Common Sense* paraphrased the discussion of the origins of government in Priestley's *Essay on the First Principles of Government*.[33] The two works do indeed have much in common. "We must

30 Paine, *Common Sense*, 1: 4–9, 16, 27–29, 37–38, 45; *American Crisis VII*, 1: 144; *American Crisis III*, 1: 84; Paine to Franklin, 24 October 1778, 2: 1153–54.

31 Paine, *Rights of Man, Part 2*, 1: 406n; Aldridge, "Thomas Paine and the New York *Public Advertiser*," p. 377. Ironically, Paine's denial of influence may actually reflect the influence of rhetorical theories which rejected appeals to established authorities and which stressed that an argument must come from the head and the heart. For Benjamin Franklin's and William Godwin's views on this question, see Ginsberg, "Rhetoric of Revolution," p. 151, and Mercer, "Rhetorical Method of Thomas Paine," p. 65.

32 On Paine's receptiveness to popular opinions in 1775, see Adams, *Diary and Autobiography*, 3: 330. For his discussions with Rush and Rittenhouse, see Rush, *Letters*, ed. Butterfield, 2: 1008, and Paine, *The Forester's Letters*, 2: 67. Franklin's offer of materials "towards completing a history of the present transactions" is mentioned in Paine, *American Crisis III*, 1: 88n.

33 Gilbert, "The English Background of American Isolationism," p. 157. In Gilbert's view, "Paine's passages [on the development of representative government] are nothing but a paraphrase of Priestley's words; whoever reads the respective sections of the two books side by side will be inclined to assume that Paine wrote *Common Sense* with Priestley's pamphlet on his desk."

suppose," wrote Priestley, "a number of people existing who experience the inconvenience of living independent and unconnected; who are exposed, without redress, to insults and wrongs of every kind, and are too weak to procure themselves many of the advantages which they are sensible might easily be compassed by united strength." Paine made the same point in much the same language: "Let us suppose," he wrote, "a small number of persons settled in some sequestered part of the earth, unconnected with the rest: they will then represent the first peopling of any country, or of the world."

Like Priestley, Paine continued that the need to overcome the inconveniences and insecurities of the state of nature would impel people to form their own society and government. And where Priestley envisaged direct democracy giving way to rule by representatives as society became more complex, Paine wrote of the transition from a "first parliament [in which] every man by natural right will have a seat" to a legislature "managed by a select number chosen from the whole body, who are supposed to have the same concerns at stake which those have who appointed them, and who will act in the same manner as the whole body would act were they present." Step by step, Paine's argument followed that of Priestley.[34]

Yet the differences between the two men are also instructive, since they reveal much about Paine's attitude to America and his transformation of Priestley's Real Whig philosophy. While Priestley viewed the state of nature purely as a logical abstraction, Paine wrote as if the peaceful and rational progression from the state of nature to society and government had actually occurred in America. For Paine, the state of nature was a "colony" carved out of the "wilderness" and peopled by "newly arrived emigrants." But when he discussed the origin of government in the Old World, he shifted from an implicitly Lockean to an implicitly Hobbesian view, in which the "quiet and defenceless" were ground down by "ruffians" and "plunderers." The inner contradictions remained unexplored, but were closely related to Paine's basic assumptions about the New World and the Old. Even on a subliminal level, Paine tapped a sense of America's distinctiveness and virtue.[35]

34　Priestley, *Essay on the First Principles of Government*, pp. 199–200; Paine, *Common Sense*, 1: 5–6.

35　Priestley, *Essay*, p. 201; Paine, *Common Sense*, 1: 5–6, 13–16. This is not to argue that Paine actually read Locke (or Hobbes, for that matter) on the state of nature. In

Although both men started from similar premises, Paine's conclusions were much more radical than those of Priestley. According to Priestley, republics were only possible in "exceeding small states," and in countries like England the representatives of the people must share power with the king and "hereditary lords"; without such a balance, the polity would collapse in chaos. Paine, as has been seen, completely rejected the mixed constitution. To ensure that "the *elected* might never form to themselves, an interest separate from the electors," he wanted all representatives to be elected by the people, without giving specific social orders special political status. In short, Paine transformed Priestley's philosophical justification of reform into an argument for revolution.[36]

If Paine's arguments about the origins of government drew on and transcended those of Priestley, his discussion of monarchy and hereditary succession was almost certainly based on John Hall's revolutionary Civil War pamphlet, *The Grounds and Reasons of Monarchy Considered* (1650). Paine's indebtedness to Hall was first recognized by Charles Inglis, who dismissed Paine's "crudities" on hereditary succession as a plagiarized version of Hall's "small treatise."[37] Hall's pamphlet had been reprinted in London in 1771, and would thus have been readily available to Paine. Despite Paine's claims to originality, the evidence supports Inglis; there are remarkably close parallels between Hall's and Paine's ideas.[38] This being the case, Paine's writings provide an important link in the transmission of English Civil War republican ideology to the radical edge of the American Revolution.[39]

1807 he commented: "I never read Locke nor ever had the book in my hands, and by what I have heard of it from *Horne Tooke*, I had no inducement to read it. It is a speculative, not a practical work, and the style of it is heavy and tedious, as all Locke's writings are" (quoted in Aldridge, "Thomas Paine and the New York *Public Advertiser*," p. 377). Leaving aside Paine's willingness to pronounce judgment on a book he said he had never read, we cannot be certain whether or not he is telling the truth. But the point remains that Lockean ideas, filtered through men like Priestley, were commonplace in Britain and America during the eighteenth century.

36 Priestley, *Essay*, pp. 200, 203; Paine, *Common Sense*, 1: 6.

37 Inglis, *True Interest of America*, p. 22.

38 Paine claimed in 1807 that he knew of "no author, nor of any work before Common Sense and Rights of Man appeared, that has exposed and attacked hereditary succession on the grounds of illegality, which is the strongest of all grounds to attack it on" (Aldridge, "Thomas Paine and the New York *Public Advertiser*," p. 380).

39 As Christopher Hill wrote, "it is unlikely that the ideas of the seventeenth-century radicals had no influence on the Wilkesite movement, the American Revolution, Thomas

In Hall's view, monarchy was founded on force or fraud. If people
looked back far enough, he argued, they would discover that monarchy arose from "some savage unnatural intrusion, disguiz'd under
some forc'd title or chimerical cognition, or else some violent alteration, or possibly some slender oath or articles, hardly extorted and
imperfectly kept." In principle, he continued, monarchy could only
be established through election, force of arms, or inheritance. If it
originated in election, then it followed that kings were subordinate
to the will of the people. "And here comes in another fallacy, with
which the assertors of royalty have so flourish'd," he added, "that an
agreement between a people and one man should descend to his
posterity." If monarchy arose out of force, it lost all claims to legiti-
macy, and kings should be "remember'd with horror and detestation,
than have that undue reverence with which they commonly meet."
And inheritance which derived from force, Hall concluded, was "merely
illegal, and apt to be shaken off with the first conveniency."[40]

Paine took the same approach and reached the same conclusions.
Just as Hall believed that monarchy began with conquest or chicanery,
Paine asserted that "could we take off the dark covering of antiquity
and trace them [kings] to their first rise, we should find the first of
them nothing better than the principal ruffian of some restless gang;
whose savage manners or pre-eminence in subtilty obtained him the
title of chief among plunderers." Where Hall argued that the basis
of monarchy lay in election, force, or inheritance, Paine wrote that
kings first came about "either by lot, by election, or by usurpation."
Like Hall, he maintained that if monarchy was initially established by
lot or election, a precedent had been set for subsequent generations,
since "to say, that the right of all future generations is taken away, by
the act of the first electors, in their choice not only of a king but of
a family of kings for ever, hath no parallel in or out of scripture but
the doctrine of original sin." The view that each generation has the
right to choose its own governors reached back to Hall and looked

---

Paine or the plebeian radicalism which revived in England during the 1790s. Unlikely:
but such influence is difficult to prove" (Hill, *World Turned Upside Down*, p. 308, and
"Republicanism after the Restoration," pp. 46–51). While the influence of Hall's pamphlet on *Common Sense* cannot be definitively proved, the connections are close enough
to strengthen Hill's argument about the long-term impact of seventeenth-century
radicalism.

40 Hall, "Grounds and Reasons of Monarchy Considered," pp. 6, 9–11.

forward to the *Rights of Man*. Similarly, Paine ruled out monarchy by usurpation as being illegitimate—"and that William the Conqueror was an usurper," he noted, "is a fact not to be contradicted." One can understand Inglis's sense of *déjà vu*.[41]

What is particularly fascinating is the way in which republican arguments from the Civil War could be applied to America's position in 1776. Both Paine and Hall fought against the "prejudice" and "superstition" which buttressed monarchy, and both men believed that the supporters of monarchy could be categorized into the credulous and ignorant, the timid, and the ambitious or powerful who benefitted from tyranny.[42] Over a century before *Common Sense*, Hall anticipated Paine's attack on the parent-child metaphor as a justification for monarchy. And both Paine and Hall argued that monarchy contradicted the "rights of nature" in which all men possessed an equal share of liberty.[43] This is not to say that Paine needed to read Hall to pick up arguments about prejudice, the parent-child metaphor, or the equal rights of nature; such views were becoming common in the Thirteen Colonies during 1775 and 1776. But it is clear that the kind of arguments expressed by Hall in 1650 were increasingly acceptable to radical colonists, including Paine, on the eve of independence.

There were other links between seventeenth-century republicanism and *Common Sense*. As Paine himself admitted, his attempt to show that monarchy was incompatible with the scriptures was taken directly from John Milton.[44] Just as Milton used the Book of Samuel to demonstrate that God was really a republican, Paine argued from the same passage that "all anti-monarchical parts of scripture, have been smoothly glossed over in monarchical governments. . . . That the Almighty hath here entered his protest against monarchical government is true, or the scripture is false."[45] It is also possible that Paine's plan of government for an independent America was modelled on James Harrington's *Oceana*, with "such alterations as he conceived would adapt it to America." This, at any rate, was Charles Inglis's view.[46]

41 Paine, *Common Sense*, 1: 13–16.

42 Hall, "Grounds and Reasons," pp. 3–4; Paine, *Common Sense*, 1: 13, 17–18.

43 Hall, "Grounds and Reasons," p. 11; Paine, *Common Sense*, 1: 10.

44 Paine discussed his use of Milton in a conversation with John Adams shortly after the publication of *Common Sense*. See Adams, *Diary and Autobiography*, 3: 333.

45 Milton, *Defence of the People of England*, 4: 344, and *Tenure of Kings and Magistrates*, 3: 206–7; Paine, *Common Sense*, 1: 10, 12.

46 Inglis, *True Interest of America*, p. 54. Although it is true that Hall's pamphlet

Although much of the force of *Common Sense* lay in its powerful response to the particular issues facing America in 1776, Paine's discussion of the Anglo-American connection rested on certain basic assumptions about the origins of government and the nature of monarchy and hereditary succession. In these areas, the influence of British Real Whigs and republicans was vitally important. Paine's analysis of the origins of government echoes that of Priestley, although Paine's attack on the balanced constitution went well beyond the confines of traditional Real Whig ideology. Paine's arguments about the illegitimacy of hereditary succession virtually repeated those of Hall. And Paine's scriptural attack on monarchy was based on Milton's religious republicanism. Drawing on radical British thought, Paine established the theoretical foundations of his argument for an independent, republican, and democratic United States of America. As he himself commented: "It was in a great measure owing to my bringing a knowledge of England with me to America that I was enabled to enter deeper into politics, and with more success, than other people."[47]

III

The impact of *Common Sense* hinged not only on its place in the "radical conceptualization" of British Real Whig ideas in America, but also on the language in which Paine expressed his political arguments. There was nothing particularly original about Paine's views; his great strength lay in his ability to articulate increasingly popular ideas in a clear and forceful writing style. *Common Sense* was written in the new rhetoric, the style Paine had developed in England's scientific and literary circles, the style in which he felt most comfortable, and the style Americans were increasingly accepting.

Once again, the transatlantic perspective is crucial. Partly as a result of the transmission of British rhetorical theory to the New World, and partly as a result of the internal dynamics of New England Puritanism, there was a "revolution in style" in America during the

---

was bound together with Harrington's works and that Paine's scheme of rotation of offices recalls that of Harrington, the notion of rotating offices was widespread in Anglo-American Radical circles.

47 Paine to Nathanael Greene, 9 September 1780, 2: 1189.

eighteenth century.[48] Colonial ministers began to criticize "affected diction, abounding with *great swelling words of vanity*, and those pompous high-flown metaphors, which under the pretence of containing some very sublime mysteries and profound sense, are only a jingle and play of words."[49] In the American universities this trend towards the plain style began to register during the 1740s.[50] William Small transmitted Scottish theories of rhetoric to students at William and Mary in the early 1760s, while John Witherspoon (with whom Paine worked on the *Pennsylvania Magazine*) taught the new rhetoric at Princeton between 1768 and 1794. In Witherspoon's view, the plain style was characteristic of republican states where the "manners of a people are little polished," in contrast to the "obsequious subjection" and "pompous swelling" of language in monarchical and aristocratic regimes.[51] William Duncan's *Elements of Logick* was circulated in the colonies, and almost certainly shaped the rhetorical structure of Jefferson's Declaration of Independence.[52] And Benjamin Franklin's contempt for "the false Glosses of Oratory," together with his insistence that effective writing must be "*smooth, clear*, and *short*," clearly expressed the changing outlook.[53] The rhetoric Paine brought from England was perfectly suited to an American audience; the plain style was becoming the dominant one in America.

Both the organization and the language of *Common Sense* reflected new rhetorical principles. The actual arguments of the pamphlet were conducted in four separate but related sections, of which the first two addressed the broader "theoretical" question of government. In these sections, Paine adopted a synthetic argumentative structure, and based his argument on supposedly self-evident first principles. He began with a discussion of "the origin and design of government in general, with concise remarks on the English constitution."[54] After describing

48 H. M. Jones, "American Prose Style," pp. 117, 133; P. Miller, *New England Mind*, pp. 331–62.

49 Quoted in Jones, "American Prose Style," p. 130.

50 The gradual transition in rhetoric in American universities is described in Perrin, "Teaching of Rhetoric," and Guthrie, "Development of Rhetorical Theory."

51 Quoted in Howell, *Logic and Rhetoric*, p. 680.

52 Howell, "Declaration of Independence," pp. 464–83.

53 Franklin, *Papers*, 1: 264, 329. See also Jorgenson, "Sidelights on Benjamin Franklin's Principles of Rhetoric," pp. 208–22.

54 Paine, *Common Sense*, 1: 4.

the progression from the state of nature to representative government in language reminiscent of Priestley, Paine established his basic premises. The purpose of government, he maintained, was to provide freedom and security. "And however our eyes may be dazzled with show, or our ears deceived by sound; however prejudice may warp our wills, or interest darken our understanding," he wrote, "the simple voice of nature and reason will say, 'tis right." This paved the way for his second premise. "I draw my idea of the form of government," continued Paine, "from a principle in nature which no art can overturn, viz. that the more simple any thing is, the less liable it is to be disordered, and the easier repaired when disordered."[55] In reasoning from such principles, Paine was following the method which had been recommended by Duncan and which Priestley himself had advocated in his own lectures on rhetoric.[56]

If mathematicians could attain certainty through proceeding from incontrovertible descriptive axioms, Paine believed he could achieve the same results in politics through proceeding from incontrovertible prescriptive maxims.[57] With these maxims in mind, he examined the "much boasted Constitution of England" to demonstrate that it was not only "exceedingly complex" but also "imperfect, subject to convulsions, and incapable of providing what it seems to promise."[58] Through this approach, Paine attempted to break down the wall of respect for the constitution which threatened to imprison the revolutionary movement in 1776. Americans should recognize that the constitution was fundamentally irrational, he concluded, and re-establish government according to the simple and straightforward principles of reason and nature.

The second section of *Common Sense* dealt with monarchy and hereditary succession; this was the part that drew heavily on John Hall and John Milton. Adopting the premise that men "were originally

55 Ibid., 1: 6.

56 For Priestley's theory of rhetoric, see Howell, *Logic and Rhetoric*, pp. 632–47.

57 A classic eighteenth-century example of a self-evident proposition in mathematics was "the whole is greater than any one of its parts"; there is, of course, a fundamental qualitative difference between such a statement and the political maxim that "the purpose of government is freedom and security." The former describes what is; the latter describes what ought to be. Moreover, the political maxim begs questions about the nature of and relationship between "freedom" and "security," and about the potential consequences of its application in a particular historical and social setting.

58 Paine, *Common Sense*, 1: 6–7.

equals in the order of creation," Paine inquired "how a race of men came into the world so exalted above the rest" and argued that hereditary rule violated the "equal rights of nature" and the "will of the Almighty." At the same time, he examined the practical consequences of monarchy to discover whether kings were "the means of happiness or of misery to mankind." Standing on its head the traditional view that hereditary succession provided peace and stability, he baldly asserted that monarchy had produced "no less than eight civil wars and nineteen rebellions" in England alone, and had laid the world in "blood and ashes." Examining hereditary rule on the grounds of reason and utility, Paine found it wanting on both counts.[59]

Having attempted to shatter America's increasingly fragile attachment to the mixed constitution and monarchy, Paine turned his attention to the particulars of Anglo-American relations. He had, as he put it, "no other preliminaries to settle with the reader"; he had established the principles of his argument and would now "offer nothing more than simple facts, plain arguments, and common sense." The rest of the pamphlet was conditioned by his response to the immediate issues facing Americans in the winter of 1775–76; the mode of argument shifted from the synthetic to the analytic.

Presenting a lawyer's brief for independence, the third section ("on the present state of American affairs") confronted and rejected the central arguments in favour of reconciliation. Against the view that colonial prosperity and security depended on the union with Britain, Paine argued that America "would have flourished as much, and probably much more, had no European power taken any notice of her," and that the imperial connection only embroiled the New World in the dynastic squabbles of the Old. Against the notion that Britain was the mother country, Paine commented that "even brutes do not devour their young," and added that "the persecuted lovers of civil and religious liberty from *every part* of Europe" had fled "not from the tender embraces of the mother, but from the cruelty of the monster." And against the position that Britain could be persuaded to treat the American colonies with justice, Paine maintained that "America is only a secondary object in the system of British politics," that Britain "consults the good of this country no further than it answers her own purpose," and that Britain's "own interest leads her to suppress the growth of ours in every case which doth not promote her advantage."

59 Ibid., 1: 9–16.

"To bring the matter to one point," he stated, "Is the power who is
jealous of our prosperity, a proper power to govern us? Whoever says
No, to this question, is an Independent. . . ."[60]

After clearing the ground for independence, he then outlined a
plan for an American constitution which would enshrine fundamental
principles such as freedom of conscience and security of property,
establish an annually elected and unicameral Congress, and rotate the
presidency among men from each colony. It was characteristic of Paine
not to leave things hanging; where there was room for concrete proposals, he would supply them.

The same practical approach informed the fourth section of the
pamphlet, which attempted to demonstrate that America had the
ability to emancipate itself from colonialism and which insisted that
"the present time is preferable to all others." This was Paine at his
most pragmatic; he bent in his favour all the evidence he could find
to argue that America could sustain the cost of war, draw on its natural
resources to defend itself, raise its own fleet, and defeat the Royal
Navy. Carrying the reader along by the sheer pace of his arguments,
Paine left a trail of contradictions behind him. When examining America's strengths, he counted the absence of a national debt as an advantage; but when acknowledging that war with Britain would involve
heavy expenditures, he cheerfully remarked that "no nation ought to
be without a debt" since it acted as a "national bond."[61] Or again, the
man who had written in 1775 that America "has now outgrown the
state of infancy" informed his readers in *Common Sense* that "the infant
state of the colonies . . . is an argument in favour of independence"

60 Ibid., 1: 17–21, 25–26. In the Appendix to *Common Sense*, added six weeks after
the first edition, Paine approached the question of independence or reconciliation from
the angle of first principles. The notion that British and American interests were
irreconcilable, he argued, was a "self-evident position," since "no nation in a state of
foreign dependence, limited in its commerce, and cramped and fettered in its legislative
powers, can ever arrive at any material eminence." He also returned to his principle
of simplicity to argue that independence was easier and more practicable than reconciliation. "He who takes nature for his guide," wrote Paine, "is not easily beaten out of
his argument, and on that ground, I answer generally—*That* independence *being a
single simple line, contained within ourselves; and reconciliation, a matter exceedingly perplexed
and complicated, and in which a treacherous capricious court is to interfere, gives the answer
without a doubt.*" Paine, *Common Sense*, 1: 41, 43. For Paine, the "theoretical" and "practical" arguments for independence were in perfect harmony.

61 Ibid., 1: 31–32.

because the growth of commerce sapped the spirit of patriotism and military defence.[62]

Intellectual coherence was a secondary consideration; the point was to marshall every available argument to persuade Americans that the time was ripe for independence. In keeping with this pragmatic approach, Paine concluded the pamphlet not with a peroration to liberty, but with a summary of the practical case for a Declaration of Independence, including the argument that such a declaration would enable America to receive much needed assistance from France and Spain.[63] While the first half of *Common Sense* had reasoned from first principles to establish the case for republicanism, the second half moved from a practical and pragmatic discussion of the details to argue that independence was desirable, necessary, and possible.

Not only the structure but also the style of *Common Sense* corresponded to the new rhetoric. Presenting his views in clear, straightforward prose, and insisting that language must reflect the facts, Paine criticized his opponents for hiding weak arguments behind dazzling eloquence. Consider, for example, his remarks on the rhetorical justification of Britain's balanced constitution. "It will always happen," he wrote, "that the nicest construction that words are capable of, when applied to something which either cannot exist, or is too incomprehensible to be within the compass of description, will be words of sound only, and though they may amuse the ear, they cannot inform the mind."[64]

Rejecting the customary glorification of Britain's system of government, Paine portrayed himself as someone who conveyed plain truth in plain language, exposing and exploding the myths that enslaved mankind. The mixed constitution, he argued, was actually a confusing and contradictory form of government behind which the monarchy steadily increased its power. The king checked the Commons, on the principle that he was more trustworthy than the Commons, yet the Commons also checked the king on the principle that he was less trustworthy. Once the rhetorical smokescreen had been penetrated, Paine argued, the "miraculous" constitution could be seen in its true light—a "mere absurdity." For Paine, the essence of common sense

62 Paine, "Utility of this Work Evinced," 2: 1109; *Common Sense*, 1:36.
63 Paine, *Common Sense*, 1: 39.
64 Paine, *Common Sense*, 1: 8.

was to make rhetoric correspond to reality rather than distorting it. Once this was accomplished, the "local or long standing prejudices" which warped men's wills would be cleared away to make room for Reason.[65]

Together with the appeal to reason, Paine also attempted to engage the feelings of his readers. Feelings, he wrote, "distinguish us from the herd of common animals. The social compact would dissolve, and justice be extirpated from the earth, or have only a casual existence were we callous to the touches of affection." After one of the most heated passages of *Common Sense* ("Hath your property been destroyed before your face? Are your wife and children destitute of a bed to lie on, or bread to live on? Have you lost a parent or a child by their hands. . . ?"), Paine immediately paused to explain himself. "This is not inflaming or exaggerating matters," he commented, "but trying them by those feelings and affections which nature justifies, and without which we should be incapable of discharging the social duties of life, or enjoying the felicities of it." Adopting the position that benevolent affections cemented the social compact, Paine argued that Britain's actions at Lexington and Concord had irrevocably broken the feelings of friendship which must unite a political community. Quoting Milton's *Paradise Lost* (actually from the words of Satan, much to his opponents' delight), Paine concluded that "never can true reconcilement grow where wounds of deadly hate hath pierced so deep."[66]

At all the key points—in its organization, its style, its assumption that language must correspond to the facts, and its attempt to balance reason and feelings—*Common Sense* belonged to the new rhetorical tradition. But if the revolution in rhetoric helps to explain the form of *Common Sense*, it cannot account for the tone. The sense of anger in the pamphlet sprang directly from Paine's experiences in England. The anger may have been controlled and disciplined, but it was no less real. Releasing the pent-up frustrations of his past, Paine attacked sacred political institutions in a tone of political blasphemy.[67] His approach to monarchy in England was typical: "A French bastard landing with an armed banditti and establishing himself king of England against the consent of the natives," he wrote, echoing popular notions

65 Ibid., 1: 7–8.

66 Ibid., 1: 30, 22–23. See also Wills, *Inventing America*, p. 315.

67 For the reactions of Paine's contemporaries to the anger of *Common Sense*, see Inglis, *True Interest of America*, p. 43; Rationalis, "Appendix to *Plain Truth*," p. 39; Cato [William Smith], *PL*, 30 March 1776, 13 April 1776, 20 April 1776, 27 April 1776.

of the Norman yoke, "is in plain terms a very paltry rascally original."[68]
The irreverent attitude, intended to shock his readers into their senses, was matched by an irreverent sense of humour.[69] "In England,"
argued Paine, "a king hath little more to do than to make war and
give away places; which, in plain terms, is to impoverish the nation
and set it together by the ears. A pretty business indeed for a man to
be allowed eight hundred thousand sterling a year for, and worshipped into the bargain! Of more worth is one honest man to society,
and in the sight of God, than all the crowned ruffians that ever lived."[70]
The technique was effective; Paine attempted to make his readers
laugh with him at the expense of monarchy, and then abruptly switched
his tone to assert the value of "usefulness" and "honesty" against the
parasitic corruption of hereditary rule.

Elsewhere in the pamphlet, the humour was dropped altogether.
After Lexington and Concord, Paine told his audience, he "rejected
the hardened, sullen-tempered Pharoah of England for ever; and
disdain the wretch, that with the pretended title of FATHER OF HIS
PEOPLE can unfeelingly hear of their slaughter, and composedly sleep
with their blood upon his soul." This kind of language electrified the
colonies; the phrases still rang in John Adams's mind nearly thirty
years later, and must have sharpened the impact of *Common Sense* in
1776.[71]

As in his earlier American writings, the obverse of Paine's anger
with the British government was his hope for the American people.
For Paine, independence was the key to the future of humankind;
Common Sense was a classic statement of America's potential to become
an Empire of Liberty. He repeatedly referred to the country as a
"sanctuary" or "asylum" for the "persecuted lovers of civil and reli-

68 Paine, *Common Sense*, 1: 14. On the myth of the Norman yoke, see Hill, *Puritanism
and Revolution*, pp. 50–122.

69 Paine was acutely aware of the shock-value of strong language. "It is necessary
to be bold," he wrote in 1802. "Some people can be reasoned into sense, and others
must be shocked into it. Say a bold thing that will stagger them, and they will begin to
think." Paine to Elihu Palmer, 21 February 1802, 2: 1426. See also Paine, *Rights of
Man, Part 2*, 1: 421.

70 Paine, *Common Sense*, 1: 16.

71 Ibid., 1: 25. In 1802, Adams recalled that "the phrases, suitable for an Emigrant
from New Gate, or one who had chiefly associated with such Company, such as 'The
Royal Brute of England,' 'The Blood Upon his Soul,' and a few others of equal delicacy,
had as much Weight with the People as his Arguments" (Adams, *Diary and Autobiography*,
3: 333).

gious liberty" in Europe, and believed that "a race of men, perhaps
as numerous as all Europe contains, are to receive their portion of
freedom from the events of a few months." This was not just a tactical
statement, intended to fire the spirits of the colonists to fight for
independence. His conviction that freedom depended on the fate of
America remained with him long after the colonists had shaken off
British political rule.

Paine was a secular prophet; America was the Promised Land. *Common Sense* outlined a blueprint for the Empire of Liberty, with a democratic constitution, a strong continental government, a powerful navy
for defence and commerce, and a national debt serviced by the western lands. An independent America would still be a city on a hill; in
fact, it would become, because of independence, *the* city on a hill.
Through *Common Sense*, Paine called on Americans to renounce their
political and emotional ties with the Old World and to fulfil the potential of the New, where it was now possible *"to begin government at
the right end."*[72]

IV

As might be expected, Paine's arguments for independence and his
vision of America's future generated intense controversy in the colonies. "We ought not now to be debating whether we shall be independent or not," he wrote in the appendix to *Common Sense*, "but
anxious to accomplish it on a firm, secure, and honourable basis."[73]
His pamphlet forced a debate not only over independence itself, but
also over the form it should take. On the question of independence,
Common Sense provoked a Loyalist literary counter-offensive spearheaded by James Chalmers, William Smith, and Charles Inglis.[74] As
for the nature of an independent America, Paine's arguments opened
up divisions between the patriots which had previously remained beneath the surface.

In the Loyalist view, Paine was a dangerous Utopian who wanted
to impose abstract theories of republicanism and democracy on the

72 Paine, *Common Sense*, 1: 19, 21, 30–37, 42–44. See also Paine, *To the Citizens of the United States*, 2: 956.

73 Paine, *Common Sense*, 1: 46.

74 The William Smith referred to here was the provost of the College of Philadelphia and should not be confused with William Smith of New York, the Loyalist lawyer who later became chief justice of Quebec.

complex realities of American society. Against his constitutional icon-
oclasm and his anti-historical outlook, Paine's Loyalist opponents argued that Britain's balanced constitution was a source of stability,
peace, and prosperity which embodied the wisdom of ages.[75] Although
it was true that problems had occurred, these lay in human frailty
rather than the system itself; Smith commented that Paine argued
"from the *abuse* of things against the *use* of them," and Chalmers
believed that the constitution was "as near to perfection as human
kind can bear."[76] Paine's attack on monarchy and hereditary succession, according to the Loyalists, could not be justified on either theoretical or practical grounds. All the Loyalist replies to *Common Sense*
stressed that Paine's arguments flew in the face of accepted eighteenth-
century constitutional thought. William Smith astutely turned Real
Whig writings against Paine, and defended the balanced constitution
by quoting "those who are acknowledged to have stood foremost in
their opposition to the encroachment of monarchy."[77] And Smith was
right; Paine had indeed travelled far beyond the original British Real
Whig position.

Turning from theory to practice, the Loyalists contended that independence would plunge America into anarchy; without the guiding
hand of Britain, it was argued, America would tear itself apart, paving
the way for a latter-day Cromwell to impose a military dictatorship.
Moreover, an independent America would be dangerously vulnerable
to the older European empires; lacking adequate means of defence,
America ran the risk of replacing mild British rule with Bourbon
tyranny. From this perspective, Paine—the "stranger intermeddling
in our affairs"—had to be stopped in his tracks before he brought
disaster to the Thirteen Colonies.[78]

Yet while Paine's adversaries regarded independence as unnecessary, impractical, and dangerous, they were less certain about how to
reconcile the conflict between Britain and America. Chalmers simply
side-stepped the issue completely; Inglis and Smith wanted negotiations, presumably on the basis of Lord North's proposals. As Inglis
put it, "America should insist that the claim of parliamentary taxation

75 Inglis, *True Interest*, pp. 18, 52–53; Chalmers, *Plain Truth*, p. 34; Rationalis,
"Appendix to *Plain Truth*," p. 40; Smith, *PL*, 20 April 1776. For a stimulating study
of Loyalist thought, see Potter, *Liberty We Seek*.

76 Smith, *PL*, 20 April 1776; Chalmers, *Plain Truth*, p. 19.

77 Smith, *PL*, 27 April 1776.

78 Smith, *PL*, 23 March 1776, 30 March 1776; Chalmers, *Plain Truth*, pp. 9, 35.

be either explicitly relinquished; or else, such security given as the case will admit, as may be equivalent to a formal relinquishment, that this claim shall not be exerted." In Smith's view, "the true interest of America lies in *reconciliation* with Great Britain, upon *constitutional principles*, and I can truly say, I wish it upon no other terms."[79]

But what if reconciliation upon constitutional principles could not be obtained? Inglis refused to admit such a possibility. Smith thought it unlikely, but noted that if Britain attempted to subvert American liberties in the future, the colonists could fall back on the resistance methods they had developed during the Stamp Act crisis. In the event, the choices actually made by Smith and Inglis were very different. Smith eventually decided that reconciliation upon constitutional principles was impossible, reluctantly came to accept independence, and in later life tried to suppress his writings of early 1776. Inglis, in contrast, wound up in exile as the Church of England bishop of Nova Scotia, finding Paineites under every bed. Men who were united against *Common Sense* could and did take opposite sides when weighing the balance of risks between independence (the threat from within) and continued dependence (the threat from without). At any rate, it was clearly possible to entertain the idea of independence despite, rather than because of, Paine's arguments.

Two other points need to be made about the Loyalist response to *Common Sense*. First, there is no doubt that the Loyalists had been forced on the defensive. Before January 1776, independence had been, as Paine put it, "a doctrine scarce and rare"; after *Common Sense*, the onus was on the Loyalists to discredit Paine.[80] Reacting to events rather than shaping them, the Loyalists conducted the debate over independence in Paine's terms of reference, and implicitly conceded the enormous influence of *Common Sense* on colonial consciousness.

Second, in a wider context, the controversy over *Common Sense* was in some respects a dress rehearsal for the Paine-Burke debate during the French Revolution. Burke's reverential attitude to the British constitution was remarkably similar to that of the Loyalists, while Paine's position in the *Rights of Man*, that Britain did not even possess a

---

79 Inglis, *True Interest*, p. 62; Smith, *PL*, 16 March 1776.

80 Paine, *American Crisis III*, 1: 87. Paine also commented that before January 1776 "it would have been unsafe for a man to have expressed independence in any public company and after the appearance of that pamphlet [*Common Sense*] it was as dangerous to speak against it" (Paine, "To a Committee of the Continental Congress," 2: 1229).

constitution, was first expressed during his literary conflict with William Smith.[81] Similarly, Burke shared the Loyalists' sense of the importance of tradition, while Paine's subsequent insistence on the right of each generation to act for itself had its roots in *Common Sense*.[82] And Paine's emphasis on first principles, together with the Loyalist view that Paine's "fine-spun political theories" were like the "quackeries of mountebank doctors," would reappear in 1791 and 1792.[83] The difference was, of course, that arguments which were so influential in America failed to dislodge the "political nation" in Britain. From his exile in Nova Scotia, Charles Inglis must have watched the outcome of the Paine-Burke debate with deep satisfaction.

Apart from challenging the Loyalist position, *Common Sense* also raised new questions about the structure of government in an independent America. The main area of contention centred on Paine's constitutional proposals, particularly his support of unicameral assemblies. People who welcomed the anti-colonial elements of *Common Sense* disagreed over his plan of government; some argued that it concentrated too much power in Congress, while others gave Paine their full support. Such differences, at a time when Patriot leaders emphasized the need for unity, clearly worried John Adams. "Common Sense," argued Adams, "by his crude, ignorant Notion of a Government by one Assembly, will do more Mischief, in dividing the Friends of Liberty, than all the Tory Writings together."[84] To counter Paine's proposals and to unite the colonists behind a sounder scheme, Adams published his *Thoughts on Government* in the spring of 1776. Fearing that an unchecked assembly would produce capricious, cumbersome and arbitrary government, Adams insisted that the legislative, executive, and judicial powers should be balanced against one

81 In May 1776 Paine wrote that "in Pennsylvania, as well as in England, there is *no Constitution*, but only a *temporary form of government*"; in a footnote he added that *"this distinction will be more fully explained in some future letter"* (Paine, *Forester's Letters*, 2: 85). As Aldridge has recently argued, Paine "fully explained" his position shortly afterwards in the hitherto unattributed *Four Letters on Interesting Subjects* (Aldridge, *Thomas Paine's American Ideology*, pp. 219–39).

82 Thus one of Paine's main objections to hereditary succession was that "the right of all future generations [to elect their leaders] is taken away" (Paine, *Common Sense*, 1: 14).

83 Compare, for example, Rationalis, "Appendix to *Plain Truth*," p. 40 and Inglis, *True Interest*, pp. 52–53, with Bowles, *Protest Against T. Paine's "Rights of Man*," pp. 6–7, and "A Farmer," *Plain and Earnest Address to Britons*, pp. 6, 11.

84 Quoted in A. King, "Thomas Paine in America," pp. 99–100.

another. In this way, he argued, Americans could prevent the emergence of tyranny from above or below.[85]

Beneath these constitutional arguments lay deeper questions of the relationship between power and liberty, and the collective identity of the new American republic which Paine and Adams envisioned. Paine was as aware as other colonists that the "mob" posed dangers to liberty, but he believed that a democratic constitution would involve the people, respond to their needs, and ensure stability, prosperity, and humanitarian reform.[86] Adams, on the other hand, was convinced that an unchecked democracy would result in "confusion and every evil work."[87] One senses that the same fears of "democratic tyranny" expressed by the Loyalists haunted the mind of Adams, although of course he felt that such problems could be overcome. Yet the deeper questions remained, and the debate over America's identity reverberated right through to the 1790s, when Paine's *Rights of Man* further divided Americans and when Cobbett emerged as the chief opponent of Paineite democracy.

This is to look ahead, however. Immediately after *Common Sense*, Paine's central task was to establish and consolidate the American Empire of Liberty. As the conflict with Britain escalated into full-scale war, and as the Patriot cause suffered severe setbacks, Paine responded with his *American Crisis* papers. Military defeat, the retreat into Valley Forge, the danger from internal enemies of the Revolution, inflation, bankruptcy—all these issues prompted Paine to use his pen to boost morale. By 1783, he was able to proclaim victory. America, he wrote, had effected "the completest and greatest revolution the world ever knew," and "need never be ashamed to tell her birth, nor relate the stages by which she rose to empire."[88] Nevertheless, the task of combining the revolution for liberty with the rise to empire continued to pose acute problems for American Patriots. After *Common Sense*, Paine's commitment to liberty found its clearest expression in his support for the Philadelphia Radicals who pushed through the remarkably democratic Pennsylvania Constitution of 1776. But his commitment to empire impelled him to support a strong and united

85 J. Adams, "Thoughts on Government," *Life and Works of John Adams*, ed. C. F. Adams, 4: 189–200.

86 Paine, *Common Sense*, 1: 27–30.

87 J. Adams, *Diary and Autobiography*, 3: 333.

88 Paine, *American Crisis XIII*, 1: 230–31.

central government, together with a national bank—policies that alienated many of his former Radical allies.

Initially, Paine viewed continental unity primarily as a defensive measure against British military aggression and attempts to choke off trade between the United States and the West Indies. Such unity was, he wrote, "our Magna Charta—our anchor in the world of empires."[89] Yet he also believed that a powerful central government had a positive, dynamic, and creative role in building America's own empire through opening up international markets and establishing a cohesive national economy. Although he did not address the matter systematically, it is clear that Paine envisaged a symbiotic relationship between political unity and economic growth. A national government, in his view, could secure conditions favourable to commercial enterprise, and commercial enterprise would in turn harmonize the discordant elements of American society. Through commerce, the various sectional interests of the United States would be linked together; income from the New England fisheries, for example, would pay for grain from the middle states and tobacco from the south, while the tobacco states themselves would benefit from the breaking of the British monopoly of their trade. "Wealth like water soon spreads over the surface, let the place of entrance be ever so remote," Paine argued; "and in like manner, any portion of strength which is lost or gained to any one or more States, is lost or gained to the whole." The reciprocal benefits of commerce, along with the operations of "social affections," would act as a centripetal force on Americans of different backgrounds, religions, languages, and customs, and thus strengthen the political coherence of the new republic.[90]

With this outlook, Paine supported the Bank of North America as a means of establishing the infrastructure for commercial growth. "The whole community derives benefit from the operation of the bank," he wrote. "It facilitates the commerce of the country. It quickens the means of purchasing and paying for country produce, and hastens on the exportation of it." The bank, he continued, not only established sound credit, kept specie in the country, and increased the quantity of circulating cash, but also enabled Americans to promote "several great improvements, such as inland navigation, building

89 Paine, *Six Letters to Rhode Island*, 2: 341; see also *Common Sense*, 1: 44.
90 Paine, *Peace, and the Newfoundland Fisheries*, 2: 191, 200–201; *Public Good*, 2: 305;. *Rights of Man, Part 2*, 1: 357–60.

bridges, opening roads of communication . . . and other matters of a public benefit." In short, Paine regarded the bank as an integral part of the rising American empire.[91]

Paine's view of empire was unequivocally expansionist; the United States, he insisted, must assert itself in the Atlantic and must fulfil its destiny to conquer the continent. Thus he argued during the War of Independence that the republic should claim its "right" of access to the Newfoundland fisheries to promote American commerce and provide a "Nursery for Seamen" to strengthen America's naval power. The Newfoundland fisheries issue, he maintained, was a "great political question, involving with it the means and channels of commerce, and the probability of empire."[92] He also argued that if Nova Scotia and Canada became more populous (an event he considered unlikely), they would become more and more Americanized, paving the way for their emancipation from Britain and absorption into the Empire of Liberty.[93] Turning his attention to the west, Paine pressed hard for central control over the new lands. The establishment of additional states, he argued, would spread the principles of representative government, while the profits from selling new land would be "capable of defraying the expenses of empire."[94] To modern minds, American expansionism is often equated with American aggression; for Paine, nothing could have been further from the truth. The whole point of the exercise, in his view, was to make still more "room upon the earth for honest men to live in."[95]

In pursuing his empire-building strategy, Paine made many enemies. If his vision of liberty, his political egalitarianism, his unicameralism, and his support for the Pennsylvania Constitution alarmed conservative American Patriots, his approach to empire offended many of the Radicals. Paine's commitment to free enterprise (after a brief flirtation with price controls in 1779) and his defence of the bank led him into an alliance with former antagonists like the conservative financier Robert Morris, much to the surprise and anger of the anti-aristocratic Constitutional Party in Pennsylvania. Similarly, Paine's be-

91 Paine, *Dissertations on Government*, 2: 397, 413.
92 Paine, *Peace, and the Newfoundland Fisheries*, 2: 199, 202.
93 Paine, *Letter to the Abbé Raynal*, 2: 257–59.
94 Paine, *Public Good*, 2: 327, 330.
95 Paine, *American Crisis IV*, 1: 105.

lief in strong central government—a stance that led him to support the Federal Constitution of 1787 despite some reservations—disturbed those democrats who feared that such a concentration of power would undermine liberty in America. And Paine's argument that the national government should control the west was not well received by Virginia politicians who insisted that their own state had prior claims on the continent. To many American Radicals, Paine's position on these matters must have seemed at best perverse and at worst a form of betrayal. Walking the tightrope between Empire and Liberty, Paine never recaptured the degree of Patriot support which his attack on monarchy brought him in 1776.[96]

As some of his contemporaries pointed out, Paine was most effective at the moment of revolution, shattering old beliefs, values, and attitudes, and inspiring his readers with a new vision of a new world.[97] Although he made a significant contribution to the debate on the Empire of Liberty, it remains true that by the early 1780s, when the revolution had clearly triumphed, his importance in American political life was gradually diminishing. After the War of Independence, Paine displayed a certain restlessness; he planned a history of the American Revolution which he never wrote, he reminded Congress that he had donated most of his royalties to the cause, and he tried with mixed success to receive financial recognition for his services.

Without the catalyst of crisis, Paine became increasingly preoccupied with his earlier scientific interests. It was his plan to build a new, single-arch iron bridge, and not politics, which took him back to France and England in 1787. He only intended to stay for a year; in fact, he remained for fifteen. Far from drawing to a close, Paine's political career took a dramatic new turn under the impact of the French Revolution. Defending the French Revolution from its conservative enemies, and writing the most popular political work Britain had ever

96 The best analysis of Paine's republicanism between 1776 and 1787 is that of Foner, *Tom Paine*, pp. 107–209. It should be noted that despite his claims that he did not write for money, Paine was paid by Morris for writing in defence of the bank. As David Hawke remarked, "Paine could be, and would be, bought" (Hawke, *Paine*, p. 102, 123–26, 133–35). Hawke also pointed out that Paine did not change his views for money.

97 See, for example, John Adams to Abigail Adams, 19 March 1776, in *Adams Family Correspondence*, 1: 363, and the comments of Madame Roland quoted in Foner, *Tom Paine*, p. xvi.

seen, Paine transmitted the democratic republican ideology he had developed in America back to his native country. Just as *Common Sense* had been part of the transformation of Real Whig ideology in America, the *Rights of Man* became part of the transformation of political Radicalism in Britain.

III

The Rights of Man, *1791–92*

WHEN PAINE returned to England in 1787, he was warmly welcomed by Real Whigs who had sympathized with the American cause and absorbed American revolutionary ideology. A source of inspiration rather than a model to be imitated, the American Revolution opened up fundamental questions of rights, representation, and constitutionalism which were directly relevant to Britain.[1] While Edmund Burke tried to shift the ground away from such "theoretical" issues, men like John Cartwright and the Earl of Abingdon began to combine American revolutionary thought with older forms of British Radicalism.[2]

Under the influence of America, Cartwright rejected the notion that liberty existed in "custom and usage" or among "mouldy parchments," and argued instead that "*personality* is the *sole* foundation of the *right* of being *represented*." Yet he refused to embrace republicanism, and insisted that the purpose of reform was to restore the British constitution to its pre-Norman purity.[3] Similarly, Abingdon followed American ideology in arguing that the constitution was separate and distinct from Parliament and that "the *Constitution* . . . [was] anterior to the Law," but he also maintained that the fundamental principles

1 The relationship between the American Revolution and English Radicalism is discussed at length in Bonwick, *English Radicals and the American Revolution*, and Sheps, "English Radicalism and Revolutionary America." See also Sheps, "The American Revolution," pp. 3–28.

2 For Burke's attempt to move the debate away from abstract questions of rights, see Burke, *Letter*, pp. 46–57. Abingdon immediately replied in his *Thoughts on the Letter of Edmund Burke*.

3 Cartwright, *American Independence*, pp. 7–9, 27, 63–68, and *Take Your Choice!*, pp. 22, 61–77.

of the constitution were enshrined in the Magna Carta.[4] Such appeals to the past gave Radicalism a form of respectability; the rationale for reform remained rooted in precedent. It was not until the *Rights of Man* that a popular Radical work refused to compromise with history and attempted to apply fully the lesson of America to Britain.[5]

The chief point of contact between Real Whig thought during the American Revolution and the new popular Radicalism of the 1790s was the Society for Constitutional Information (SCI) founded in 1780 in reaction to the government's policies in both Britain and America. Although the SCI's entrance fee of one guinea limited membership to the propertied, the organization flooded the country with cheap political pamphlets supporting the American Patriots and pressing for parliamentary reform. By 1787, when Paine himself was made a member, the society had issued as many as 100,000 copies of Real Whig works.[6] One such publication, Cartwright's *Give us our Rights!* (1782), which echoed Abingdon's constitutional views, was discussed at the first two meetings of the popular democratic London Corresponding Society (LCS) in 1792.[7] Thomas Hardy, the founder of the LCS, was strongly influenced by the writings which the SCI had distributed, and had been converted to Radicalism by Richard Price's pro-American *Observations on the Nature of Civil Liberty.*[8]

Yet it took the French Revolution to bring this process of popular politicization into the open. The French Revolution not only revitalized a fading SCI but also precipitated the entry of the "people" into politics. As Thomas Hardy put it, in 1792 "another class of reformers started up unknown to those who preceded them—they were of the lower and midling class of society *called the people.*"[9] Inspired by the democratic radicalization of the French Revolution and angry about "the heavy pressure of the daily accumulating taxes, and the consequent rise in the prices of all the necessaries of life," the popular

4 Abingdon, *Thoughts on the Letter of Edmund Burke*, p. 52.

5 This is not to argue that Paine was the only Radical to break with the notion that Britain must return to its original constitution. Welsh Radical David Williams argued in 1790 that a British constitution had never existed. But Paine was the first to transmit this view to a wide audience.

6 Walvin, "English Democratic Societies," pp. 9–12.

7 Cartwright, *Give us our Rights!*, esp. p. 24. For its influence on the LCS, see PP, Add. Ms. 27814, ff. 85–86.

8 Price, *Observations on the Nature of Civil Liberty*; Hardy, *Memoir*, pp. 8–9, 12, 102.

9 PP, Add. Ms. 27814, f. 36, Hardy, "A Sketch, of the History of the London Corresponding Society."

democrats injected a new tone of egalitarianism and a new social content into British Radicalism.[10] With their low weekly subscriptions, their predominantly artisan roots, and their deep distrust of "leaders," the new democratic clubs and societies marked a qualitative shift in the Radical movement.[11]

At the same time, there were also elements of continuity between the Radicalism of the 1780s and that of the 1790s. Because the French Revolution was such a powerful presence in British political controversy after 1789, the Anglo-American ideological origins of British popular Radicalism can easily be overlooked. Yet popular Radical demands for universal manhood suffrage and annual parliaments had already been expressed and publicized by the SCI during the American Revolution. And while many members of the SCI were frightened away by the new popular Radicalism they had unwittingly helped to create, those who stayed in the society distributed Paine's writings and helped to co-ordinate the emergence of a national popular democratic movement in 1792 and 1793. Drenched in the language of the French Revolution and motivated primarily by economic hardship and a sense of social injustice, many artisans believed that the solution to their problems lay in political reforms which were rooted in Anglo-American Radical traditions. Paine's *Rights of Man* was perfectly suited to the new situation. Not only was the book occasioned by the French Revolution and written by a man who himself had been an artisan; it was also grounded in Paine's American experiences. Indeed, the *Rights of Man* had at least as much to do with the American Revolution as the French. The relation of the *Rights of Man* to the French Revolution and Burke's *Reflections on the Revolution in France* has long been recognized; the American dimension, however, deserves further consideration.

I

In Paine's own view, the *Rights of Man* applied the principles of *Common Sense* to English conditions. The only difference between the two works, he argued, was that "one was adapted to the local circumstances

10 Hardy, *Memoir*, p. 10.

11 For some general accounts of the popular democratic movement, see Thompson, *Making of the English Working Class*, pp. 18–203; G. A. Williams, *Artisans and Sans-Culottes*, pp. 1–18, 58–80, 95–114; Walvin, "English Democratic Societies," and Goodwin, *Friends of Liberty*.

of England, and the other to those of America."[12] As early as 1778,
he had been planning to repeat the success of *Common Sense* on English
ground. In his seventh *American Crisis* paper, addressed "To the People of England," Paine maintained that the interests of the "caterpillar
circle of the court" were diametrically opposed to those of the "mer-
cantile and manufacturing" community in England. The king and
ministers, according to Paine, wanted to siphon off America's wealth
to buttress the corrupt system of domestic patronage; Britain's merchants and manufacturers, on the other hand, could only benefit from
free trade with an increasingly prosperous American republic. "Your
present king and ministry," he had written, "will be the ruin of you;
and you had better risk a revolution and call a congress, than be thus
led on from madness to despair, and from despair to ruin. America
has set you the example, and you may follow it and be free."[13] With
such arguments in mind, he decided to "convey himself secretly" to
England and produce a "well timed and well composed publication"
against the war. In the end, the fear of being executed as a spy made
him drop this plan.[14]

Nevertheless, Paine's idea of writing a democratic work in England
persisted well after the War of Independence. When the French Revolution broke out, Paine seized the opportunity and began what became the *Rights of Man*. The book was not originally intended to be
a reply to Burke's *Reflections*; Paine was already writing before he was
even aware that Burke opposed the revolution. But after the *Reflections*
appeared in 1790, Paine integrated his earlier work into an attack on
Burke.[15] The French Revolution and Burke provided the occasion;
but the assumptions and arguments of the *Rights of Man* derived from
Paine's American experience. In arguing for the "sovereignty of the
present generation," natural and civil rights, the need to establish a
real Constitution, and the practical benefits of republican government,
Paine drew on the radical conceptualization of Real Whig ideology

12 Paine, *To the Citizens of the United States*, 2: 910.
13 Paine, *American Crisis VII*, 1: 152–53, 155. See also *American Crisis II*, 1: 72, and
American Crisis III, 1: 84, 86.
14 Paine, *To a Committee of the Continental Congress*, 2: 1231–33; *Rights of Man, Part
2*, 1: 407n.
15 In January 1790, when Paine still thought that Burke supported the French
Revolution, Lafayette informed George Washington that "Common Sense is writing a
book for you." (*Letters of Lafayette to Washington*, ed. Gottschalk, p. 346). Paine dedicated
the *Rights of Man, Part 1* to Washington.

which had occurred in America, and in which *Common Sense* had played such an important part.

Paine opened the *Rights of Man* by confronting what he called Burke's "sepulchre of precedents."[16] Against Burke's view of government as a "partnership not only between those who are living, but between those who are living, those who are dead, and those who are to be born," Paine spoke in the political present tense. "Every age and generation must be as free to act for itself, *in all cases*," he wrote, "as the ages and generations which preceded it. . . . I am contending for the rights of the *living*, and against their being willed away, and controlled and contracted for, by the manuscript assumed authority of the dead."[17]

This argument, central to the *Rights of Man*, had American antecedents. One catches a glimpse of it in *Common Sense*, but it was not fully articulated until 1786. During his defence of the Bank of North America in that year, Paine commented that "as we are not to live forever ourselves, and other generations are to follow us, we have neither the power nor the right to govern them, or to say how they shall govern themselves. It is the summit of human vanity, and shows a covetousness of power beyond the grave, to be dictating to the world to come."[18] Two years later, Paine and Jefferson discussed the concept of an autonomous political generation and found themselves in substantial agreement.[19] When Paine read Burke's *Reflections* he had already developed a theoretical basis from which he could attack custom and precedence. Grounding his argument on the principle that each generation possessed sovereignty, he simply dismissed a full quarter of Burke's book as being "null and void."[20]

Paine's emphasis on the "rights of the *living*" demanded a definition of rights as well as the notion of an autonomous political generation. And here again, Paine repeated arguments that had grown out of his American experience. In Paine's view, government must be based on

16 Paine used the phrase in *Rights of Man, Part 2*, 1: 386.

17 Burke, *Reflections*, pp. 194–95; Paine, *Rights of Man Part I*, 1: 251–52.

18 Paine, *Common Sense*, 1: 14; *Dissertations on Government*, 2: 395.

19 Jefferson, *Papers*, ed. Boyd, 11: 112–16; 13: 4–7; 15: 392–97; Koch, *Jefferson and Madison*, pp. 81–88. See also Paine, *Letter Addressed to the Addressers*, 2: 509. Jefferson, working through bills of mortality, defined a generation as 19 years; Paine suggested 21 years.

20 Paine, *Rights of Man, Part 1*, 1: 254. Paine believed that in only four pages he had demolished "almost one hundred pages" of Burke's argument.

both the natural and the civil rights of man. Natural rights were "those which appertain to man in right of his existence," such as freedom of thought and "all those rights of acting as an individual for his own comfort and happiness, which are not injurious to the natural rights of others." Civil rights were those which were beyond the power of any one individual, such as security and protection, and which were deposited in the "common stock" of society. "Every civil right," Paine wrote, "has for its foundation some natural right pre-existing in the individual, but to the enjoyment of which his individual power is not, in all cases, sufficiently competent."

From these premises, Paine argued that civil power must be founded on those natural rights which are exchanged for civil rights, that this power "cannot be applied to invade the natural rights which are retained in the individual," and that any other kind of power was illegitimate.[21] It was not a new position. Back in 1777, Paine had made exactly the same distinction between natural and civil rights in almost exactly the same language.[22] And in 1788, when he was in Paris discussing the American Federal Constitution with Jefferson and Lafayette, Paine once more raised the issue of natural and civil rights in the course of his argument for strong central government in the United States.[23]

Both Paine's arguments about rights and the sovereignty of the present generation were at the heart of the *Rights of Man*; they were the fundamental premises on which the book was based.[24] As far as Paine was concerned, these arguments were really different ways of saying the same thing, since rights could only be possessed by the living, and the living could not alienate those rights to past or future generations. But the essential point is that these premises had been formulated by Paine in America. At one level, the *Rights of Man* can

21 Ibid., 1: 275–76.

22 Paine, *Candid and Critical Remarks on a Letter Signed Ludlow*, 2: 274–75.

23 Paine to Jefferson, February 1788, 2: 1298–99; Foner erroneously dates this letter in 1789. See Jefferson, *Papers*, ed. Boyd, 13: 4–5, and Gottschalk, *Lafayette between the American and the French Revolution*, p. 374. The practical conclusion which Paine drew from his discussion of natural and civil rights in 1788 was that "I consider the individual sovereignty of the States retained under the act of confederation to be of the second class of right [ie. civil rights]. It becomes dangerous because it is defective in the power necessary to support it. It answers the pride and purpose of a few men in each State, but the State collectively is injured by it." Paine to Jefferson, 2: 1299.

24 Paine, *Rights of Man, Part 1*, 1: 272–78.

be seen primarily as a response to the French Revolution. But beneath the surface, America resonated deeply in Paine's consciousness.

A similar pattern emerges when we consider Paine's views on constitutions in the *Rights of Man*. Although he spent much of *Part One* comparing the French constitution to the "English Government," Paine's concept of constitutionalism had been formed during the American Revolution. As we have seen, the notion that governing institutions should be subject to constitutional principles, and that a written constitution was needed to define those principles, arose out of America's ideological revolution between 1763 and 1776. In 1776, Paine had taken precisely this position in the debate over the Pennsylvania Constitution; in the *Rights of Man* he brought his message directly to an English audience.[25] "A constitution," he wrote in 1791, "is not a thing in name only, but in fact. It has not an ideal, but a real existence; and wherever it cannot be produced in a visible form, there is none. A constitution is a thing *antecedent* to a government, and a government is only the creature of a constitution." From this viewpoint, Paine argued, it followed that in England "no such thing as a constitution exists, or ever did exist, and consequently that the people have yet a constitution to form."[26]

The implications of this position were revolutionary. Rather than going back to Anglo-Saxon myths, rather than venerating Magna Carta, and rather than calling for constitutional reform, Paine demanded a complete overhaul of the system of government. The Americans had pointed the way: the Pennsylvania Constitution of 1776 and the Federal Constitution of 1787 were founded by conventions representing the *"authority of the people,"* and had established the conditions under which the process of government was conducted. More immediately, in the context of 1791–92, the French had followed the American lead. The National Assembly, wrote Paine, was "a *convention*, to make a constitution." It was now Britain's turn. "The right of reform," Paine insisted, "is in the nation in its original character, and the constitutional method would be by a general convention elected for the purpose. There is, moreover, a paradox in the idea of vitiated

---

25 Paine, *Common Sense*, 1: 7–8, 28–29; *Forester's Letters*, 2: 85; *Four Letters on Interesting Subjects*, p. 18; *American Crisis VII*, 1: 152. He made similar comments during the regency crisis of 1788–89. See Paine to Thomas Walker, 16 January 1789, and Paine to Jefferson, 26 February 1789, 2: 1283.

26 Paine, *Rights of Man, Part 1*, 1: 278.

bodies reforming themselves."[27] Such an argument not only alarmed the government, but also went too far for many democrats who welcomed the *Rights of Man* but drew back from its constitutional position to the more familiar ground of the Saxon constitution and the "people's Alfred."[28]

Paine's American experience influenced his approach to the structure as well as the principles of constitutional government. His immersion in Pennsylvania politics made him rethink his earlier support for a unicameral legislature, and by 1786 he was arguing that when "party differences" overrode the public good "a single legislature, on account of the superabundance of its power, and the uncontrolled rapidity of its execution, becomes as dangerous to the principles of liberty as that of a despotic monarchy."[29] Although Paine never actually advocated bicameralism, his awareness that a single assembly might "act with too quick an impulse" prompted him to suggest in the *Rights of Man* that an assembly be divided into two or three parts, and that proposed legislation should be discussed separately by each part before the whole assembly debated and voted on the bill in question.[30] Nevertheless, the general principles remained more important than the specific arrangements. After all, the Age of Revolution had only just begun, and the art of constitution making was still in its infancy. "The best constitution that could now be devised consistent with the conditions of the present moment," he wrote in 1792, "may be far short of that excellence which a few years may afford."[31]

This sense of optimism ran right through the *Rights of Man*. Taken together, Paine believed that events in America and France were opening up a new era of liberty. In this respect, his view was similar to that of Richard Price, who told an audience of Real Whigs in 1789

---

27 Paine, *Rights of Man, Part 2*, 1: 375–81, 385; *Rights of Man, Part 1*, 1: 280.

28 See, for example, Fennessy, *Burke, Paine and the Rights of Man*, p. 228; Thompson, *Making of the English Working Class*, pp. 95–97. For the reaction of some members of the LCS to Paine's position, see PP, Add. Ms. 27812, f. 11, and PP, Add. Ms. 27812, ff. 17–18, *Address from the L.C.S. to the Inhabitants of Great Britain*.

29 Quoted in Aldridge, "Some Writings of Thomas Paine," p. 835. See also Paine, *Dissertations on Government*, 2: 390, 409–10. Compare *Common Sense*, 1: 28–29, for Paine's initial views on this subject.

30 Paine, *Rights of Man, Part 2*, 1: 390. This notion first appeared in Paine's *Answer to Four Questions*, 2: 526–27, written in the previous spring.

31 Paine, *Rights of Man, Part 2*, 1: 396. For this reason, he maintained that a constitution must contain within itself the means of remedying its own defects. See also Paine, *Answer to Four Questions*, 2: 532.

that "the light you have struck out, after setting AMERICA free, reflected to FRANCE, and there kindled into a blaze that lays despotism in ashes, and warms and illuminates EUROPE!"[32] For Paine, as for Price, the French Revolution was directly connected to the American. The American Revolution, argued Paine, had stimulated a "spirit of political inquiry" already begun by the *philosophes* and helped produce the "mental revolution" necessary to the political one. The Franco-American alliance had directly exposed Frenchmen to the revolutionary doctrines of "the natural rights of man, and justified resistance to oppression." The financial collapse of the *ancien régime* provided the opportunity to put the theory into practice; before long, Paine would envisage a similar combination of national bankruptcy and democratic ideology occurring in Britain itself. The world would never be the same again: "The opinions of men, with respect to government, are changing fast in all countries," he wrote. "The revolutions of America and France have thrown a beam of light over the world, which reaches into man."[33]

America and France, argued Paine, had revolutionized the very concept of revolution, transforming it from a cyclical to a linear and progressive approach to change. "What were formerly called revolutions," he wrote, "were little more than a change of persons, or an alteration of local circumstances. They rose and fell like things of course, and had nothing in their existence or their fate that could influence beyond the spot that produced them. But what we now see in the world, from the revolutions of America and France, is a renovation of the natural order of things, a system of principles as universal as truth and the existence of man, and combining moral with political happiness and national prosperity."[34] Once revolutions were seen in this way, it would only be a matter of time before another new phenomenon, the professional revolutionary, appeared on the

32 Price, *A Discourse*, p. 50.

33 Paine, *Rights of Man, Part 1*, 1: 298–301, 320. When Paine sent the key of the Bastille to Washington, he commented "that the principles of America opened the Bastille is not to be doubted; and therefore the key comes to the right place" (Paine to Washington, 1 May 1790, 2: 1303). For other examples of this attitude, see Paine to Washington, 21 July 1791, 2: 1319; *Address to the People of France*, 2: 539.

34 Paine, *Rights of Man, Part 1*, 1: 341–42. In some of his earlier writings, Paine himself occasionally used the word "revolution" in its traditional cyclical sense. See, for example, Paine, *American Crisis II*, 1: 59, *American Crisis V*, 1: 108 and *American Crisis VII*, 1: 149.

political scene. Indeed, in some respects Paine himself, with his dedication to the democratic revolution, anticipated this aspect of the
nineteenth-century European revolutionary tradition.[35]

Although Paine praised both the American and French revolutions,
he presented himself first and foremost as an American who had
personal experience of the practical benefits of democratic republicanism. When he wrote the *Rights of Man*, France was still a constitutional monarchy; America, in contrast, was the "only real republic
in character and practice" in the world. Establishing his credentials
as a disinterested friend of liberty by citing his American career, Paine
identified himself with the New World of the rights of man, cheap
government, and economic abundance. Free from the "greedy hand"
of hereditary rule, the United States was not ground down by taxation,
Paine argued; low taxes enabled the "productive classes" to prosper,
and this prosperity laid the foundations for American progress and
improvement. An admirer of Adam Smith's *Wealth of Nations*, Paine
believed that America enjoyed both political liberty and the benefits
of a self-regulating laissez-faire economic system. In Paine's view,
economic and political liberty were inseparable.[36]

After associating American political liberty with economic prosperity and a broad social egalitarianism among the "productive classes,"
Paine then discussed the practical improvements that Britain could
expect from a democratic republican government. The result was the
famous "social chapter" of the *Rights of Man*, in which Paine addressed
himself directly to the problems of the "common people" in a new
departure in eighteenth-century British Radicalism. What Paine did
was to give traditional political demands a direct and immediate social
content. Britain had never seen anything quite like it before.

Almost inevitably, his chief targets were hereditary government and
taxation. Arguing that excessive taxation served only the narrow self-
interest of a parasitic aristocracy, Paine estimated that in practice

35 This argument must not be pushed too far. While the professional revolutionaries of the nineteenth century, such as Philippe-Michel Buonarroti and Auguste Blan-
qui, consciously plotted to bring about revolution through seizing power in the name
of the people, Paine was above all an ideologue of revolution. The whole question of
the changing definition of revolution and the emergence of the professional revolutionary is worth a volume in itself.

36 Paine, *Rights of Man, Part 1*, 1: 326; *Rights of Man, Part 2*, 1: 370, 406n–7n. See
also *Rights of Man, Part 2*, 1: 354, 355, 358, 360, 371–72, 374–75. Paine spoke highly
of Smith's *Wealth of Nations* in *Rights of Man, Part 1*, 1: 282.

roughly £1.5 million was sufficient to cover the actual expenses of government, leaving a surplus of £6 million. With this money, Paine would abolish the poor rates which pressed so heavily on the "middling orders," and apply the rest to areas of genuine social need. He advocated a child allowance scheme, old age pensions ("not of the nature of charity, but of a right"), educational assistance for the children of the poor, and employment centres for the "casual poor." The army and navy would be cut back, since democratic republican nations would, he convinced himself, solve problems by reason rather than force. Disbanded soldiers and sailors would receive pensions, while those who remained in service would get pay increases.

To undermine primogeniture and thus the economic foundation of landed aristocracy, he proposed a steeply progressive income tax which would make taxes "more equal than they are" and which would break vast "hereditary estates." That still left him with £1 million "surplus taxes" which could be used, among other things, to benefit the "inferior clergy" and—not forgetting his first cause—to increase the salaries of excise officers. "Ye who sit in ease and solace yourselves in plenty," he wrote, "and such there are in Turkey and Russia, as well as in England, and who say to yourselves, 'Are we not well off,' have ye thought of these things?"[37]

The idea was not social "levelling," in the sense of equality of property, but rather the creation of conditions in which political and economic liberty would flourish as he believed it flourished in America. His ideal society was a democracy of small-scale property owners, without extremes of wealth and poverty, a society in which laissez-faire economics would allow men of talent to realize their potential, but not at the expense of their fellow men. The best way to raise workmen's wages, he argued, was to allow market forces to operate without regulation. Opposed to landed wealth, Paine also felt that "it would be impolitic to set bounds to property acquired by industry" and believed that "the probable acquisition to which industry can extend" could not exceed £23,000 a year. The possibility and implications of industrial capital accumulation quite simply did not occur to him. Paine had no conception that he was living through the world's first Industrial Revolution.[38]

37 Paine, *Rights of Man, Part 2,* 1: 410–42, 431–32.
38 Ibid., 1: 439–40, 434–35. See also Kramnick, "Tom Paine: Radical Democrat," pp. 127–38.

It is true, of course, that Paine was a consistent "advocate for commerce," which he believed would promote peace, internationalism, and "universal civilization."[39] The American and French revolutions, he argued, marked the beginning of a secular millenium which would be characterized by political democracy, economic liberty, and commercial growth. When England and Holland joined the democratic revolution, wrote Paine, they could unite with the United States and France to "propose, with effect, to Spain, the independence of South America, and the opening those countries, of immense extent and wealth, to the general commerce of the world." Democracy would emancipate Europe's colonies and provide Europe with "an immense field for commerce, and a ready market for manufactures." "The present age," he wrote, "will hereafter merit to be called the Age of Reason, and the present generation will appear to the future as the Adam of a new world."[40]

Yet this new world was essentially a projection into the future of the values and aspirations of the eighteenth-century Anglo-American "productive classes"; it was a world of small producers in which competitive market forces would apparently ensure a broad egalitarianism. Paine never considered the possibility that economic growth might ultimately threaten his notion of political democracy. He had a strong sense of class conflict between the "productive classes" and the aristocracy, between tax-payers and tax-eaters, but the concept of serious class conflict arising within the "productive classes" themselves was outside the scope of his ideology. Precisely because Paine seems so "modern" in his support for democracy, his faith in commercial progress, and his proposals for social welfare, we must remind ourselves that he lived in the eighteenth century, and could not know the nineteenth.

II

In the early 1790s, Paine's arguments impressed large numbers of people outside Britain's "political nation." As in *Common Sense*, his literary style was central to his success. In his rhetorical method as much as his political ideology, Paine was a transatlantic Radical. He participated in the growing movement towards new rhetoric in Brit-

39 Paine, *Rights of Man, Part 2*, 1: 400–401.
40 Ibid., 1: 448–49.

ain, came into his own as a writer in America where the plain style predominated, and brought the approach back home with remarkable effect. Although the new rhetoric had been nurtured in Britain, it still competed there with older forms. Even a cursory glance at eighteenth-century British pamphlets and sermons indicates that much political and religious discourse continued in the grand style. Paine was conscious of this; the new rhetoric, in his view, was the language of the New World. The *Rights of Man,* he argued, not only transmitted American ideas back to Britain, but did so "in a style of thinking and expression different to what had been customary in England."[41]

As Wilbur Howell has pointed out, the battle between Paine and Burke was, among other things, a battle between the new and old rhetoric.[42] Paine expressed himself in plain speech with the same belief that language must correspond to the facts and the same concern for the right balance between reason and feelings which had characterized his earlier writings. From this perspective, Burke's *Reflections* appeared to be full of "gay and flowery" language, style without substance, and unintelligible "learned jargon."

In Paine's view, Burke's famous "age of chivalry" passage in the *Reflections* epitomized everything that was objectionable about the grand style:

As to the tragic paintings by which Mr. Burke has outraged his own imagination, and seeks to work upon that of his readers, they are very well calculated for theatrical representation, where facts are manufactured for the sake of show, and accommodated to produce through the weakness of sympathy, a weeping effect. But Mr. Burke should recollect that he is writing history, and not *plays*; and that his readers will expect truth, and not the spouting rant of high-toned declamation.

When we see a man dramatically lamenting in a publication intended to be believed, that, "*The age of chivalry is gone*! that *The glory of Europe is extinguished forever*! that *The unbought grace of life* (if any one knows what it is), *the cheap defense of nations, the nurse of manly sentiment and heroic enterprise, is gone,*" and all this because the Quixotic age of chivalric nonsense is gone, what opinion can we form of his judgment, or what regard can we pay to his facts?[43]

41 Ibid., 1: 348.

42 Howell, Review of *The Language*, p. 522. See also Howell, *Logic and Rhetoric*, p. 647n.

43 Paine, *Rights of Man, Part 1*, 1: 258–59.

Burke, according to Paine, had employed lofty and grandiloquent prose in which theatre was substituted for history, in which the attempt to move the passions of the readers took precedence over truth, and in which the rhapsodies of the imagination became more important than the understanding of events. For Paine, such an approach contradicted every principle of clear and effective writing.

Although the "age of chivalry" passage Paine ridiculed was not representative of the *Reflections* as a whole, it is true that Burke's theory of rhetoric alloted a much more important role to the passions than that allowed by Paine. The rhetorical theory underlying the *Reflections* had actually been elaborated by Burke thirty-three years earlier, when he wrote in his *Philosophical Enquiry into the Origins of Our Ideas of the Sublime and Beautiful* that

we do not sufficiently distinguish, in our observations upon language, between a clear expression, and a strong expression. . . . The former regards the understanding; the latter belongs to the passions. The one describes a thing as it is; the other describes it as it is felt. . . . there are words, and certain dispositions of words, which being peculiarly devoted to passionate subjects, are always used by those who are under the influence of any passion; they touch and move us more than those which far more clearly and distinctly express the subject matter. We yield to sympathy, what we refuse to description.[44]

The difference between Burke's and Paine's outlook can be clearly seen in each man's use of the word "sympathy." In Burke's view, powerful writing directed towards the passions could make the readers "yield to sympathy"; for Paine, Burke's rhetoric was unacceptable precisely because it attempted to play on the "weakness of sympathy" instead of the understanding. Paine did believe that there was an important place for "imagination" and "passion" in persuasive writing, but maintained that emotion must be subordinated to reason. In 1783, he had argued that the elevation of the passions over the judgment would result in a "pantomime of the mind"; it is thus not surprising that in 1791 he likened Burke's *Reflections* to a "dramatic performance" and condemned its "theatrical exaggerations." As far as Paine was concerned, Burke's attempt to manipulate the passions was a kind of literary fraud, the counterfeit of compassion. "Not one glance of

44 Burke, *Philosophical Enquiry*, pp. 338–39.

compassion," commented Paine, "not one commiserating reflection . . . has he bestowed on those who lingered out the most wretched
of lives, a life without hope, in the most miserable of prisons. . . . He
is not affected by the reality of distress touching his heart, but by the
showy resemblage of it striking his imagination. He pities the plumage,
but forgets the dying bird." From the standards of the new rhetoric,
Burke's language was a species of mystification, a "jingle of words that
convey no ideas"; the *Reflections* was seen as a "frenzy of passion,"
which finished with "music in the ear, and nothing in the heart."[45]

On the same grounds, Paine attacked the *Reflections* for its apparent
lack of order and criticized Burke for presenting his readers with "a
wild, unsystematical display of paradoxical rhapsodies." "His intention," wrote Paine of Burke, "was to make an attack on the French
Revolution; but instead of proceeding with an orderly arrangement,
he has stormed it with a mob of ideas tumbling over and destroying
one another."[46] In contrast, Paine emphasized the importance of organizing his work around certain principles. "Before anything can be
reasoned upon to a conclusion," he stated, "certain facts, principles,
or data, to reason from, must be established, admitted, or denied."[47]
At the core of the *Rights of Man* lay a straightforward pattern of
reasoning: government must be founded on the natural and civil
rights of the present generation; the English system of government
was in fact based on power and precedent; therefore the English
system of government must be replaced by one that accorded with
first principles. It all seemed so simple; it all seemed so obvious.

The structure of the *Rights of Man, Part One*, was largely conditioned
by Paine's triple purpose of demolishing Burke's arguments, establishing his own position, and incorporating his earlier writings on the
French Revolution into his reply to the *Reflections*. The result was a
measure of unevenness; the organization was too flexible, and one
senses that Paine himself realized that it tended to meander.[48] In *Part*

45 Paine, *Letter to the Abbé Raynal*, 2: 214; *Rights of Man, Part 1*, 1: 249, 255, 260,
267–68; *Rights of Man, Part 2*, 1: 372.

46 Paine, *Rights of Man, Part 1*, 1: 272, 281, 318.

47 Paine, *Rights of Man, Part 1*, 1: 272.

48 His attitude when introducing his "Miscellaneous Chapter," for example, was
noticeably defensive; he was anxious to ensure that "variety might not be censured for
confusion," and attempted to deflect any criticism by adding that "Mr. Burke's book
is *all* Miscellany" (Paine, *Rights of Man, Part 1*, 1: 318).

Two, however, he imposed a much tighter framework on his material. It was divided into five chapters, the first four of which "endeavoured to establish a system of principles as a basis on which governments ought to be erected"; in the final chapter he moved from principles to practice as he developed his plans for social reform.[49] But in both parts of the book, Paine strove self-consciously for order, even if his results were mixed. And in both parts, he combined synthetic and analytic methods of arrangement; he travelled from general propositions to particular conclusions in matters of political theory, and proceeded from the particular to the general in matters of political practice. The *Rights of Man*, like *Common Sense*, can be placed squarely within the modern approach to the disposition of arguments.

The *Rights of Man* also shared with *Common Sense* a tone of humorous defiance and unnerving self-confidence. If anything, Paine's attitude was even more assertive and abrasive in the *Rights of Man* than in *Common Sense*; he had beaten monarchical government once, America and France had shown that nations could will their own freedom, and the English system of government was unlikely to survive the onslaught of Reason. "I become irritated," he wrote with uncharacteristic understatement, "at the attempt to govern mankind by force and fraud, as if they were all knaves and fools. . . ." Aristocrats were "drones"; the idea of hereditary legislators was as "absurd" as that of hereditary mathematicians; aristocratic titles were meaningless, childish gewgaws; monarchy was "all a bubble, a mere court artifice to procure money." "What is called monarchy," he wrote, "always appears to me a silly, contemptible thing. I compare it to something kept behind a curtain, about which there is a great deal of bustle and fuss, and a wonderful air of seeming solemnity; but when, by any accident, the curtain happens to open, and the company see what it is, they burst into laughter." In his social chapter, the laughter gave way to a mounting sense of anger; the resources of the country were "lavished upon kings, upon courts, upon hirelings, imposters, and prostitutes," leaving the poor as "the exposed sacrifice of vice and legal barbarity," compelled through taxation to "support the fraud that oppresses them." With his frontal assault on deference, his sense of disgust and his conviction that revolution was imminent, Paine struck a formidable pose. "In taking up this subject," he told his readers, "I seek no recompense—I fear no

49 Paine, *Rights of Man, Part 2*, 1: 398.

consequences. Fortified with that proud integrity that disdains to triumph or to yield, I will advocate the Rights of Man."[50]

Clearly, then, Paine challenged not only the political but also the literary standards of Burke's *Reflections*. In many respects, the difference between Burke's and Paine's approach to rhetoric can be related to the wider differences between an aristocratic and an emerging democratic culture. As George Chalmers commented in his hostile biography of Paine, "classical writing was not to be expected from a mere stay-maker, a mere grocer, a mere exciseman; but . . . he is the true orator, who gains his end by affecting, and convincing"; there was insight in the insult.[51]

Other gentlemen of polite learning took a similar position. Samuel Cooper, for example, wrote a pamphlet in support of Burke which was full of learned allusions, Latin quotations, and elaborate metaphors. "Even strip him [Burke] of all his eloquence, which kills at every stroke, and leave him only his wisdom," ran a typical passage, "he would still be but like Pallas robbed of her spear, but whose Aegis alone will strike her opponents dumb in confusion, horror, and dismay."[52] Such language was unlikely to appeal to those without a classical education. Far from being struck dumb, however, Burke's opponents who inhabited the same scientific and literary culture as Paine responded by treating the grand style with contempt. Thus Joseph Priestley dismissed Burke's "age of chivalry" passage as "a great pomp of *words* with but few *ideas*," while Mary Wollstonecraft criticized Burke's "empty rhetorical flourishes" which "foster every emotion till the fumes, mounting to your brain, dispel the sober suggestions of reason." "If the passion is real," commented Wollstonecraft, "the head will not be ransacked for stale tropes and cold rodomontade."[53]

50 Paine, *Rights of Man, Part 1*, 1: 277, 286–87, 289; *Rights of Man, Part 2*, 1: 366, 373–74, 404–5.

51 Chalmers, *Life of Thomas Pain*, p. 52.

52 Cooper, *First Principles of Civil and Ecclesiastical Government*, p. 8. Examples of replies to Paine written in the grand style include *Letter from a Magistrate*; *Cursory Remarks*; Elliot, *Republican Refuted*; and Hervey, *New Friend*.

53 Priestley, *Letters to Edmund Burke*, pp. 29–30; Wollstonecraft, *Vindication of the Rights of Man*, pp. 63, 6, 60. Wollstonecraft also attacked Burke's *Enquiry into . . . the Sublime and Beautiful*, arguing that "truth, in morals, has ever appeared to me the essence of the sublime; and, in taste, simplicity, the only criterion of the beautiful" (Ibid., p. 2). It should be added, however, that Wollstonecraft frequently failed to

But there was no clear-cut connection between culture, politics, and literary style. One finds hard-line Tories expressing their views in plain speech, one finds self-professed moderates condemning the language and logic of the *Rights of Man* for sinking to the level of shoemakers and barbers, and one sometimes finds shoemakers and barbers writing in the grand style. Nor should it be assumed that Paine himself wrote in the plain style because he wanted to reach a new audience of artisans and labourers. For most of his career, he wrote as a member of an Anglo-American "proto-intelligentsia" rather than a "proto-proletariat," and he directed his arguments towards the "productive classes" in general rather than the "lower orders" in particular.

Paine did not specifically address himself to artisans and labourers until the *Rights of Man, Part Two*, sixteen years after he became a political writer. As Gwyn Williams points out, the *Rights of Man, Part One*, initially sold for 2s.6d. Had Paine been primarily concerned with reaching artisans and labourers, he would not have priced them out of the market before 1792. Once the grass-roots impact of *Part One* became clear, Paine geared *Part Two* to his new, unprecedented audience. "Paine, like a good American," concludes Williams, "adjusted the product to the market and received monopoly political profit." In this sense, the work which is frequently taken to be classic Paine was actually the exception, not the rule, in his writings.[54]

III

Deriving much of their inspiration from Paine, thousands of artisans emerged from their "vegetable sleep" into new forms of political consciousness during the early 1790s. Initially, *Part One* was transmitted to a wide audience by socially respectable Radical organizations such as the SCI and the Manchester Constitutional Society. By the end of 1791, however, the first signs appeared that Paine's influence was registering among the common people. In December, the first popular democratic society was formed in Sheffield, and began at once to publish the *Rights of Man*. Hard on the heels of Sheffield, the LCS got

---

follow her own rhetorical advice; see, for example, her encomium on Richard Price, pp. 34–35.

54 Boothby, *Observations on Mr. Paine's Rights of Man*, p. 98; Wills, Review of *Tom Paine* by Foner, p. 22; Paine, *Letter Addressed to the Addressers* 2: 486; G. A. Williams, "Atlantic Revolution," pp. 2–3.

going in January 1792, and in March the United Constitutional Societies of Norwich wrote enthusiastically about Paine. "Things wear a
very threatening aspect" in Norwich, one alarmed observer informed
the government later in the year as the town developed into one of
the major regional centres of popular Radicalism. Meanwhile in Sheffield Colonel De Lancey "found that the seditious doctrines of Paine
and the factious people who are endeavouring to disturb the peace
of the Country, had extended to a degree very much beyond my
conception." Reports came through of over a dozen clubs at Ipswich,
"to which the common ignorant people are invited, and a *Reader* is
elected in each, and explains Pain's Pamphlet to those ignorant people
who can neither write nor read." In Rainham, Paine's works were
being sold to "the lower people," while in Leicester Richard Phillips
was accused of distributing the *Rights of Man* among the soldiers. The
list goes on and on; it is no wonder that the government was worried.[55]

Some people read Paine and joined the clubs; others joined the
clubs and read Paine. In any case, the societies shared Paine's notion
of political equality, his absolute faith in political democracy as the
answer to Britain's problems, and his expectation of social benefits
from political change. Popular Radicals believed that with full representation and annual parliaments they would see

liberties restored, the press free, the laws simplified, judges unbiased, juries
independent, needless places and pensions retrenched, immoderate salaries
reduced, the public better served, taxes diminished and the necessaries of
life more within the reach of the poor, youth better educated, prisons less
crowded, old age better provided for, and sumptuous feasts, at the expense
of the starving poor, less frequent.[56]

Paine's social chapter was beginning to grip the minds of popular
Radicals; social grievances were becoming politicized. The *Rights of
Man* helped people to clarify and articulate ideas that had previously
only been dimly felt. Writing to the LCS in March 1792, the secretary
of the Sheffield society described how its members had a deep-rooted
dislike of aristocracy and how "with these sentiments, and perusing
Mr. Paine's 'Rights of Man,' maturely considering the force and weight
of argument therein contained, by degrees became confirmed in a

55 HO, 42/20, ff. 47, 167, 176; 42/22, f. 305; 42/23, ff. 10–17.
56 PP, Add. Ms. 27812, ff. 17–18.

judgment, that Pride, Ambition, luxury and oppression, with every vice, appeared to be at the height or nearly at the utmost stretch." "We have derived more true knowledge from the works of MR. THOMAS PAINE, entitled RIGHTS OF MAN, Part the *First* and *Second*," declared the Sheffield democrats, "than from any other author on the subject."[57] And throughout the 1790s, other popular Radical writers, such as Daniel Isaac Eaton and John Thelwall, continued to convey Paineite politics—including Paine's "scheme of progressive taxation" and his proposed social reforms—to this new public.[58]

This is not to argue that all popular Radicals accepted all of Paine's ideas. For many, Paine's republicanism and his rejection of the British constitution were too much to take. But, whatever doubts and reservations the democrats may have had, the fact remains that the *Rights of Man* was the central text of popular Radicalism in the 1790s. Thomas Hardy recalled in 1799 that Paine's work "seemed to electrify the nation, and terrified the imbecile government of the day into the most desperate and unjustifiable measures."[59]

The peak of Paine's popularity was 1792; by March the following year, Hardy informed a correspondent that the *Rights of Man* continued to be sold "in great numbers, but privately."[60] By that time the government's so-called "desperate and unjustifiable" measures were taking effect, and the popular Radicals were on the defensive. The Royal Proclamation of May 1792, directed principally against Paine's writings, the successful prosecution of Paine *in absentia* for seditious libel that December, the Loyalist backlash of 1792–93, and the outbreak of war between Britain and France in February 1793 all severely damaged the democratic movement in Britain. Under these circumstances, Paine's name moved away from the centre of political debate, although Paineite principles continued to permeate popular Radicalism. The democratic societies managed to survive the Loyalist campaign and the treason trials of 1794 to reach a new height in the near-famine year of 1795, until repressive legislation drove the movement underground.[61] The *Rights of Man* politicized and polarized the coun-

57 *Report of the Committee of Secrecy, 1794, Appendix D*, p. 48; Rickman, *Life of Thomas Paine*, p. 16.

58 Eaton, *Revolutions without Bloodshed*; Thelwall, *Sober Reflections*.

59 Hardy, *Memoir*, p. 20.

60 PP, Add. Ms. 27814, f. 186, Thomas Hardy to Mr. Bogue, 22 March 1793.

61 For a thorough analysis of these developments, see Goodwin, *Friends of Liberty*, pp. 208–358.

try; the immediate effect of polarization, however, was the isolation of the Paineites as the government rallied its supporters against the menace of democracy.

Contrary to Hardy's point of view, the government's response to the *Rights of Man* was not "imbecile"; from Pitt's perspective, strong counter-measures were essential to check this threat from below. Indeed, it can be argued that the greatest testament to the impact of the *Rights of Man* came from its opponents. Governmental action against Paine, the Loyalist movement, and the flood of anti-Paineite literature indicate that Britain's ruling class was smitten by fear. There was, of course, a risk in adopting repressive policies; by focusing attention on Paine, the government could actually increase his political importance. And it seems that something like this in fact happened."Thomas Paine has been honoured with so much abuse in both houses," one observer noted, "as to have become quite a man of consequence."[62] Paine himself shared this view, and believed that the Royal Proclamation and his trial for seditious libel could easily backfire on the government.[63] And at the height of the Loyalist campaign, it was reported in Lewes that "the late conviction of Paine has occasioned his book to be rather more than less sought after by our peasantry, who are almost daily applying for it; and it is not a little laughable to see them express their disapprobation of our refusal, by a most significant shake of their sapient noddles."[64]

There was a risk, but it was one the government felt was well worth taking. Faced with a rapid "change in sentiment" towards Paineite principles, confronted by a book that was "printed at a very low price, for the express purpose of its being read by the lowest classes of the people," and mindful of events in France, the government felt that it could not stand still.[65] After the Royal Proclamation, Colonel De Lancey reported that at least some sellers of the *Rights of Man* had

62 Metropolitan Toronto Library, William Dummer Powell Papers, Henry Motz to William Dummer Powell, 24 June 1792. I would like to thank Dana Johnson for providing me with this reference.

63 Paine to William Short, 2 November 1791, 2: 1320; *Letter Addressed to the Addressers*, 2: 499.

64 *SWA*, 31 December 1792.

65 For Paine's awareness of this "change in sentiment," see Paine to John Hall, 25 November 1791, 2: 1322; *Letter Addressed to the Addressers*, 2: 499. The comments about the price of the *Rights of Man* are those of Attorney General Sir Archibald MacDonald in explaining the decision to prosecute Paine (*Trial of Thomas Paine*, pp. 6–7).

been scared off. By the end of 1792, the author himself had fled to France to escape prosecution. Rumours circulated that Paine's trial was only the beginning of a massive legal offensive against popular Radicals; the *Morning Chronicle* reported that "there are no fewer than two hundred indictments prepared by the Crown officers."[66] But in fact, the government's main strategy was to encourage the mobilization of public opinion against what John Reeves's Loyalist Association called the "nefarious designs as are meditated by the wicked and senseless reformers of the present time."[67]

Not that Paine's opponents needed much encouragement. The *Rights of Man* provoked a series of ritualistic Paine-burning ceremonies, barroom brawls between "aristocrats" and "democrats," "parochial associations" to sift out local Paineites, and no less than forty angry replies from supporters of Britain's "miraculous constitution."[68] Nightmares of social revolution haunted the Loyalists. John Bowles believed that Paine's exploitation of the "worst passions" and manipulation of "minds entirely uncultivated" amounted to a "catechism of sedition and disloyalty for the lower orders of the people." Other writers dreaded the effects of Paine's attack on deference. "Mr. Payne's book," commented one Loyalist, "is perhaps one of the most dangerous publications that ever appeared on any subject;—calculated to seduce the weak and encourage the disaffected, and written expressly to destroy every existing sentiment of duty, affection and respect."[69] Both Paine and his opponents realized that the existing political and social order rested to a considerable degree on the cultural hegemony of the ruling class: hence Paine's blasphemous tone, and hence the emphasis on ceremony and ritual in the Loyalist backlash of 1792–93.

As in America, Paine's Loyalist enemies regarded him as an impractical "visionary" who wanted to reshape society according to abstract first principles. But in Britain during the French Revolution, the practical consequences of such theories seemed particularly horrifying. In Bowles's words, Paine's ideas

66 Quoted in Werkmeister, *Newspaper History of England*, p. 199.

67 Quoted in Mitchell, "Association Movement," p. 58.

68 Thompson, *Making of the English Working Class*, pp. 113, 122–26; for some examples of how this process worked in and around Lewes, see *SWA*, 12 December 1792, 17 December 1792, and 24 December 1792.

69 Bowles, *Protest against T. Paine's "Rights of Man,"* p. 9; Hervey, *New Friend*, p. 18.

really point to action, and that of the most pernicious and criminal nature—they lead not to any practicable good, but to turbulence and general commotion. If they were to have their desired effect, the Constitution would be annihilated; our lives, our liberties, and our property, would be deprived of legal protection; Government would be overturned; and in vain might we look into the darksome void of futurity to catch even a faint and dubious glimpse of security against unbridled licentiousness and unrestrained violence.[70]

To such writers, Paine's "social chapter" was simply "an advertisement for general pillage, and for a division, by scramble, of the revenues of Britain."[71] Time and again Paine was depicted as a "plunderer" of private property. Acutely aware of developments in revolutionary France, the British Loyalists equated democracy with the Terror. "The late transactions in France," argued one writer, "are the best comment, and the most satisfactory reply" to the "fine-spun speculations of the 'Rights of Man.' " "I have property," he continued, "and I do not chuse to live where the first beggar I meet may, with the sword in one hand, and *Rights of Man* in the other, demand a share of that which a good government tells me is *my own*. . . . Let those who are fond of French politics and French government, transport themselves to France, like their friend PAINE. . . . If they are fond of scenes of horror and distress, they may indulge their propensities to the utmost."[72] When the Committee of Public Safety arrested Paine in 1793, Britain's Loyalists doubtless felt that he was only reaping what he had sowed.

At times the fear generated by the *Rights of Man*, popular Radicalism, and the French Revolution reached quasi-hysterical proportions; some writers went to any length to discredit Paine. One of his enemies argued that Paine was "actuated by the same infernal spirit of envy which prompted the *Devil* to enter Eden and blast the felicity of our first parents," and went on to portray Paine quite literally as an agent of Satan in the earthly paradise of Britain. Others felt that the best reply to Paine was the hangman's noose, while still more attempted to attack him through *ad hominem* arguments. In his biography of Paine, George Chalmers characterized him as "the dishonest stay-

70 Bowles, *Protest*, pp. 6–7.
71 Thomas Hardy, D. D., *Patriot*, p. 73. Thomas Hardy, Doctor of Divinity, is not to be confused with Thomas Hardy, shoemaker, of the LCS.
72 "A Farmer," *A Plain and Earnest Address to Britons*, pp. 6, 11.

maker, the swindling tradesman and the cruel husband." But the most extreme example of personal invective came from one Charles Elliot, who in lurid detail accused Paine of gross and unnatural sexual acts involving his "*maiden* wife" and a cat. If Paine's writings could elicit that kind of response, it was clear that he had damaged some highly sensitive nerves.[73]

Yet British Loyalism was more than a panic-stricken reaction to the *Rights of Man*. The political challenges of the early 1790s forced the Loyalists to clarify and articulate their long-held views about the nature of government and society, and to reaffirm their faith in the balanced constitution which had "stood the test of ages" and brought security, prosperity, and liberty to the country.[74] From what has since become known as a Burkean perspective, the Loyalists attacked Paine's basic premises about the sovereignty of the present generation and about natural and civil rights. Paine's definition of a generation, they argued, imposed a static and mechanistic concept onto a fluid and evolving situation; besides, the revision of all laws at the end of a fixed period would produce perpetual instability and insecurity. It was also contended that Paine's notions of rights would replace real liberty and the practical wisdom of experience with the Utopian fantasies and dangerous ambitions of a propertyless democracy.[75]

Within these broad anti-Paine assumptions there existed a wide variety of political positions; Loyalism cannot be seen in monolithic terms. At one extreme we find the arguments of John Riland that the British constitution existed by divine right; at the other we find writers who felt that "our representation in Parliament is very defective" but who wanted gradual reforms rather than wholesale revolution.[76] Despite these differences, however, the Loyalists were firmly united against the "completely hostile and destructive" theories of Paine.[77]

---

73 *Letters to a Friend*, pp. 158, 151–87; *Rod in Brine*; Chalmers, *Life of Thomas Pain*, p. 25; Elliot, *Republican Refuted*, pp. 4–5.

74 See, for example, Hey, *Happiness and Rights*, p. 37; Bowles, *Protest*, p. 19; *Letters to Thomas Paine*, pp. 80–81; *Address to the Inhabitants*, p. 6. The latter anonymous author reminded Paine of Samuel Johnson's definition of a constitution as "the established form of government and system of laws and customs."

75 *Defence of the Rights of Man*; *Rights of Citizens*; Hawtrey, *Various Opinions of the Philosophical Reformers Considered*.

76 Riland, *Rights of God*, p. 6; Jepson, *Letters to Thomas Payne*, p. 23; *Cursory Remarks on Paine's Rights of Man*, p. 16.

77 Macleod, *Letters to the People of North Britain*, p. 11.

IV

The fear, hope, and passion generated by the *Rights of Man* existed under the shadow of the French Revolution. Everywhere in Britain, people approached politics in terms of their acceptance, qualification, or rejection of events in France. But by focusing on the influence of France, historians have largely ignored the important role that America, or the myth of America, played during these controversies. In Paine's view, the United States was the only real example of republican government in the world. When his political enemies accused him of being an impractical dreamer whose schemes would inevitably produce terror and tyranny, when William Pitt argued that if a government based on the *Rights of Man* "began at noon, it would end at night," Paine answered with one word: America. "But it is needless now to talk of mere theory," Paine told Home Secretary Henry Dundas, "since there is already a government in full practice, established upon that theory; or in other words, upon the 'Rights of Man,' and has been so for almost twenty years."[78]

Paine's writings in England in 1792 repeatedly returned to this theme; there is no doubt that America was much more important than France in Paine's defence of the *Rights of Man*. "I have also seen," he wrote in a letter intended for the people of Lewes, "a system of government rise up in that country [the United States], free from corruption, and now administered over an extent of territory ten times as large as England, *for less expense than the pensions alone in England amount to*; and under which more freedom is enjoyed, than under any other system in the world."[79] This, above all, was the lesson of the American Revolution; republican government worked.

Although Paine's opponents generally preferred to connect Paine with political instability in France, a significant number realized that his American experience was central to the *Rights of Man*. "The old hackneyed, confuted, worn-out objections which were extracted from

78 Paine, *To Mr. Secretary Dundas*, 1792, 2: 447–48. He continued with a comparison of government in Britain and America and concluded the letter with the statement that "I am, Mr. Dundas, Not your obedient humble servant, But the contrary, Thomas Paine" (2: 457).

79 Paine, *To the Sheriff of the County of Sussex*, 2: 464. Paine wanted this letter to be read at the meeting held on 4 July 1792 to discuss the Royal Proclamation; instead it was "cast unopened upon the table, and torn to pieces with distinguished marks of contempt" by the sheriff (*SWA*, 9 July 1792).

the republican writers by the American pamphleteers," commented
one writer, "are by Mr. Paine hashed up again with the aid of a little
French cookery manqué, which is the worst of all mixtures." Another
Loyalist, equally aware of the transatlantic nature of Paine's Radicalism, attacked "this American interloper, who wants to cram French
cooking down English throats."[80]

Having recognized the pivotal role of America in Paine's thought,
many Loyalists attempted to turn his American experiences against
him. Ransacking *Common Sense* and the *Letter to the Abbé Raynal* for
suitable quotations, the "friends of government" argued that Paine
was motivated by a "rooted hatred" and a "deep rooted malice of
sixteen years continuance against the constitution and people of this
country of all ranks and orders."[81] The British people, commented
John Bowles, "are not so short-sighted as to believe, that in 1792 the
man would counsel them to their good, who a few years before was
labouring at their destruction."[82] Paine's American writings branded
him as a traitor before he even put pen to paper in England. Moreover,
just as some American Loyalists argued that as an Englishman he had
no business to be meddling in the internal affairs of the colonies, his
British enemies presented Paine as a "foreign emissary" who should
keep his nose out of the internal affairs of Britain.[83] There were
certain disadvantages in being a citizen of the world. Besides, one
writer added, "if America is a free country; if it is the land flowing
with milk and honey, why are Bancroft, Paine, and many other Americans lurking in this country?"[84] The Loyalists already knew, or thought
they knew, the answer: Paine's American career clearly demonstrated
that he was a disloyal troublemaker whose influence had to be checked.

As well as using Paine's American background against him, the
Loyalists also attempted to undercut the entire concept of America
as a land of liberty destined to illuminate the Old World. It was
essential, they felt, to show that America was not the republican paradise portrayed in the *Rights of Man*. For some, the United States was

---

80 *Letter from a Magistrate*, p. 71; *British Freeholder's Address*, p. 13.

81 Boothby, *Observations*, pp. 98–106; Bowles, *Protest*, pp. viii, 3; Hunt, *Rights of
Englishmen*, p. 5; J. Jones, *Reason of Man: Part Second*, p. 5; Hardy, D. D., *Patriot*,
pp. 2–3.

82 Bowles, *Protest*, p. 5.

83 *British Freeholder's Address*, p. 5; Hardy, D. D., *Patriot*, pp. 2–3.

84 *Defence of the Constitution*, p. 9.

simply too primitive and immature to furnish any kind of example to Europe. "America was born but the other day," argued William Lewelyn, "and is hardly out of her cradle yet: she knows nothing therefore, what she is or does. There have been already many shifts and shiftings; and there will be a great deal more."[85] Any attempt to apply the standards of the cradle to the more complex and sophisticated societies of Europe was seen as an invitation to disaster. "Those who misled the French by endeavouring to make them imitate America," William Playfair wrote, "have much to answer for."[86]

Other Loyalist writers conceded that America did enjoy more liberty than Britain, but insisted that this was a product of environmental factors rather than republican government. Because America was relatively isolated from the designs of foreign powers, the argument ran, she was not burdened with a standing army, which was both a drain on resources and a serious threat to liberty. And because America was blessed with an abundance of land, the United States would enjoy prosperity and "the means of preserving a certain degree of equality among their citizens, for a much longer period than is ever likely to be attainable in Europe." According to this viewpoint, the structure of government in America was of secondary importance. Paine's attempt to make America a model for Britain was thus seen as misguided and misleading.[87]

Leaving aside such environmental considerations, men like Bowles and Thomas Hardy D.D. believed that the American system of government was actually an argument against Paine's democratic republicanism. Discussing the Federal Constitution of 1787, Bowles maintained that America was gradually moving towards the kind of balanced government that had worked so well in Britain. "After a trial for several years of the pure democratical representative system," he argued, America "has found it necessary to adopt both Monarchy and Aristocracy: for the President, under that denomination, is invested with monarchical prerogatives; and the Senate constitutes a Middle

85 Lewelyn, *Appeal to Men*, 2: 88.

86 Playfair, *Inevitable Consequences*, pp. 16–17. Compare with Jepson, *Letters to Thomas Payne*, p. 46: "nor is it very extraordinary," wrote Jepson, "that, from a country where all are nearly on a level, you should transplant your levelling principles into others, to which they are in no wise adapted."

87 *Considerations on Mr. Paine's Pamphlet*, pp. 14–17; *Answer to the Second Part of Rights of Man*, p. 16.

Chamber: so that even American experience contradicts all Mr. Paine's notions of Government." It was only a matter of time, he concluded, before the presidential office would become hereditary.[88]

Hardy agreed, emphasizing the deep sectional conflicts within the United States and arguing that only the monarch-like figure of George Washington held the country together. "At any rate," wrote Hardy, "as soon as America shall become a manufacturing country, and a land of cities, one of two events must follow: either that the states must separate, and exhibit the vices, and experience the miseries, of republics in such circumstances, or they must resort to a mixed government, in which a monarchy, and a nobility, may consolidate and balance the political system." Many democratic republicans, including Paine himself, would soon express Bowles's and Hardy's hopes as their own fears.[89]

Not only Paine's view of America as "the admiration and model of the present," but also his image of the New World as an asylum of virtue and liberty was strongly attacked in the Loyalist literature.[90] The notion that America was in any way superior to Britain provoked Paine's opponents into some of their most heated language. "In a word," wrote Lewelyn, "all the refuse of the nations, the issues and sweepings of the prisons, the nuisance of society, and the scum of kingdoms have there met, and collected into a national body. . . . America therefore, or Botany Bay, for they are the same, must not be proposed as places from whence the perfection of government is to be expected. For to hear a collection of convicts, bankrupts, run aways, vagabonds and prodigals, say that they are the first people of good sense and decorum that ever appeared in the world, is insulting. . . ."[91] The treatment of American Loyalists during the Revolution and America's refusal to pay its debts to Britain were regarded as

88 Bowles, *Protest*, pp. 20–21.

89 Hardy, D. D., *Patriot*, pp. 52–53. For Paine's fears about such possible tendencies, see his *Letter to George Washington*, 2: 692–93, 695–96, and *To the Citizens of the United States*, 2: 916–17. In the former, Paine commented that "as the Federal Constitution is a copy, though not quite so base as the original, of the form of the British Government, an imitation of its vices was naturally to be expected" (*Letter to George Washington*, 2: 693). Fearing monarchical tendencies in the executive and aristocratic tendencies in the Senate, he specifically wanted a plural executive and a shorter duration of the Senate.

90 Paine, *Rights of Man, Part 2*, 1: 372.

91 Lewelyn, *Appeal to Men*, 2: 125–26.

sufficient commentaries on American "virtue" and "honesty." But what else was to be expected, asked one writer, from "the sink into which England . . . poured all its filth?"[92] This was hardly a flattering picture; Paine's idealization of America had simply been stood on its head.

Such arguments made no impact on popular Radical perceptions of America; the principal participants in the "debate" over the *Rights of Man* were talking to themselves rather than to each other. Almost all British democrats shared Paine's positive image of the New World. Popular Radicals drank toasts to the United States as the land of liberty, and printed handbills comparing English and American taxation. Charles Pigott's *Political Dictionary* ("Explaining the True Meaning of Words") defined America as "a bright and immortal example to all colonies groaning under a foreign yoke, proving the invincible energy and virtue of freedom, and enjoying a state of prosperity, since she has thrown off her dependence on Great Britain, hitherto unknown in the nations of Europe."[93]

Before the birth of popular Radicalism in Britain, moderate reformers such as Christopher Wyvill had praised America as an example of the benefits of moderate reform; after 1791, egalitarian democrats praised America as an example of the benefits of egalitarian democracy. Paine played a major part in this shift of emphasis, and contributed to popular Radical notions of America as a "beacon of freedom." Right through to the Chartist era, the United States came to symbolize the benefits and demonstrate the practicability of political liberty: universal manhood suffrage, the secret ballot, cheap government, freedom of the press, separation of church and state, and the reform of public finance. In 1839, a leading Chartist newspaper believed that "the inhabitants of the United States are governed on the principles of Chartism, the consequence of which is that all legislation is bent towards the welfare of the many, and not of the few."[94]

A good example of Paine's "American" influence on popular Radicals is provided by William Winterbotham, a "Jacobin" Baptist preacher from Plymouth who in 1793 got four years' imprisonment for his "seditious" sermons. Winterbotham's four-volume *Historical, Geo-*

---

92 *Considerations on Mr. Paine's Pamphlet*, p. 14; *Defence of the Constitution*, p. 16.

93 HO, 42/19, f. 397; *Explanation of the Word Equality*, p. 1; Pigott, *Political Dictionary*, pp. 2–3.

94 Quoted in Lillibridge, *Beacon of Freedom*, p. 49.

graphical, Commercial and Philosophical View of the American United States
was "published in numbers and generally read by the members" of
the LCS; it helped educate a new political generation.[95] Arguing that
"the latest and acutest of our political philosophers are more than
suspected of being the disciples only of Paine and Barlow, whose
knowledge is notoriously the produce of the American school," Winterbotham intended his own work to become part of the process through
which the New World would regenerate the Old.

In his view, America represented the victory of reason, liberty, and
the rights of man over "superstition" and "despotism," and demonstrated that political liberty was inseparable from a broadly egalitarian
society. America, for Winterbotham, was the land where the productive classes had come into their own. "There are few, indeed," he
wrote, "whose incomes will reach two thousand pounds sterling per
ann. and the number nearly as small, and perhaps smaller, who are
reduced to a dependent situation. . . . A man is respected and admired
more for the variety, ingenuity and utility of his handywork, than for
the antiquity of his family." The social benefits of republican democracy, which Paine described in the *Rights of Man*, already existed in
America. Once the British people came to their senses and threw off
the oppressive yoke of hereditary government, they could expect similar benefits; the Old World would remodel itself on the image of the
New.[96]

And yet, as long as "old corruption" remained in Britain, as long
as Winterbotham could get four years for his radical sermons, or
someone like Thomas Muir could get fourteen years' transportation
for disseminating Paine's writings, America served another, more immediate function: it could become a place of refuge for the persecuted, "where they may almost say, the wicked cease from troubling,
and the weary are at rest."[97] With every tightening of the anti-Jacobin
screw, more and more British democrats crossed the Atlantic to the
"land of liberty." Writing of the Loyalist campaign of 1792 and 1793,
Thomas Hardy recalled that "all that hubbub and noise throughout

95 *Trial of William Winterbotham*; Winterbotham, *Historical . . . View*; PP, Add. Ms.
27808, f. 113.
96 Winterbotham, *Historical . . . View*, 1: iv; 3: 281, 286, 298, 331. Another Anglo-
American Radical work, Barlow's *Advice to the Privileged Orders*, was read by British
democrats, while Barlow himself maintained close links with the SCI and LCS. See
HO, 42/21, f. 665, and PP, Add. Ms. 27812, f. 23.
97 Winterbotham, *Historical . . . View*, 1: v.

the country disorganized the *London Corresponding Society* very much—many of the members were also alarmed and fled to different parts of the country—some went to America."[98] More went to America after the treason trials of 1794 and the Two Acts of 1795.[99] Pigott's dictionary in 1795 defined an emigrant as "one who, like Dr. Priestley, or Thomas Cooper, is compelled to fly from persecution, and explore liberty in a far distant land, probably America, the states of Europe for the most part, France excepted, being rank despotisms."[100]

Tired of repeated failure in their own country, many leading British democrats left for America in the 1790s. They included not only Priestley and Cooper (who wound up as a slave-owning South Carolina judge), but also men like Joseph Gales, editor of the radical Sheffield newspaper the *Isis*; Daniel Isaac Eaton, democrat, free-thinker, writer, and publisher; Citizen Richard Lee, one of London's more extreme Jacobin publishers, and Morgan John Rhees, the Welsh Baptist and Jacobin who attempted to establish a Welsh freedom settlement in the New World.[101] There were many lesser-known figures, who were hostile to the British system of government and whose heads were full of Paine's and Winterbotham's notions of America. One such figure was an obscure ex-soldier who crossed the Atlantic late in 1792. His name was William Cobbett.

98 PP, Add. Ms. 27816, f. 43.

99 On the Two Acts, which restricted the right of free speech and public meeting, see Goodwin, *Friends of Liberty*, pp. 387–90.

100 Pigott, *Political Dictionary*, pp. 17–18.

101 See Durey, "Transatlantic Patriotism," pp. 7–31, and Twomey, "Jacobins and Jeffersonians."

PART TWO

Cobbett

The most dangerous arguments of the infamous Paine, and the other seducers of the people, were built on their impudent mistatements respecting America . . .
Cobbett, *PG*, 26 October 1799

You remember PAINE, baptized "TOM"; for our aristocracy and money mongers are so frugal that they cannot afford a word so long as "Thomas" in such a case. Our old friend "TOM," who gave tyranny harder knocks than any man that ever lived, concluded his dedication (which he addressed to WASHINGTON) to that thunder-bolt, the first part of the *Rights of Man*, in these words: "That the *new world may regenerate the old*, is the fervent prayer of your most obedient servant, THOMAS PAINE."

This prayer of our old friend "TOM," who was born, let it be remembered, at THETFORD, in Norfolk, is very likely now to be fulfilled. You have been at work *in the regenerating of us*, ever since you raised the standard of *"liberty, property and no stamp act."* The sousing which you gave to our long list of heroes in the last war, did still more towards our regeneration. The cheapness of your government is continually working our regeneration. But, *now*, you seem to have set about finishing the good work; for, if you root out the accursed, and ever accursed paper money, we are regenerated indeed. If you destroy the accursed thing, we cannot keep it? and, then, freedom will once more be safe in this world.
Cobbett to the people of the U.S.A., *PR*, 1 February 1834

IV

From Ploughboy to Paineite, 1763–92

IN CONTRAST to Paine, who rarely mentioned his early life in England, Cobbett often wrote about his upbringing. He penned his autobiography when he was only thirty-three and filled the pages of the *Political Register* with anecdotes about his youth.[1] The trouble is that Cobbett on Cobbett is not a reliable witness. Because he used his past to contrast a romantic Old England with a distinctly unromantic present, and because he idealized his personal life and achievements, it is difficult to distinguish between Cobbett the self-made man and Cobbett the self-made myth.[2]

In another sense, however, Cobbett's self-perception reveals a great deal about the man and his politics. Just as he tried to become the ideal to which he aspired, to live out his own mythology, he approached politics as a confrontation between the ideal and the "real," between the way things should be and the way they were. This tension between "is" and "ought" operated in a transatlantic context: Cobbett's experience of the United States turned him from a Paineite republican into a High Tory, in much the same way that his subsequent experience of English politics turned him from a Tory into a Radical. To understand this process, it is necessary first to examine Cobbett's attitude and beliefs as they unfolded in England and New Brunswick, before he established himself as a political writer in the United States.

---

1 Cobbett, *Life and Adventures of Peter Porcupine*; for an excellent compilation of Cobbett's numerous autobiographical writings, see *Autobiography of William Cobbett*, ed. Reitzel.

2 The gap between Cobbett's day-to-day existence and his idealized self-image is brought out by Spater, "Quest for William Cobbett," pp. 12–13.

I

Cobbett, twenty-six years younger than Paine, was born at Farnham, Surrey, in 1763. The son of a small farmer and innkeeper who taught him the rudiments of reading, writing, and arithmetic, Cobbett spent his first years working as a ploughboy and a gardener's assistant. In the England of his youth, Cobbett recalled, honesty, thrift, and hard work won respect and a good farm; his own father's modest success was proof of that.[3] Cobbett remembered the fairs ("we had a great many holidays"), the cricket matches, hunting, adventure, and healthy work of an upbringing characterized by "Honest pride, and happy days!" This nostalgic image of Old England was not entirely fanciful; behind it lay a core of reality.

Cobbett's Farnham was, in fact, a prosperous hop-growing centre, close to some of the best soil and most beautiful scenery in the country. But, ultimately, it was the myth of Farnham that mattered; the imagination of his youth became a unifying symbol in Cobbett's thought, against which he would judge either American Jacobinism or English corruption. His later writings represented an attempt to reshape nineteenth-century realities into eighteenth-century memories. "I wish to see," he wrote in 1807, "the poor men of England what the poor men of England were when I was born."[4]

It is impossible to disentangle Cobbett's early attitudes from his later recollections. He presented himself as an inquisitive, impressionable boy who went without supper to buy Jonathan Swift's *Tale of a Tub*, and who experienced a "sort of birth of intellect" after reading the book. He remembered how the American Revolution had brought "politics" into the countryside, and recalled how he had been impressed by his father's heated and tenacious defence of the Patriots; "had my father been on the other side," he added, "I should have been on the other side too." He wrote about his "astonishment and admiration" at the sight of the fleet off Spithead, and of his desire to become a sailor. (Unlike Paine, who served as a privateersman during

3 Cobbett recalled that his father, possessing "experience and understanding" and being "honest, industrious and frugal," rose from poverty to become the owner of a "good farm" (Cobbett, *Life and Adventures*, pp. 11–12).

4 *PR*, 28 February 1807. For Cobbett's description of his youth in rural England, see *Autobiography of William Cobbett*, pp. 9–21, and Cobbett, *Life and Adventures*, pp. 9–21. On the influence of the Surrey countryside on Cobbett's later outlook, see Sambrook, *William Cobbett*, pp. 31–36, and Green, *Great Cobbett*, pp. 24–37.

the Seven Years' War, Cobbett was unsuccessful in his attempt to run away to sea).

Apart from such memories, indicating an early fascination with Swift's satire, a vague hostility to "oppression" as defined by his father, and a strong patriotic pride in the navy, little is known of Cobbett's outlook at this time. The fact that he ran away from home three times demonstrates that the reality of Farnham was less idyllic and more constricting for Cobbett than subsequently he would suggest. By 1783, his impulse to see more of the world took him to London, where he wound up working fifteen hours a day as an attorney's clerk. Detesting this job, but unwilling to return home, Cobbett joined the army. Just over a year later, after completing his training at the Chatham Depot, he crossed the Atlantic to join his regiment in Nova Scotia and New Brunswick.[5]

Despite the harrowing experience of hunger while at Chatham— an experience he never forgot—and despite his unfavourable impression of Nova Scotia, Cobbett developed a strong "bond of attachment" to the army and an overwhelming sense of pride in his own record. "In my regiment," he boasted, "I was every thing: the whole corps was under my controul: I rendered services, not only in the regiment, but in the provinces where we were stationed, such as no one but myself would have thought of. . . . the fame of my service and talents ran through the whole country."[6] His list of self-proclaimed achievements was remarkable. According to his later writings, Cobbett handled all the administrative work of the regiment, wrote a short book on arithmetic for his fellow soldiers, designed and supervised the building of a barrack for four hundred men, taught the regiment David Dundas's *Principles of Military Movements,* and wrote up a report on "the state of the provinces of Nova Scotia and New Brunswick."

If he was exaggerating, it was not by much. His rapid promotion to regimental sergeant major ("over the heads of thirty Sergeants") indicates his worth to the army; his arithmetic book has recently been

5 Cobbett, *Life and Adventures,* pp. 14–15, 18.

6 Ibid., p. 28; *PR,* 17 June 1809, 6 December 1817, 22 November 1828; Cobbett, *Advice to Young Men,* para. 47. Green puts considerable emphasis on Cobbett's experience of hunger at the Chatham Depot, arguing that those who are "suddenly and unexpectedly" forced to feel hunger "will never again be able to take food for granted, nor will they be able to accept, without anger, the proposition that it is part of the human condition that some part of mankind must always starve" (*Great Cobbett,* pp. 51–54).

discovered, and it seems plausible that he helped introduce to the regiment Dundas's system of drilling and weapon handling.[7] The report to which he referred was connected with the Loyalist Claims Commission of 1785–87; Cobbett probably analysed and arranged the extensive material collected by the commissioners, but since the report has disappeared, it is impossible to be certain of his contribution.[8]

Yet Cobbett's greatest and most lasting accomplishment during his army years was his painful, frustrating, and ultimately successful attempt to master English grammar. During his year in Chatham, Cobbett began his long battle with Bishop Lowth's *Grammar*. "I was a young man, a private soldier," he recalled, "animated with the double ambition of shining as a scholar and as a soldier, and who clearly saw that grammar was absolutely necessary to give me even *a chance* of being a man of any weight in the world. . . . Yet, even with these motives and this character, I was, a hundred times, upon the point of committing the Bishop's book to the flames." And after allowing for all Cobbett's self-dramatization about his struggle for learning in the barracks at Chatham and "amidst the woods and snows of Nova Scotia and New Brunswick," his achievement was indeed impressive— as he himself was fully aware. For the rest of his life, Cobbett would frequently judge the moral worth and intelligence of his opponents by the quality of their grammar.[9]

Cobbett not only studied grammar while in the army, he also read anything he could get his hands on. At Chatham he subscribed to a circulating library, and devoured "novels, plays, history, poetry. . . . with equal avidity." It is also possible that he became familiar at this time with Isaac Watts's influential *Logick* and Hugh Blair's recently published *Lectures on Rhetoric*, works he referred to later in life. Yet even if this was the case, Cobbett remained unimpressed with these

7 Cobbett's arithmetic book, "Of Vulgar Fractions," is now at Yale University. See Brown, "William Cobbett in the Maritimes," pp. 448–62. Dundas's *Principles of Military Movements* was not in general use until 1792, but was probably introduced to particular regiments before then. For the argument that Cobbett simply invented the story about teaching Dundas's system to the regiment, see *Rival Imposters*, pp. 31–34.

8 *PR*, 5 December 1817, 22 November 1828. Because he stated that one of the commissioners was called Dundas, it is clear that Cobbett was writing about the commission of Thomas Dundas and Jeremy Pemberton to compensate those Loyalists who had fled from the Thirteen Colonies to what is now Canada.

9 *PR*, 21 November 1818, 6 December 1817; see also his own *Grammar of the English Language*.

treatises on logic and rhetoric. He believed that grammar was much more important than rhetorical theory, argued that "logic and rhetoric are found in men's thoughts; nature gives them, in a greater or less degree, to all persons who are not idiots," and criticized Blair for failing to live up to his own standards of plainness and clarity. Cobbett's writing style did take shape in these years, but apparently owed more to the literary example of people like Swift and Goldsmith than to the precepts of Watts and Blair.[10]

As he developed his talents and acquired a local reputation for his accomplishments, Cobbett's self-confidence began to expand into a staggering sense of superiority. A strong-willed, hard-working, and self-righteous soldier, he quickly came to despise the "profound and surprizing ignorance" of the "*Epaulet* gentry." His officers, he wrote in 1809, "were, in every thing except authority, my inferiors; and ought to have been commanded by me." To make matters even worse, some of them were also corrupt. When he discovered that certain officers were practising peculation, and when his complaints met with a cool reception, Cobbett decided to prepare secretly a case against four officers, get safely out of the army, and then take legal action against them. Here, in New Brunswick, we catch the first glimpse of Cobbett's lifelong conflict with corruption and the misuse of power.[11]

It is not clear whether or to what extent Cobbett's attitude to the abuse of authority assumed political dimensions. He later commented that he had been more concerned with specific grievances than wider issues. "My head was filled with the corruptions and the baseness in the army," he wrote. "I knew nothing at all about politics." Not everyone in the army agreed; there were reports in 1792 that before his discharge Cobbett had drunk a toast to "*the destruction of the House of Brunswick.*" "I had talked pretty freely, upon the occasion alluded to," Cobbett replied; "but I had neither said, nor thought any thing against the king, and, as to the *House of Brunswick*, I hardly knew what it meant."[12] Whatever one makes of those accusations—and there are good grounds to be sceptical about them—Cobbett's declaration of

10 Cobbett, *Life and Adventures*, p. 25; *PR*, 21 November 1818; *Grammar of the English Language*, esp. paras. 171–73. As well as reading Swift's *Tale of a Tub*, Cobbett was impressed with Goldsmith at this time; see *PR*, 23 June 1832. For Watts's and Blair's respective places in new logic and new rhetoric, see Howell, *Logic and Rhetoric*, pp. 331–45, 647–71.

11 *PR*, 17 June 1809, 6 December 1817.

12 *PR*, 17 June 1809.

political ignorance is unconvincing. It certainly does not fit with Cobbett the voracious reader, or the Cobbett who told his children that he had written a *History of the Kings and Queens of England* before he joined the army. But if Cobbett was not as ignorant as he later claimed, what kind of political leanings did he have while stationed in the "Loyalist Elysium" of New Brunswick?

An important clue—but one which has been completely overlooked by his biographers—is provided by Cobbett's later comments about the nature of New Brunswick politics during the 1780s. When he arrived at Saint John in 1785, the pioneer town was split between the Loyalist élite and the rank and file over the distribution of land and provisions. The colony which Edward Winslow hoped would become "the most Gentlemanlike one on earth" was rocked by charges that the élite had indulged in "gross partialitys" at the expense of the poorer refugees. With ordinary Loyalists fearing that they would be reduced to tenants (or "slaves") of a few large landowners, and with the élite viewing any challenge to its position as a threat to the orderly, hierarchical "model" society which it intended to establish in New Brunswick, Saint John became a bitterly divided community.

Things came to a head in November 1785, when the colony's first election was fought between the government candidates, or "Upper Covers" as they were known, and the popular party, or "Lower Covers." When it appeared that the Upper Covers were going to lose, their leaders tried to give the soldiers the vote, assuming that the soldiers would follow the lead of their officers and support the government candidates. Writing about these events in 1817, shortly after his conversion to adult male suffrage, Cobbett stated that:

Our *Officers* were, of course, of the Upper Cove party; but it was far different with us, who had canvassed and discussed the whole thing as amply as it had ever been discussed by the Governor and his Council. . . . It was odd enough, that we should have had this unanimous feeling in favour of the popular party in the Province; but we had it, and all the cats o'nine tails at the command of the Holy Alliance would not have rooted it out of our hearts.[13]

According to Cobbett, the Upper Covers dropped their demands to enfranchise the soldiers when it became clear that the soldiers could

13 *PR*, 13 December 1817. On the political divisions within New Brunswick, see Bell, *Early Loyalist Saint John*, and Wright, *Loyalists of New Brunswick*, pp. 125–26.

not be relied upon. In the event, the Upper Covers lost the election but managed to reverse the result by demanding a scrutiny and disqualifying sufficient numbers of Lower Cove voters. Having suppressed dissent, the Loyalist élite set out to make New Brunswick the "envy" of the American states.[14]

Although Cobbett may have been manipulating his past to win an argument in 1817 about the importance of enfranchising soldiers, it is more likely that in the 1780s he had genuine sympathies with the Lower Covers. His dissatisfaction with his officers in New Brunswick was real enough, and it is significant that in both his later Tory and Radical phases Cobbett ridiculed the pretensions of "those who called themselves the gentry" among the Upper Cove supporters. New Brunswick, he wrote in 1796, contained "thousands of captains and colonels without soldiers, and of squires without stockings or shoes."[15] In his first political encounter, Cobbett probably took the "popular" side against an élite whose abilities and ambitions he did not respect. At any rate, the view that Cobbett was essentially non-political at this time must be called into question. And it is quite conceivable that a combination of factors, from his father's support for the American Revolution to Cobbett's experience of corruption in the army and hostility to the Loyalist élite in the Saint John election, predisposed him towards some form of political Radicalism before he returned to England in November 1791.

II

He arrived in England just as the popular Radical movement was gathering momentum under the impetus of the French Revolution and the writings of Paine. During the four months Cobbett spent there, before leaving for France, the first democratic societies were attracting more and more people who were reading the *Rights of Man*, especially *Part Two* which came out in February 1792. In this atmosphere, Cobbett, having left the army, was trying to bring his former officers to justice at a court martial, and was finding serious obstacles in the way.[16] And in this atmosphere, he produced his first political

14 This theme is developed in Condon, *Envy of the American States*.

15 *PR*, 13 December 1817; *Life and Adventures*, p. 28. See also the discussion in Bell, *Early Loyalist Saint John*, pp. 142–43.

16 For Cobbett's account of his unsuccessful attempt to court-martial his former

pamphlet, *The Soldier's Friend.* Just as Paine's *Case of the Officers of Excise* illuminates Paine's attitudes on the eve of his American career, *The Soldier's Friend* reveals a great deal about Cobbett's outlook just before his own career in the United States.

The immediate occasion for Cobbett's pamphlet was the debate over the army estimates in the House of Commons in February 1792, when the government requested extra money to raise the soldier's pay to three shillings a week. In theory, soldiers already received that amount of money; in practice, however, peculation had sharply driven down their wages. According to the Mutiny Act, any officers found guilty of such practices would be court-martialled; this is why Cobbett had already brought his own case to the attention of secretary at war, George Yonge, the previous month. When he now discovered that Yonge knew of corruption in the army, was prepared to gloss it over, and would rather restore the three shillings wage through raising taxes than rooting out corruption, Cobbett was incensed. If he had earlier believed that corruption in the army was the exception rather than the rule, his experiences in England, at a time of radical political and ideological change, quickly changed his mind.

In its style and tone, *The Soldier's Friend* anticipated much of Cobbett's later political writing. Consider, for example, his response to Yonge's comment that it had "so happened" that soldiers were only receiving half their official pay.

It has "so happened!" and for years too! Astonishing! It has "so happened" that an act of Parliament has been most notoriously and shamefully disobeyed for years, to the extreme misery of thousands of deluded wretches (our countrymen), and to the great detriment of the nation at large; it has "so happened," that not one of the officers have been brought to justice for this disobedience, even now it is fully discovered; and it has "so happened," that the hand of power has made another slice into the national purse, in order— not to add to what the soldier ought to have received; not to satisfy *his* hunger and thirst; but to gratify the whim or the avarice of his capricious and plundering superiors.[17]

The use of repetition, the rhythm of the argument and the rising

---

officers, see *PR*, 17 June 1809; for the views of one of his later opponents, see *Rival Imposters*. Spater discusses the affair in *William Cobbett*, pp. 30–36.

17 Cobbett, *The Soldier's Friend*, pp. 8–9.

sense of anger and indignation would all become characteristic of Cobbett. So too would the plain style and blunt language of the pamphlet. Like Paine, Cobbett attempted to cut through "plausible delusions" to arrive at the plain truth. Cobbett even "rewrote" Yonge's speech in the "language of truth," making Yonge conclude that "it is certainly much better to tax the people to their last farthing than to wound *the honour* of our *trusty and well beloved* Officers of the Army, by any ordinary and *ungentlemanlike* investigation of their conduct." This kind of sarcasm, used by Cobbett to expose and undermine political hypocrisy, would also pervade his later writings.[18]

The Soldier's Friend was firmly grounded in Cobbett's own experiences in the army. He wrote of "the little knowledge People in general have of military affairs," and explained the mechanics of peculation to his civilian readers. Against popular perceptions of "those jovial, honest looking fellows, the Officers of the Army," Cobbett drew on his recent past. "I could mention characters in this *honourable* profession," he wrote, "that would shine amongst the *Seed of Abraham*, or do honour to the society of Stock Jobbers." This was the first sign of the anti-Semitism and the hostility to high finance which came to characterize his work in the *Political Register*.

Together with contempt for corrupt officers went Cobbett's sympathy for the common soldier. "I would have you know," he told the soldiers, "that you are not the servant of *one man* only; a British soldier never can be that. You are a servant of the whole nation, of your countrymen, who pay you, and from whom you can have no separate interests. I would have you look upon nothing that you receive as a *Favour* or a *Bounty* from Kings, Queens, or Princes; you receive the wages of your servitude; it is your property, confirmed to you by Acts of the Legislature of your Country, which property, your rapacious Officers ought never to seize on, without meeting with a punishment due to their infamy." Driven by an elementary sense of justice, Cobbett quite simply wanted soldiers to be treated as men, not "Beasts."[19]

But in 1792, Cobbett's critique of corruption was no longer directed only at particular army officers; it was now broadened to embrace the

---

18 Ibid., pp. 4, 18–19. Paine himself employed the technique of rewriting his opponents' speeches later in 1792, in response to the House of Commons debate on the Royal Proclamation against seditious writings; see Paine, *Letter Addressed to the Addressers* 2: 472–74.

19 Cobbett, *The Soldier's Friend*, pp. 4, 12–13, 21–22.

government itself, perceived as being run by and for "gentlemen" at the expense of the common people. The government's refusal to remedy abuses in the army, wrote Cobbett,

points out in the clearest light the close connection that exists between the *ruling Faction* in this Country and the military Officers: and this connection ever must exist while we suffer ourselves to be governed by *a Faction*. If any other body of men had thus impudently set the laws of the land at defiance, if a *gang of robbers*, unornamented with red coats and cockades, had plundered their fellow citizens, what would have been the consequence? They would have been brought to justice, hanging or transportation would have been their fate; but it seems, the Army is become a *sanctuary* from the power of the law.

While the "ruling Powers" looked after themselves, argued Cobbett, the burden of looking after the ordinary soldier fell on the "nation." With this kind of officially sponsored corruption, it was no wonder that there existed an "enormous load of taxes, that press out the very vitals of the People."[20]

Cobbett kept quiet about *The Soldier's Friend* during his years as a Tory, and one can see why. One can also see why the government in the 1790s reacted strongly against the pamphlet. It was republished at the price of 2d. in 1793, and may well have had a large circulation; the government was sufficiently alarmed to take legal action against James Ridgway, its publisher.[21] Lord Melville (formerly Home Secretary Henry Dundas) later wrote that the pamphlet was "fraught with ten times more mischief than Paine's Rights of Man," and "was a considerable source of the naval mutiny at the Nore."[22] George Chalmers, the government's biographer of Paine, even speculated that Paine himself wrote *The Soldier's Friend*.[23] This is not really surprising; William Cobbett in 1792 sounded very like Tom Paine.

It must be remembered that Cobbett wrote his pamphlet at the same time that he was reading the *Rights of Man, Part Two*. In that

20 Ibid., pp. 4, 17, 20–21.
21 On the impact of the pamphlet and the general question of political Radicalism in the army at this time, see Emsley, "Political Disaffection," pp. 230–45, esp. 232. Ridgway in 1793 was sentenced to four years for publishing Paineite and other Radical literature; see Goodwin, *Friends of Liberty*, p. 272.
22 The accusation is quoted in *PR*, 5 October 1805.
23 Chalmers, *Life of Thomas Pain* (7th ed., 1793), p. 25.

work, Paine had linked poor treatment of soldiers with the aristocratic system of government and written that, with democratic government, "the oppressed soldier will become a free man." "As soldiers have hitherto been treated in most countries," argued Paine, "they might be said to be without a friend. Shunned by the citizen on an apprehension of their being enemies to liberty, and too often insulted by those who commanded them, their condition was a double oppression. But when genuine principles of liberty pervade a people, everything is restored to order; and the soldier civilly treated, returns the civility."[24]

Such words must have captured Cobbett's imagination. Indeed, Cobbett provides a classic example of the process by which the *Rights of Man* made such a remarkable impact. Paine articulated the kind of grievances Cobbett had directly experienced, and Paine located those grievances within the wider political system. The intention was clearly to politicize discontent. And there is no doubt that early in 1792 Cobbett became politicized. As he wrote several years later,

previous to my leaving England for France, previous to my *seeing* what republicanism was, I had not only imbibed its principles, I had not only been a republican, but an admirer of the writings of PAINE. The fault, therefore, if there was any, was in the head, and not in the heart; and, I do not think, that even the head will be much blamed by those who duly reflect, that I was, when I took up PAINE's book, a novice in politics, that I was boiling with indignation at the abuses I had witnessed, and that, as to the powers of the book itself, it required first a proclamation, then a law, and next the suspension of the *habeas-corpus* act, to counteract them.[25]

One may doubt his claim that he was a Paineite because of political ignorance; Cobbett repeatedly dismissed his earlier views as the product of ignorance or naïvety.[26] But the general thrust of his statement rings true. His own experiences interlocked with Paine's arguments to turn Cobbett into a Radical. "Under such circumstances," he added, "it would have argued not only a want of zeal, but a want of sincerity, and even a want of honesty, not to have entertained sentiments like those expressed in the *'Soldier's Friend.'* "[27]

24 Paine, *Rights of Man, Part 2,* 1: 449–50.

25 *PR,* 5 October 1805.

26 Thus in 1820 Cobbett the Radical explained away his American Toryism by saying that he "understood little at that time" (*PR,* 19 February 1820).

27 *PR,* 5 October 1805.

As a good Paineite republican, Cobbett was also at this time an admirer of the United States. The country had fascinated him since his youth, when news of the American Revolution first filtered through to Farnham. A few years later, he read Abbé Raynal's "flattering picture" of the United States and decided to see it for himself.[28] This positive image of the new republic was reinforced by the *Rights of Man, Part Two*, with its glowing description of New World liberty.[29] When England became too dangerous for him, it is not surprising that he fled to republican America by way of revolutionary France.

Little is known about his six months in France; there is no evidence, however, that he involved himself in politics or that his experiences turned him against republican principles.[30] On his arrival in the United States in October 1792, Cobbett's views remained unchanged. "I had imbibed principles of republicanism," he told his American readers four years later, "and . . . I thought that men enjoyed here a greater degree of liberty than in England; and this, if not the principal reason, was at least one, for my coming to this country."[31] And one of the first things he did when he reached America was to contact Secretary of State Thomas Jefferson about employment possibilities. "Ambitious to become the citizen of a free state," he wrote, "I have left my native country, England, for America. I bring with me, youth, a small family, a few useful literary talents, and that is all."[32]

At this stage, Cobbett seems to have been typical of the many British Radicals who chose to live in America at least partly for political reasons. One might have expected him to follow the path of those other "ideological immigrants" who committed themselves to democratic republicanism in the 1790s.[33] But almost two years after writing his letter to Jefferson, Cobbett resurfaced as an aggressive conservative writer whose denunciations of democracy surpassed in their

28 Cobbett, *Life and Adventures*, p. 33; *PR*, 5 October 1805. See also Raynal, *Revolution of America*.

29 *PR*, 5 October 1805.

30 He had just married in February 1792; his time in France, which he later described as "the six happiest months of my life," seems to have been taken up improving his French, studying continental fortifications, and, of course, on honeymoon. See Spater, *William Cobbett*, p. 36–37.

31 Cobbett, *Life and Adventures*, p. 33.

32 Quoted in M. Clark, *Peter Porcupine in America*, p. 7. Jefferson replied: "Public offices in our Government are so few, and of so little value, as to offer no resources to talents" (Ibid., pp. 7–8).

33 The phrase is from Sheps, "Ideological Immigrants," pp. 231–46.

ferocity even those of Bowles and Burke. Cobbett's progress from ploughboy to Paineite had been abruptly halted, as he moved in new directions which led him to High Toryism in America and eventually to a form of Tory Radicalism back in England. It would be a mistake, however, to dismiss his early Paineite viewpoint merely as a passing phase, for it holds an important clue to both Cobbett's conversion to Toryism and the intensity with which he held his new Tory convictions.

V

The Tory in America, 1792–1800

IN JULY 1796, William Cobbett, or Peter Porcupine as he now called himself, set up his own publishing and bookselling shop in Philadelphia. Determined to "excite rage in the enemies of Great Britain," he not only painted his new shop a Tory blue, but exhibited in the windows portraits of George III and his ministry, together with a large engraving of Lord Howe's naval victory over the French in 1794. Another part of the display coupled pictures of leading American Patriots with those of extreme French sansculottes; Franklin, for example, was carefully placed next to Marat. To do this in democratic Philadelphia was, as Cobbett realized, both unprecedented and dangerous. "Such a sight had not been seen in Philadelphia for twenty years," he wrote. "Never since the beginning of the rebellion, had anyone dared to hoist at his windows the portrait of George the Third." And when his landlord received an anonymous letter threatening to destroy the shop unless its new tenant was evicted, Cobbett happily generalized from the particular and portrayed all democrats as being intolerant, violent men who believed that "the press is free for them, and them alone."[1]

His defiant opening of the shop symbolized Cobbett's continued commitment to strengthen the consciousness of Englishness among Americans, to fight against "all the hell of democracy," and to bind the United States as closely as possible to its former mother country.[2]

1 *PW* 4: 3–4; *PR*, 5 October 1805; Cobbett, *The Scare-Crow*, p. 19.
2 Cobbett, *An Antidote for Tom Paine's Theological and Political Poison*, p. 52. The phrase deliberately recalls Paine's declaration of war against "all the hell of monarchy" (Paine, "To the Abbé Sieyès" 2: 520).

He had made this commitment back in 1794. The occasion of Cobbett's entry into American politics was the arrival in New York of Joseph Priestley, the Unitarian, chemist, and democrat who had been driven out of England after a Birmingham Church-and-King crowd destroyed his house and laboratory.[3] Attacking Priestley as a deluded "visionary" whose ideas would in practice produce a revolutionary bloodbath, Cobbett abandoned his earlier democratic and republican sympathies and found his voice as a Tory in America. The contrast with his views in 1792 could not have been more striking; the same man was talking in a completely different political language. What had made him change his mind? And what was the character of Cobbett's newly acquired conservatism in America?

I

Cobbett's own explanation was deceptively simple; his conversion, he argued, was primarily an instinctive patriotic response to persistent democratic attacks on his country. As he put it in 1798, he had "long felt a becoming indignation at the atrocious slander that was continually vomitted forth against Great Britain; and the malignancy of Priestley and his addresses at New-York brought it into action."[4] At a time when many Americans embraced the style and slogans of the French Revolution, viewed Britain as the centre of counter-revolutionary oppression and complained about British depredations on American commerce, Cobbett, so he told his audience, could only remember that he was an Englishman. "Though I had been greatly disgusted at the trick played me in England, with regard to a court-martial," he recalled, "I forgot every thing when the honour of England was concerned."[5] Even when he changed his political beliefs again in later life, he never felt any reason to apologize for his patriotism in America. He might state that he had been ignorant about the British "system," and he might eventually shake hands with his old American adversaries, but he remained proud of his patriotism. The problem, he wrote in 1817, was that he had confounded "the *government* of my country with *my country herself*."[6]

3 See Rose, "The Priestley Riots of 1791," pp. 68–88.
4 Cobbett, *Democratic Judge*, p. 7.
5 *PR*, 19 February 1820.
6 *PR*, 4 January 1817. Ironically, Cobbett in 1798 attacked Noah Webster for

His patriotism need not be doubted; indeed, it remained a central and permanent feature of his outlook. But the question remains— why did Cobbett choose in 1794 to identify love of his country with love of his country's government? To understand his conversion, it is necessary to go beyond straightforward patriotism, and to examine Cobbett's changing perceptions of republicanism shortly after he arrived in the United States.

Much of the change in his position was generated by events or reports of events in revolutionary France. As a teacher of English to French *émigrés*, Cobbett moved among men whose direct experience of revolutionary "excesses" probably made him question his earlier Paineite leanings. Similarly, his translation in early 1793 of a pamphlet on Lafayette's impeachment made Cobbett aware of the dark side of the French Revolution: judicial persecution and "mob" violence in the name of liberty. He had already spoken out against the abuse of power in England; now it must have seemed to him that republican democracy was even worse than the system it opposed.

His initial reaction was one of political withdrawal. "Every time the newspapers arrive," he wrote to a friend in July 1793, "the aristocrats and democrats have a decent quarrel to the admiration of all the little boys in town. . . . God preserve you from the political pest. Let them fight and tear one another's eyes out; take care of your business, and let the devil and them decide their disputes."[7] Only when he had become thoroughly disillusioned with republicanism was it possible for Cobbett to break with his Paineite past and move through passivity to his Loyalist brand of patriotism.

Yet this disillusionment was more than a reaction to the French Revolution. Central to Cobbett's conversion was the tension between his ideal image of America and his perception of the reality. He had arrived in the United States *"brim full of republicanism,"* strongly influenced by Paine's description of the country as the land of liberty,

---

making precisely such a distinction between the British government and the British nation. "This is a true French distinction," he wrote, "a separation of *the government* from *the people*. But, wretch, wretch, are not the army and navy composed of Britons? are not the parliament and ministry also composed of Britons? and is not the King a Briton? And in abusing all these, all that gives union, strength, activity, character, consequence, and even existence to the British nation, in abusing and vilifying all these, do you not, I say, abuse the *British nation*?" (*PW*, 9: 44–46).

7 Quoted in M. Clark, *Peter Porcupine in America*, p. 6.

virtue, and simplicity.[8] The trouble was that America as it actually existed fell far short of the America of Cobbett's imagination. In fact, his early impressions were almost uniformly negative.

The country, he informed an English friend, was "Exactly the contrary of what I expected it. The land is bad, rocky. . . . The seasons are detestable. . . . The people are worthy of the country—cheating, sly, roguish gang."[9] And as reality failed to live up to his expectations, Cobbett increasingly turned against Paine and his myth of American republicanism. "The truth is," wrote Cobbett in 1805, "the change in my way of thinking was produced by experience. I had an opportunity of *seeing* what republican government was; this experience overcame prejudice; I followed the dictates of truth and reason. Instead of that perfect freedom, and that amiable simplicity, of which PAINE had given me so flattering a description, I found myself placed under a set of petty, mean, despots, ruling by the powers given them by a perversion of the law of England."[10] Somewhere on the road to Philadelphia, Cobbett realized that he had been worshipping a false god.

Disillusionment bred in Cobbett a sense of anger, a sense of betrayal. His experience of republicanism in the United States, he wrote in 1800, "convinced me of my error, admonished me to repent of my folly, and urged me to compensate for the injustice of the opinions I had conceived."[11] This "compensation"—perhaps "overcompensation" would be more accurate—lay behind most of Cobbett's writings in America. By 1794, he believed that such freedom as there was in the United States existed despite, not because of, Paineite principles. He maintained that some Americans, the most conservative ones, were "amongst the best of mankind," but felt that the republican element of the population was corrupt, immoral, and dishonest. As a repented republican sinner, he relentlessly attacked those who saw the American nation as the living embodiment of democratic republican ideals. Determined to correct the "errors" which he himself had once believed, Cobbett repeatedly cited instances of American corruption, gleefully labelling each one "a pretty little specimen of *republican purity*." "I shall not like to be told when I return to England," he wrote after

8 *PG*, 12 August 1799.

9 Cobbett to Rachel Smither, 7 July 1794, in *Life and Letters of William Cobbett*, ed. Melville, 1: 87.

10 *PR*, 12 October 1805.

11 Cobbett, *Prospectus of a New Daily Paper*, p. 7.

cataloguing numerous instances of crime in the United States, "that 'America is totally free from those vices which abound in monarchical governments.' "[12]

The main elements in Cobbett's conversion, then, were patriotism, hostility to the abuse of power, which he associated with republican government in France and to a lesser extent in the United States, and the tensions between the ideal and the "real" in his perceptions of the American republic. These elements remained consistent in Cobbett's world view. In 1794, the conjunction of these attitudes impelled him towards an extreme anti-republican position. As his ideal image of America became tarnished, as he began to "make a comparison" between America and Britain, Cobbett began to develop a new ideal, that of "Old England." Pitt and Burke, viewed as the principal defenders of traditional English liberty, replaced Paine and Winterbotham as Cobbett's heroes. For the rest of his American career, Cobbett did everything in his power to make America and the world safe from democracy, and to strengthen the position of England in the Atlantic and on the North American continent.

II

Both Cobbett's attacks on democracy and his attempt to forge close Anglo-American ties must be placed in the broader context of America's international position during the 1790s. When he arrived in the United States, republican government was still in its infancy, Americans were still searching for a sense of identity in the face of internal tensions and external vulnerability, and American political leaders believed that their policies would decisively affect the future shape of their country. The United States was confronted with the increasingly restrictive mercantilist empires of the Old World, and had to come to grips with Britain's economic and naval control of the Atlantic. Against the background of the French Revolution and the outbreak of war between Britain and France in 1793, conflicting American interests and ideologies interlocked with the imperialist rivalries of Britain, Spain, and France.[13]

12 *PR*, 12 October 1805; *PG*, 26 September 1797, 4 October 1797.

13 For some general treatments of the dilemmas and conflicts facing Americans during the 1790s, see Buel, *Securing the Revolution*; J. Miller, *Federalist Era*; Nelson, "Hamilton and Gallatin"; Howe, "Republican Thought," pp. 147–65.

In this struggle between rival imperialisms, Britain was particularly powerful. With an economic hammerlock on the United States and with fur trade interests threatening to block American expansion in the northwest, Britain in the early 1790s was well placed to exert political influence on the new republic.[14] Meanwhile, in Louisiana and the Floridas, the weaker but ambitious Spanish empire supported the Creek and Cherokee Indians as a barrier to American continentalism, refused to grant Americans access to the Mississippi and New Orleans, and encouraged secessionist tendencies in the west.[15] The "shadow empire" of the French also began to make its presence felt, as Edmund Genêt played on pro-French feeling in the United States to organize expeditions against Spanish and British territory and to attack British shipping in the Atlantic.[16]

Caught between these conflicts, the United States had its own imperialist thrust, with its vision of continental domination, maritime power, and political liberty.[17] To establish itself as an Empire of Liberty, the United States had to overcome its neo-colonial relationship with Britain, break the encirclement of the older powers in the west, and develop sound republican institutions to consolidate the achievements of the Revolution. In the process, Americans had to face a deeper question: how could the requirements of the rising American empire be reconciled with the spirit of liberty? Much of the political tension generated in the United States during the 1790s hinged on precisely this issue, as Federalists and Republicans grappled with the problem of defining America's destiny.

The Federalists, in power until 1800, laid the foundations of the American empire. Acutely aware of America's external vulnerability and fearing that the greatest internal threat came from the influence of the "people" on the government, the Federalists attempted to build a strong central authority based on the rule of the wealthy and respectable members of society. Their fiscal policies, which included

14 Britain's influence was such that Alexander Hamilton, the first secretary of the treasury and one of the founding fathers, actually figured as number 7 on the British secret service list; see Boyd, *Number 7*.

15 Spain's position is discussed in Bemis, *Pinckney's Treaty*, and Whitaker, *Mississippi Question*.

16 See Van Alstyne, *Rising American Empire*, pp. 74–76; Miller, *Federalist Era*, pp. 132–39; Palmer, *Age of the Democratic Revolution*, 2: 516–43.

17 On this question see Van Alstyne, *Rising American Empire*, and W. A. Williams, *Contours of American History*.

funding the national debt, assuming state debts, and creating a national bank, were intended to strengthen the federal government's control over revenue and taxation, and to bind rich and influential creditors to the central government. Because the revenues needed to finance their policies came largely from Anglo-American commerce, and because most of these rich and influential creditors were merchants whose livelihood depended on Anglo-American commerce, the Federalists had sound reasons to cultivate good relations with Britain. Thus in the crisis year of 1794, when British seizures of American vessels threatened to put the two countries on a collision course, the Federalists sought to ease the situation by opening negotiations with Britain.[18]

Whatever the shortcomings of the subsequent Jay's Treaty in 1794, it did succeed in defining the terms of Anglo-American trade and in breaking the British presence in the American northwest, just as Pinckney's Treaty with Spain the following year relieved the pressure in the south and west. By avoiding war or an economic showdown with Britain, the Federalists were in a strong position to win the support of the creditor class and thus to insulate the government from popular opinion, to establish a central government strong enough to hold the republic together, and to increase the prosperity of Anglo-American commerce.

But while the Federalists agreed on the importance of the Anglo-American connection, they were not united about the extent to which America should link itself with Britain. For men like Washington and Adams, Jay's Treaty was a necessary step in the development of an independent American empire. High Federalists like Alexander Hamilton, on the other hand, thought in terms of a closely integrated Anglo-American empire in which America would eventually become the senior partner. In the late 1790s, Hamilton proposed that the United States and Britain should form a full-scale alliance against France, and wanted a joint Anglo-American expedition to break open the Spanish American empire. When Adams refused to adopt such policies and attempted to improve America's relations with France, the Federalist party fell apart at the seams, leaving the way open for Jefferson's Republicans to win the election of 1800.

18 Buel, *Securing the Revolution*, pp. 1–49; Miller, *Federalist Era*, pp. 33–69, 99–125, 140–54; W. A. Williams, *Contours of American History*, pp. 162–70; Nelson, "Alexander Hamilton and American Manufacturing," pp. 971–95.

During the 1790s, the Republicans strongly challenged the Federalist approach towards building the American empire. As the Federalists strengthened the power of the central government, Republicans increasingly perceived the emergence of a political élitism which they felt was undermining American liberty. The Republicans were not necessarily opposed to strong central government itself; many, like Paine, believed that a powerful but democratic national government was essential for the American empire. But whatever their position, Republicans were convinced that the Federalists' actual use of the central power contradicted democratic and even republican principles. According to the Republicans, Federalist financial policies were creating an aristocracy of wealth in a republic supposedly of equals, were supporting Anglo-American commercial interests at the expense of domestic manufacturing, and were aligning the United States with counter-revolutionary Britain against republican France. All of these objections quickly focused on Jay's Treaty.

The Republicans argued that the treaty failed to win any significant commercial concessions from Britain, did nothing to stimulate America's industrial development, and accepted Britain's definition of neutrality to the detriment of France. In her earlier treaty with France in 1778, America had secured the principle that free ships make free goods. But in 1794, Britain successfully insisted that all French property in American ships was subject to seizure and that American naval stores bound for France would be regarded as contraband. This meant that Britain could block American ships trading with France, but that France, if she adhered to the treaty of 1778, would be unable to take corresponding measures against Anglo-American trade. The treaty, argued the Republicans, was both a slap in the face to France and a humiliating confirmation of America's neo-colonial status.

In the Republican view, Federalist policies ran counter to the spirit of American liberty and impeded the development of an independent American empire. Believing that a strong American manufacturing sector and an independent foreign policy were prerequisites for empire, Jefferson and Madison advocated commercial discrimination against Britain to break America's neo-colonial position. In the process, they argued, the government must develop a national market system with international connections to link together different economic interests and to establish the foundations for economic prosperity, social stability, and political unity. Through taking this course, believed the Republicans, America could fulfil its mission as an Empire of Liberty.[19]

Among the most vociferous supporters of the Republican approach to the Empire of Liberty were the democratic societies of 1793–95 and the transatlantic Radicals who emigrated to the United States from Britain and Ireland. With their support for the French Revolution and their strong artisan base, the democratic societies appeared remarkably similar to the popular Radical clubs in Britain. Like the Radicals of Sheffield, the democrats of Boston celebrated with processions and feasts the French victory over the Prussians and Austrians at Valmy. And like their British counterparts, American democrats adopted Jacobin styles of dress, greeted each other as "citizens," and embraced the symbols of revolutionary France.

For the democrats, events in France confirmed and continued the achievements of the American Revolution; just as America had undertaken to "begin the world over again" in the New World, the French Republic heralded a new era of liberty in the Old—it was no longer 1792, but Year I. Not surprisingly, the democratic societies attacked Federalist policies for betraying America's "sister republic" in France and for supporting Britain. Moreover, the democrats had good economic reasons for opposing the Federalists' accommodation with Britain. Drawing much of their support from artisans and manufacturers whose interests were neglected by the Federalists, and from merchants who traded outside the British Empire, the societies advocated protectionist policies to establish a strong and independent national economy.[20]

The British and Irish Jacobins who sought asylum in the United States during the 1790s reinforced the radical democratic element in American politics. Men like Joseph Gales, John Binns, Thomas Emmet, and Morgan John Rhees, who were among "the most zealous republicans in the Anglo-American world," believed that the United States could reassert its role as a model republic once the power and influence of the Federalists had been broken. Becoming active Republicans, the transatlantic Radicals pushed for humanitarian reforms, civil liberty, and a more egalitarian democracy with universal suffrage, frequent elections, rotation of offices, and accountability of representatives. They also wanted to protect domestic manufacturers and lay the foundation of an independent and interdependent econ-

19 For an excellent discussion of Republican political economy, see Nelson, "Hamilton and Gallatin," pp. 6–7, 141–211.

20 Link, *Democratic-Republican Societies*; Nelson, "Hamilton and Gallatin," pp. 181–83.

omy based on the balance of industrial, commercial, and agricultural interests. The rising American empire, in which the loosely defined "productive classes" enjoyed political and economic liberty, could thus escape from the long shadow of the British government and inspire the democratic movement of the British people.[21]

Given Cobbett's subsequent American career, it seems entirely appropriate that he was initially prodded into action when the Democratic Society of New York welcomed the transatlantic Radical Joseph Priestley to the Empire of Liberty. Writing as a born-again English Tory rather than as an American Federalist, Cobbett was incensed not only by the activities of American democrats but even more by those British and Irish "Emigrated Patriots" whom he regarded as traitors to king and country, and as the ringleaders of Jacobinism in America.[22] And while he regarded the republican ideology of liberty as "a despotism of the many over the few," in contrast to the "*real* liberty" enjoyed by British subjects, he also felt that America had the potential to become a powerful empire which would eventually tower over Europe.[23] For this reason, he attempted to harness American potential for the good of Britain. In the service of his idealized country, Cobbett supported any group whose policies he believed would strengthen British influence in America, hoped for the eventual reunion of Britain and the United States, and engaged in tough, pragmatic polemics to realize his ends.[24]

III

In an important sense, Cobbett's anti-Jacobin position lacked originality; he assimilated and articulated traditional Anglo-American Loyalist arguments, in much the same way that Paine had absorbed Anglo-

21 Twomey, "Jacobins and Jeffersonians," pp. 4, 82–170.

22 See, for example, *PW*, 10: 75. For the argument that Cobbett wrote as a Tory rather than a Federalist, see List, "Role of William Cobbett."

23 For some examples of this attitude, see *PG*, 19 August 1797; *PR, Supplement to Volume I*, 1: 1166; *PR*, 12 October 1805.

24 Evidence that Cobbett ideally wanted to reunite the old British Empire comes from Carey, *Porcupiniad, Canto I*, p. ii. Carey produced a sworn statement from John Pearce, a Philadelphia justice of the peace, that Cobbett told Pearce in private conversation that "I hope soon to see the two countries [Britain and America] united together again." Although such statements from Cobbett's political enemies must necessarily be treated with caution, they are nevertheless consistent with Cobbett's general attitude towards Britain and America at this time.

American Radical ideology. Rejecting the *Rights of Man*, Cobbett embraced Burke's *Reflections*. When Burke died in 1797, Cobbett expressed "gratitude for the pleasure and instruction I have derived from his Herculean, invaluable, and immortal labours" and pledged to carry on Burke's war against revolutionary democracy.[25] Like the conservative opponents of *Common Sense* in America and the *Rights of Man* in Britain, Cobbett argued that democracy was a Utopian attempt to impose abstract theories on complex realities, and that democrats tried to make circumstances conform to their theories instead of making their theories conform to circumstances. The Terror, in this view, was the inevitable result of such an approach. Although Paine distinguished between principles and practice in revolutionary France, arguing in 1795 that "it is not because right principles have been violated that they are to be abandoned," Cobbett insisted that the principles were directly responsible for the practice. By turning Liberty and the Rights of Man into moral absolutes, Cobbett contended, those democratic leaders who both defined liberty and acted in its name were in effect claiming absolute power; the way was open for the oppression of the people in the name of the People.[26]

Throughout his American writings, Cobbett repeated other stock conservative responses to democratic ideology. Echoing views expressed from many Anglican pulpits, Cobbett argued that the principles of atheism and deism (he did not think the difference between them amounted to much in practice) further undermined morality and created conditions under which revolutionary violence could flourish.[27] Adopting the tactics of the British Loyalist Association, he wrote long and lurid accounts of French atrocities while reminding his readers that there existed in the United States "a hardened and impious faction, whose destructive principles, if not timely and firmly opposed, may one day render the annals of America as disgraceful as those of the French Revolution."[28] And confirming Loyalist fears

25 *PG*, 5 September 1797.

26 Cobbett, *Observations on the Emigration of Dr. Joseph Priestley*, pp. 14–15, 20; Paine, *Age of Reason, Part 2*, 1: 516.

27 Cobbett, *Bone to Gnaw*, p. 13. On the employment of such arguments in British North American sermons at this time, see Wise, "Sermon Literature," pp. 3–18.

28 Cobbett, *Bloody Buoy*, pp. ix, 240–41; Cobbett's publication of Aufrer, *Cannibal's Progress*; Cobbett, *Bone to Gnaw, Part 2*, p. 42; *PC*, November 1796, p. 59. *Bloody Buoy* and *Cannibal's Progress* were among the most popular works he sold. See Gaines, "William Cobbett's Account Book," pp. 299–312. In *PW*, 8: 320, Cobbett claimed that

voiced during the American Revolution, he maintained that democratic principles were eating away political and social stability in the
United States, that a wide suffrage produced demagogic politicians,
and that the tyranny of the majority stifled freedom of expression.[29]

Cobbett also struck a familiar chord when he argued that the language of liberty was usually a smokescreen concealing narrow self-
interest. In his view, the hollowness and hypocrisy of democratic language was glaringly apparent in the institution of slavery. Like many
Federalists and like the American Loyalists before them, Cobbett ridiculed southern slave-owning democrats who spent the day "singing
hymns to the Goddess of Liberty" and spent the night with their
"*property*" under their roofs or in their beds. Advertisements in democratic newspapers for slaves brought out the anger in him: "And
these are the people, my God!" he exclaimed, "who talk about the
natural and *unalienable* rights of man—and who make such a boast of
the purity of their principles. Never was there any thing in the world,
that exhibited such a dishonourable, such a base, odious, and dis-
gusting contrast as the professions and the conduct of this race of
patriots." It should not be inferred from this that Cobbett himself
opposed slavery. On the contrary, he adopted a crude and ugly racism,
believing that "negroes . . . are made for servitude and subjection."
His purpose was not to help black slaves, but to undermine the cred-
ibility of their white democratic masters.[30]

If the general outlines of Cobbett's critique of democracy repeated
familiar themes, so too did his attitude to British liberty. He wrote
effusively about his church and king, praised the constitution for
embodying the wisdom of ages, and argued that Britain's independent
and impartial judicial system guaranteed security from oppression.[31]
He emphasized the supremacy of the king over Parliament, and saw
the constitution as a harmonious whole which safeguarded the com-

---

Cannibal's Progress, priced at three and a half cents, sold over 100,000 copies in the
United States.

29 See, for example, Cobbett, *The Democratic Judge*, p. 6; *A Little Plain English*, p.
110; *PW*, 10: 5; *PR*, 12 October 1805 and *PC*, March 1796, pp. iv–v.

30 Cobbett, *Bone to Gnaw*, p. 48; *PW*, 8: 122–23; *PR*, 28 July 1804. Cobbett's racism
makes for extremely unpleasant reading; he likened blacks to monkeys, ridiculed their
physiognomy, and wrote with disgust about mixed marriages. He continued to support
slavery and the slave trade, until as a member of parliament in 1833 he bowed to the
wishes of his constituents and advocated emancipation of slaves in the British colonies.

31 See, for example, Cobbett, *Observations on the Emigration*, p. 7, and *PW*, 8: 15.

mon interests of monarchy, nobility, and the nation. Where Paine attacked the notion of constitutional checks and balances from the left, Cobbett attacked it from the right. "Nothing is more invidious, nothing more repugnant to the principles of the monarchy, nothing more dangerous and leading to consequences more destructive," wrote Cobbett, "than this whiggish doctrine of *separate powers*, acting in opposition to each other."[32] Where Paine thought in terms of a self-regulating democratic republic in which political and economic liberty based on the rights of man would ensure the common good, Cobbett thought in terms of a hierarchical, organic society bound together by the mutual duties, obligations, and affections of king, Lords, and Commons in which prosperity, order, and harmony would prevail. Cobbett's England was the Farnham of his youth writ large, a myth which could expand in the absence of the reality; between the ages of twenty-one and thirty-seven, he spent barely four months in his native country.

On the far right of the Loyalist spectrum, Cobbett differed from someone like John Reeves not so much in ideology as in geographical location.[33] Although he initially pretended to be an American and condemned foreigners for meddling in the internal affairs of the United States, Cobbett quickly established himself as the voice of British Loyalism in America.[34] He attempted to revive pro-British sentiment which had apparently been suffocated by the American and French revolutions, and attributed his wide readership to his courage in articulating opinions which many held but few were prepared to express in public.[35] (Paine had made the same claim for his democratic republican arguments in *Common Sense*.) Adopting a thoroughly pragmatic approach, Cobbett argued that the political revolution of 1776 had not changed the fundamentally British "national character" of the United States, reminded Americans that they inherited the English legal system, and maintained that the Founding Fathers "raised a

---

32 *PG*, 24 August 1797.

33 In 1796 Pitt's government had attempted to prosecute Reeves for making comments that could be taken to support monarchical rather than mixed government. Writing in 1803, Cobbett recalled that when news of the government's action reached the United States, he was shocked, and even questioned whether it was "better to leave loyalty and Mr. Pitt to support themselves." Ultimately, however, he was "unable . . . to resist the desire of opposing the enemies of my country." *PR* 29 January 1803.

34 Cobbett, *Bone to Gnaw*, pp. 19–20, 51.

35 *PR*, 29 September 1804, 29 January 1825.

republic, as nearly representing the British government as it was possible."[36]

Everything he did not like about the United States, in contrast, was projected onto the menace of democracy. When the United States moved towards closer links with Britain, Cobbett offered his full support; after it became clear that the United States would not form an alliance with Britain, that support was withdrawn. Thus the man who in 1796 described his purpose as "keeping alive an attachment to the Constitution of the United States" could by 1802 characterize that same constitution as "impractical nonsense."[37] But Cobbett's concern to advance the cause of his country far outweighed such minor considerations as the need for consistency.

While his anti-democratic writings could feed into Federalist arguments during the 1790s and his image of England could appeal to many Americans, Cobbett's originality lay not so much in what he said as the way in which he said it; again, the parallels with Paine are striking. Like Paine, Cobbett strove for clarity of expression, arguing that "perspicuity is so essential a quality in every writer, that hardly any thing can make up for the want of it."[38] Although he felt that "tropes and figures are very useful things," he insisted that they must be used as a means to illustrate a point, rather than as ends in themselves; the idea was to produce "light, without dazzling." From this perspective, Cobbett enjoyed puncturing any examples he encountered of the grand rhetorical style. "When I see you flourishing with a metaphor," he told one unfortunate adversary, "I feel as much anxiety as I do when I see a child playing with a razor."[39]

Cobbett's American career illustrates that there was no automatic connection between one's writing style and one's politics; the plain style was not the exclusive preserve of democratic publicists. Cobbett the Tory regarded those who wrote for the common people as "popular parasites" who were prepared to "sacrifice truth, honour, justice, and even common sense, to the stupid stare and momentary huzza of the populace."[40] Yet there was a paradox in his position; he was in

36 *PC*, November 1796, pp. 61–62; Cobbett, *Observations on the Emigration*, pp. 16–17.
37 Cobbett, *Life and Adventures*, p. 52; *PR*, 10 July 1802.
38 Cobbett, *Kick for a Bite*, p. 15.
39 Ibid., p. 12.
40 Cobbett, *A Little Plain English*, p. 3.

effect appealing to the people to reduce the influence of the people on government.

At times this position pushed him in unusual directions. When he learned in 1798 that the Earl of Exeter had burned his copies of the works of Voltaire, Rousseau, Raynal, Volney, and Bolingbroke, Cobbett rejoiced and commented: "It would be a happy thing if the accursed art of printing could be totally destroyed, and obliterated from the human mind"—unorthodox opinions for a journalist.[41] Facing the power and influence of "so many [Jacobin] *printing-presses*," Cobbett felt compelled to turn democratic techniques against democrats. "The only method of opposition," he wrote in 1796, " . . . is to meet them on their own ground; to set foot to foot, dispute every inch and every hair's breadth; fight them at their own weapons, and return them two blows for one."[42] Peter Porcupine had arrived.

Along with this combative style went a fierce independence and a black-and-white approach to politics. Refusing to become a "spaniel-like sycophant" who crawled to the wishes of the *"sovereign people,"* Cobbett prided himself on his independence, and was highly sensitive to any hint of pressure from publishers, advertisers, or subscribers. Although he believed that he was in a war to the death between "Virtue and Vice, Good and Evil, Happiness, and Misery," Cobbett scrupulously avoided accepting any money or assistance from either the British or American government.[43] In one sense, Cobbett's emphasis on independence, his aggressive tone, and his tendency to think in terms of moral absolutes recall the writings of Paine. Yet Cobbett carried these tendencies to extremes rarely found in Paine's work. And Cobbett's tone was very different from that of Paine. There is nothing in Paine to match the inexhaustible stream of personal invective, the Swiftian satire, the downright vindictiveness, and the venomous character sketches that flowed from Cobbett's pen.

Believing that it was impossible to dissociate an idea from the character of the person holding that idea, Cobbett moved easily between the political and the personal. "I never could see," he wrote, "how abuses were to be corrected, without attacking those to whom they were to be attributed. If swindling and debauchery prevails, how are

41 *PW*, 9: 204.

42 *PR*, 11 December 1802; *PC*, December 1796, n.p.

43 *PC*, March 1797, p. 105; *PG*, 6 March 1797. On Cobbett's personal and financial independence, see List, "The Role of William Cobbett," pp. 83–84, 92–98.

you to check it without exposing the *swindler* and the *debauchee*? And how are you to expose them without attacking their private characters?"[44] With this outlook, Cobbett ridiculed his opponents and viewed their flawed ideology as the product of their flawed personalities.

In a Federalist literary culture whose dominant image was the Voyage to Laputa, Cobbett put his earlier enthusiasm for Swift's work to immediate and effective use.[45] "Everyone will, I hope, have the goodness to believe that my grandfather was no philosopher," Cobbett wrote in his autobiography. "Indeed he was not. He never made a lightning-rod, nor bottled up a single quart of sun-shine, in the whole course of his life."[46] The pursuit of "useful science" in America which had impressed Paine so much became a natural target for Cobbett. Benjamin Franklin, whose "projects," emphasis on self-interest, and posthumous reputation were too much for Cobbett to resist, was nicknamed "old Lightning-Rod" and described as "a whore-master, a hypocrite and an infidel."[47] Similarly, Cobbett mocked Priestley as a scientific quack who had really come to the United States to escape charges of plagiarism in England, and who "set to work bottling up his own f-rts, and selling them for superfine inflammable air."[48] With his plain English, no-nonsense, down-to-earth, anti-intellectual self-image, Cobbett kicked and laughed, inviting his audience to kick and laugh with him.

Adopting a tone of Swiftian irreverence towards "projectors," philosophers, and patriots, Cobbett delighted in needling his political and personal enemies. Benjamin Rush, the revolutionary Philadelphia doctor who believed that the American Revolution opened up a new political, moral, and medical order, was labelled "Doctor Sangrado" and accused of unleashing a medical Terror which slayed thousands of Americans through bleeding them to death.[49] Noah Webster, who developed a simplified spelling system as part of his program to eliminate American cultural dependence on Britain and to replace Old World obscurantism with New World simplicity, was not quite so bad.

44 *PW*, 10: 205–6.

45 The image of Laputa in Federalist writings is explored in Kerber, *Federalists in Dissent*, pp. 1–22.

46 Cobbett, *Life and Adventures*, p. 11.

47 Cobbett, *Scare-Crow*, p. 18; *Life and Adventures*, p. 11.

48 Cobbett, *Observations on the Emigration*, pp. 65–69, 87. Cobbett was alluding to Priestley's discovery of oxygen and to his other chemistry experiments.

49 *PG*, 18 and 19 September 1797. These and similar comments prompted Rush to introduce the libel suit which helped drive Cobbett out of the United States in 1800.

"On certain subjects he has shown that he possesses considerable talents," wrote Cobbett, moving in for the kill, "but the moment the name of Great Britain is mentioned, he seems to lose his reason; this hated name is to him what water is to one bitten by a mad dog."[50]

The list could be extended almost indefinitely. John Swanwick, one of those Philadelphia merchants who traded outside the British Empire and argued for a democratic American mercantilist empire, was ridiculed for his poetic pretensions and portrayed as a "lascivious" teacher of little girls. Samuel Bradford, one of the Bradford publishing family with whom Cobbett had fallen out, was addressed as "thou compost of die-stuff, lampblack and urine." Judge Thomas McKean of Philadelphia was viewed as a corrupt, hen-pecked alcoholic, and other leading democrats came in for similar treatment.[51] While personal invective was not new to American political writings, it had never before been carried on with such sustained intensity; doubtless the shock-effect of Cobbett's prose contributed enormously to his popularity.

Cobbett's fiercest writings, however, were reserved for those "Republican Britons" who were seen as part of an international Jacobin conspiracy with its headquarters in Paris. Thomas Muir, the Scottish democrat who had escaped from Botany Bay only to be maimed in a naval conflict, was singled out for particularly vicious treatment. "The rascal has lost one eye," Cobbett wrote when he heard the news. "So far so good; but he should have lost two. However, to be continually tormented with the sight of his '*totally disfigured*' visage may, for aught I know, be a greater punishment than blindness itself; and if so, I am glad he has got one eye left. . . . A thousand blessings on the ball that caused his wounds! May such never be wanting while there is a Jacobin traitor on earth!"[52] It is no wonder that Paine in 1802 described Cobbett's writings as a mixture of "wit" and "*blackguardism.*"[53]

Other transatlantic Radicals were subjected to Cobbett's *ad hominem* attacks. He described James Callender, who had fled to America to avoid prosecution for seditious libel in Britain, as suffering from "*the mania reformatio*; and if this malady is not stopped at once . . . , it never fails to break out into Atheism, Robbery, Unitarianism, Swindling,

50 *PG*, 16 August 1797.

51 See, for example, Cobbett, "Remarks on Pamphlets" in *Antidote*, p. 76; *PC*, March 1797; *Democratic Judge*, and virtually every issue of the *PG*.

52 *PG*, 14 September 1797.

53 Paine, *To the Citizens of the United States*, 2: 924.

Jacobinism, Massacres, Civic Feasts and insurrection."[54] Daniel Isaac Eaton, in the United States after surviving several sedition trials in Britain, was portrayed as "tramping through the dirt" with a newly acquired Indian squaw, or "yellow hided frow," for a mistress.[55] Archibald Hamilton Rowan, the United Irishman who had escaped from an English jail while awaiting charges of high treason, was reduced to selling spruce beer from a wheelbarrow, according to Cobbett.[56] And the United Irishmen in general were accused of importing into America "the dark and silent system of organized treason and massacre" which had brought so much horror and devastation to their own land.[57]

Taken together, these attacks amounted to a verbal reign of terror which attempted to make democracy appear "un-American." Through rallying public opinion against Anglo-American democrats, Cobbett hoped that they would be isolated, forced on the defensive, and politically destroyed. His writings contributed to the political atmosphere behind the Alien and Sedition Acts of 1798, which put men like Citizen Richard Lee, William Duane, Thomas Cooper, and James Callender behind bars. Characteristically, Cobbett felt that the acts did not go far enough, complaining that they were only designed to intimidate rather than to eradicate politically his democratic opponents.[58]

All the force of Cobbett's writing style—his aggressive black-and-white approach, his personal attacks, and his strident satire—was directed not only at Anglo-American Jacobins in general, but at the man at the heart of the transatlantic democratic revolution in particular: that arch traitor, "indefatigable constitution-grinder" and "Infidel Anarchist," Tom Paine.[59] Drawing on George Chalmers's biography, Cobbett attempted to discredit Paine's ideas by discrediting his personality. Paine was portrayed as "a brutal and savage husband, and an unnatural father," who personified all the vices of democrats. "Paine's humanity, like that of all the reforming philosophers of the present enlightened day, is of the speculative kind," wrote Cobbett. "It never breaks out into action. Hear these people, and you would think them overflowing with the milk of human kindness. They stretch

54 Cobbett, *Bone to Gnaw*, p. 5.
55 *PW*, 9: 258.
56 *PW*, 9: 257.
57 *PW*, 10: 17.
58 *PW*, 10: 154–55.
59 Cobbett, *Antidote*, p. 48; *PW*, 11: 354; *PW*, 10: 4.

their benevolence to the extremities of the globe: it embraces every living creature—except those who have the misfortune to come into contact with them. They are all citizens of the world: country and friends and relations are unworthy the attention of men who are occupied in rendering all mankind happy and free."[60]

Behind this character assassination of Paine lay a deeper attitude. Rooting his own politics in memories of "country and friends and relations," Cobbett shared Burke's view that "to love the little platoon we belong to in society, is the first principle (the germ as it were) of public affections."[61] Cobbett was always highly suspicious of abstract humanity and abstract liberty, even as he himself clung to an equally abstract ideal of Old English Liberty.

As well as accusing Paine of cruelty, Cobbett argued that his opponent was motivated by a deep sense of bitterness and resentment at being sacked as an excise officer. Had he been reinstated, commented Cobbett, Paine would doubtless have been "among the supplest tools of Lord North"; instead, he took his revenge on Britain by encouraging the colonies to revolt.[62] As further evidence of Paine's reprehensible character and general dishonesty, Cobbett reminded Americans that Paine had kept quiet about the *Case of the Officers of Excise* and had claimed that *Common Sense* was his first publication. "It would have looked a little awkward," wrote Cobbett, "to see that work [*Common Sense*] coming from the pen of a discarded excise officer, who had petitioned for a reinstatement in his oppressive office. Not a whit less awkward does it now appear, to hear clamours against the expenses of the British government coming from the very man who would have added to those expenses by an augmentation of his own salary."[63] One can only marvel at Cobbett's nerve; these criticisms came from a man whose own autobiography, written only four months

60 Cobbett, *Antidote*, pp. 10–11. Cobbett was the first person to republish in America Chalmers's *Life of Pain*. In his edition of Chalmers's work, Cobbett continually commented on the text. The idea was that Chalmers would wrestle Paine to the ground and Cobbett would kick him when he was down.

61 Burke, *Reflections*, p. 135.

62 It should be pointed out that Cobbett was careful to distinguish between Paine's motivation and the issue of American independence; to have done otherwise would have been to undermine his own position. "Is a man to be looked upon as regretting that America obtained its independence," he asked, "merely because he detests a cruel, treacherous and blasphemous ruffian who once wrote in favour of it?" (Cobbett, *Antidote*, pp. 16, 24).

63 Cobbett, *Antidote*, p. 17.

before this attack on Paine, said nothing at all about corruption in the army, his court-martial proceedings, or his authorship of *The Soldier's Friend*. This kettle had no scruples about calling the pot black.[64]

In the United States, Cobbett continued, Paine vented his hatred of Britain, profited from the plunder of Loyalist estates, and acquired an inflated opinion of his own importance. In Cobbett's view, the fact that Paine had magnified beyond recognition his role as the secretary of the Committee for Foreign Affairs and that he was eventually fired from his job clearly demonstrated both Paine's egotism and his inability to cope with order and responsibility.[65] Having been sacked as an excise officer by a monarchical government and dismissed as a clerk by a republican one, Paine hated all government, whether in Britain or America, maintained Cobbett. Paine's "element was confusion"; when Americans returned to order he found himself "universally despised and neglected," and thus "crossed the Atlantic to bask in the rays of the French Revolution."[66]

Cobbett warmed to his task when denouncing Paine's place in the French Revolution. He had little to say about that "manuel of Jacobinism," the *Rights of Man*, other than that it went "further than . . . [the English Jacobins] ever dreamed of," that it defended the French Constitution of 1791 which Paine himself helped to dismantle the following year, and that it "nearly cost him a voyage to the South Sea."[67] Rather than systematically criticizing Paine's ideas, Cobbett

64 See Cobbett, *Life and Adventures*. In 1805 he wrote of these omissions that "here, in the printed account of my life, there is a small chasm. When I published that account, I was in the midst of the revilers of England, and particularly of the English army; or, I should then have stated, that the primary cause of my leaving the army . . . was, the abuses, the shocking abuses as to money matters, the *peculation*, in short, which I had witnessed in it, and which I had, in vain, endeavoured to correct" (*PR*, 5 October 1805). He still denied in 1805 that he had written *The Soldier's Friend*.

65 Although Paine described himself in the *Rights of Man* as "secretary in the foreign department," in fact he had only light clerical duties and no share in policy making; in this way he was able to concentrate on his *Crisis* papers. He was forced to resign in 1779 after he accused Silas Deane of profiteering from French assistance to America and publicized confidential information on foreign affairs to back up his accusations. For a full discussion of the Deane affair, see A. King, "Thomas Paine in America," pp. 177–214.

66 Cobbett, *Antidote*, pp. 29–30; *PC*, May 1796, p. 197; *A Little Plain English*, p. 85.

67 *PC*, March 1797, p. 95; *PC*, May 1796, p. 198. Many of Paine's opponents at this time accused him of hypocrisy for defending in the *Rights of Man* the Constitution of 1791 and then helping to draft its successor in late 1792.

presented his readers with the verbal equivalent of a James Gillray
caricature and portrayed Paine as revelling in revolution:

From the thief-catchers in England Tom fled, and took his seat among the
thieves of Paris. . . . This may be looked upon as the happiest part of Tom's
life. He had enjoyed partial revolts before, had seen doors and windows
broken in, and had probably partaken of the pillage of some aristocratic stores
and dwelling houses; but, to live in a continual state of insurrection . . . to sit
seven days in the week issuing decrees for plunder, proscription and massacre,
was a luxurious life indeed! It was, however, a short life and a merry one: it
lasted but five months. The tender-hearted philanthropic murderer, Brissot,
and his faction, fell from the pinnacle of their glory: poor Tom's wares got
out of vogue and his carcass got into a dungeon.[68]

Nothing satisfied and delighted Cobbett more than Paine's imprisonment at the hands of the very revolutionaries whom his principles
had supposedly elevated to power in the first place. "There he lies!"
exclaimed Cobbett with all the malice he could muster; "manacled,
besmeared with filth, crawling with vermin, loaded with years and
infamy. . . . Here he is, fairly caught in his own trap, a striking example
for the disturbers of mankind."[69] Gloating over Paine's misery, Cobbett believed that the "old broken exciseman" was at last suffering the
same kind of treatment which his ideas had inflicted on others.
    Under these circumstances, Cobbett argued, Paine wrote the *Age
of Reason* in a desperate attempt to save his skin through flattering
the deism of his revolutionary captors. Contrasting Paine's denuncia-
tion of revealed religion in the *Age of Reason* with his scriptural justification for American independence in *Common Sense*, Cobbett scorned
his earlier "hypocritical canting professions" and insisted that the "In-

68 *PC*, May 1796, pp. 198–99.
69 Cobbett, *Antidote*, pp. 47–48. See also *Observations*, p. 13, and *PC*, May 1796, p.
198. Compare Paine's own description of his imprisonment: "During the time I laid
at the height of my illness they took, in one night only, 169 persons out of this prison
and executed all but eight. The distress that I suffered at being obliged to exist in the
midst of such horror, exclusive of my own precarious situation, suspended as it were
by the single thread of accident, is greater than it is possible you can conceive. . . .
When I take a review of my whole situation—my circumstances ruined, my health half
destroyed, my person imprisoned, and the prospect of imprisonment still staring me
in the face, can you wonder at the agony of my feelings?" (Paine to James Monroe, 18
August 1794 and 13 October 1794, 2: 1343, 1359).

fidel" could now be seen "in his true colours."[70] Cobbett made similar use of Paine's *Letter to George Washington*, in which Paine criticized monarchical tendencies in the Federal Constitution and attacked Washington for what Paine took to be his pro-British position. Juxtaposing these sentiments with Paine's support for the constitution and the president in the *Rights of Man*, Cobbett exulted that "Never, surely never, was a poor demagogue so completely detected."[71] To uphold Washington's character, Cobbett simply stated that "I will make you, Tom, defend him against yourself," and used Paine's earlier praise for Washington to undercut the "slurs" in the *Letter* of 1796.[72]

Ironically, it would not be long before Cobbett's own enemies would use the same technique against him. After he converted to Radicalism in England, his Tory opponents took great delight in rubbing Cobbett's nose in his earlier American writings.[73] It is also ironic that only a few years after accusing Paine of inconsistency towards Washington, Cobbett himself moved from defending to attacking America's first president, even accusing Washington of acquiescing in war crimes at Yorktown. Paine had broken with Washington because he considered the president pro-British; Cobbett broke with him for not being sufficiently anti-French.[74]

The composite biographical sketch of Paine that emerges from Cobbett's American writing is a fascinating mixture of distortion, satire, and insight. One can dismiss Cobbett's comments that Paine was personally inhumane, that he delighted in the Terror, and that he wrote works like the *Age of Reason* at the command of his French "masters." In other respects, Cobbett's attacks are a compendium of half-truths. It would not be accurate to say, as Cobbett did, that Paine wrote *Common Sense* simply to avenge himself on a government that had fired him as an excise officer, but Paine was partly motivated by bitterness and anger at Britain's political and social structure. It was not true, in Cobbett's sense, that Paine's "element was confusion," but it is reasonable to argue that Paine was better at inspiring revolutionary change than working out the mechanics of post-revolutionary recon-

70 *PC*, May 1796, pp. 196, 200–203; *PW*, 11: 3–6.
71 Cobbett, "Letter to the Infamous Tom Paine," in *PC*, December 1796, p. 13.
72 Ibid., p. 15.
73 For some examples, see above, p. xv n22.
74 *PR*, 30 October 1802. The first sign of his disillusionment with Washington came in 1800, probably because Cobbett heard that Washington approved of Adams' overtures to France. See Spater, *William Cobbett*, p. 272, n. 19.

struction. Cobbett could correctly point out that Paine shifted his position on the French and American constitutions as well as Washington's character, but this does not mean that Paine was being hypocritical.[75]

On the other hand, Cobbett's view that Paine used the scriptures cynically in *Common Sense* may well be valid, although it is quite possible that Paine's religious views gradually moved towards deism between 1776 and 1793. And Cobbett was undoubtedly correct that Paine was arrogant and had a conveniently selective memory; but then Cobbett was not entirely free from such traits himself. At any rate, there was just enough truth in Cobbett's anti-Paine writings to give his argument some bite, to give his position a degree of plausibility. Paine, across the Atlantic in France, did not defend himself against Cobbett's attacks; indeed, it is not clear to what extent he knew about them. In his *Letter to George Washington*, however, he did refer to certain pro-British sentiments emanating from the Philadelphia press, and used them to illustrate the real "principles of the Washington faction." Paine did not know the author of these sentiments, but believed it was someone who wrote under the name of "Peter Skunk or Peter Porcupine, or some such signature."[76]

Whether attacking Paine, transatlantic Radicals, or "American Jacobins," Cobbett developed his characteristic literary style in the United States. There is a strong continuity between his style as a Tory in America and as a Radical in England; only the targets changed. The combative language was carried through to Cobbett's Radical writings, as he declared war on England's financial system. The rigid approach to politics remained, as he came to stand for the virtuous labourer and farmer against the vice of parliamentary corruption. The irreverent, satirical tone continued, as he turned his fire against *laissez-faire* "Scotch feelosofers" rather than American "projectors," and transferred his talent for nicknames to people like George ("the Upstart") Canning and Jeremy ("Jerry the Old Rump Cock") Bentham instead

75 For Paine's views on constitutional change, see above, p. 72. In his *Letter to George Washington*, Paine still supported the Federal Constitution despite its supposed flaws because, among other reasons, it "contained the means of remedying its defects by the same appeal to the people by which it was ... established," and he added that "it is always better policy to leave removable errors to expose themselves than to hazard too much in contending against them theoretically" (*Letter to George Washington*, 2: 691).

76 Paine, *Letter to George Washington*, 2: 709–10n. At this time, Paine had heard rumours that Peter Porcupine was Phineas Bond, a British consul in the United States.

of American Patriots such as Benjamin Rush and Noah Webster. The conspiratorial mentality was maintained, as the source of evil changed from the Jacobin International to the all-pervasive "Pitt system" in England. Just as Cobbett in America had worshipped Pitt while reviling Paine, Cobbett in England increasingly praised Paine and came to despise Pitt. And throughout his American and English writings, Cobbett asserted his fierce, uncompromising spirit of independence— except that in the United States he proclaimed his independence from the "mob," while in England he proclaimed it from the government.

This is to look ahead, however. In the 1790s, Cobbett's conversion to Radicalism would have been impossible to predict. Yet there is a curious episode in 1795 which demonstrates Cobbett's ability to argue both sides of a case. Among the many replies to Cobbett's pamphlets, a particularly incisive one argued that his real intention was to "raise the interests of Great Britain" in America on the ruins of the Franco-American alliance. It accused Cobbett of grossly exaggerating the excesses of the French Revolution to discredit republican government in general, it criticized him for being insensitive to American grievances and for insulting revered American Patriots, and it attacked his tendency to substitute sarcasm for reasoned argument. And it was written by none other than Cobbett himself. The "reply" was a "puff" against Cobbett's *A Bone to Gnaw*, to increase its sales and widen the controversy; had Cobbett not fallen out with the Bradfords, his publishers in 1795, the story might never have seen the light. It shows Cobbett's skill as a polemicist; although the Radicalism was feigned, it is an eerie foreshadowing of the days to come.[77]

IV

When considering Cobbett's heated and humorous attacks on democracy and democrats, it is easy—and misleading—to see him as a magnificent political buffoon, or a belligerent John Bull trampling everything and everyone in his way. What this perspective misses is Cobbett's keen awareness of geopolitical realities and his attempt to bend those realities towards British interests. In his view, America was a potentially decisive battleground in the conflict between rival British and French imperialism. He perceived American democrats

---

77 Samuel Bradford, "A Refreshment for the Memory of William Cobbett," appended to his *Imposter Detected*, pp. 21–23.

as a French fifth column, and after 1795, when Spain reversed alli-
ances and moved towards France, he saw the Spanish empire as a
"front" for French ambitions. Between 1794 and 1800, Cobbett employed his impressive polemical skills to drive French ideology and
French interests out of the New World, and to establish closer relations
between the United States and Britain. This campaign was conducted
in two phases: the struggle to win American support for Jay's Treaty,
and the attempt to bring about a full-scale offensive and defensive
Anglo-American alliance.

Looking back on the first phase of the campaign over thirty years
later, Cobbett felt that the expression "Jay's Treaty" was a misnomer;
it should really have been called "Cobbett's Treaty," since without him
it would never have been ratified and the United States would eventually have joined the war on the side of France.[78] Although this view
says more about Cobbett's ego than Anglo-American relations, it is
true that he played an important part in mobilizing American public
opinion behind the treaty. He entered the fray in August 1795, after
the treaty had passed the Senate but when it faced mounting criticism
in the House of Representatives and the American press. Against
Republican criticisms that the treaty was unnecessary and unjust, that
it would infect the United States with British "debauchery and corruption" while strengthening "*monarchical*" elements which threatened
the republic from within, and that America was abandoning France,
Cobbett attempted to demolish systematically the assumptions and
arguments behind the anti-treaty position.[79]

Far from being unnecessary and unjust, Cobbett maintained, Jay's
Treaty was essential to regulate the United States's growing trade with
Britain, to "terminate all differences in an amicable manner," and to
open up the northwest posts which Britain had held since 1783. If
specific clauses failed to give American merchants significant access
to British colonies, he continued, the United States should remember
that it had declared independence from Britain and could not expect
to enjoy the full benefits of an empire it had rejected. Besides, as a
relatively weak republic highly dependent on British trade, the United
States could not expect better terms. In Cobbett's view, Republican

78 *PR*, 22 August 1829, 29 January 1825.
79 On the anti-treaty position, see [Dallas], *Letters of Franklin*, pp. 11, 15–16, 18–
19, 21, 52. Cobbett replied to this pamphlet, point by point, in *A Little Plain English*.

arguments that the United States could stand up to the most powerful empire in the world were the product of a deluded sense of American power and cohesion. "Now, you will observe," he wrote, "that it is not my intention to render this treaty palatable to you; I shall not insist, that the terms of it are as advantageous as you might wish, or expect them to be; but I insist that they are as advantageous as you ought to have expected."[80]

As well as discussing its specific terms, Cobbett defended Jay's Treaty on broader ideological and strategic grounds. Arguments that the treaty contradicted public opinion and would introduce monarchical principles were dismissed as irrelevant. There was nothing in the Constitution, wrote Cobbett ("the half-English Constitution," he added, rubbing it in), that compelled the president to rule according to the wishes of the ignorant mob. And to worry about insidious British influences in the New World, he continued, was to ignore the fact that American government and law already rested on British foundations. Turning Republican arguments upside down, Cobbett insisted that the real threat to American liberty and independence came from France, not Britain, and that Jay's Treaty stood as a bulwark against pernicious French influences. Even if it was disappointing, the treaty at least protected Americans from French plots to embroil them in a diversionary war against Britain, "at the expense of your prosperity, and even your very existence as a nation."[81]

Throughout the winter of 1795 and 1796, Cobbett kept up the pressure on the Republicans, reaching a new pitch of intensity in April 1796 when it seemed that the House of Representatives might refuse to vote the funds needed to implement Jay's Treaty. Participating in a massive Federalist campaign to turn back this Republican offensive, Cobbett's arguments ran along two lines: he attacked the motivation of the treaty's opponents, and he maintained that the treaty's defeat would plunge the United States into disaster. On the question of motivation, Cobbett argued that southern democrats opposed the treaty because it would make them pay their debts to British merchants, presented evidence to suggest that "French gold" had bought Republican consciences, and made caustic comments about the gullability of those who believed that Jay could have won better terms from

80 Cobbett, *A Little Plain English*, pp. 9, 48, 62.
81 Ibid., pp. 86–96.

Britain. "Thus," he concluded, "is the opposition bottomed on *dis-honesty, corruption*, or *ignorance*, and, probably, on all three together."[82] As for the consequences of the treaty's defeat, Cobbett pointed out that Britain would retain the northwest posts, the Royal Navy would seize and search American ships without compensation, and Anglo-American tensions could quickly escalate into full-scale war. Such a confrontation, he wrote, would hurt the United States much more than Britain. America's trade would be devastated, and the pressures of war would split the country between north and south, leaving an opening for the French in the continent. In short, argued Cobbett, if the treaty was rejected, the United States had nothing to gain and everything to lose.[83]

Although the Federalists did manage to break opposition to the treaty in the House, Cobbett's role in their victory must not be exaggerated. As Richard Buel points out, Federalist arguments and manoeuvres within the House were more important than the pressure of public opinion. Nevertheless, Cobbett had every reason to be triumphant. "I now bid the opposers of the treaty farewell," he wrote in May 1796; "they and I have been at war for rather better than a year; I have seen them completely beaten, and though I pretend to no other merit than the little that is due to a diligent drummer or trumpeter, I must be permitted to rejoice as well as others. Rejoice I certainly do at their downfall, and notwithstanding I think it unmanly to set my feet upon the neck of a prostrate foe, no endeavours of mine shall be wanting to prevent them from rising again."[84] As it turned out, this would be the only time in Cobbett's long political career that he was unequivocally on the winning side.

The dust had hardly settled when Cobbett moved into the second phase of his struggle against Jacobinism. The Anglo-American commercial treaty was not, for Cobbett, an end in itself. Rather, it was a step towards a political and military alliance between Britain and the United States to crush the "armed principles" of the French Revo-

---

82 *PC*, April 1796, p. 121–22, 138–40, 149–51. Cobbett's arguments about "French gold" made much use of evidence which suggested that Secretary of State Edmund Randolph had been involved in intrigues with Joseph Fauchet, the French minister in the United States. See J. Miller, *Federalist Era*, pp. 169–71, and Cobbett, *A New-Year's Gift to the Democrats*, pp. 69–70; *PC*, April 1796, pp. 144–55.

83 *PC*, April 1796, pp. 158–62.

84 *PC*, May 1796, pp. 194–95; Buel, *Securing the Revolution*, pp. 119–21.

lution.[85] Up to this point, Cobbett's interests had coincided with mainstream Federalist policies; after 1796, his public pronouncements aligned him with the extreme right wing of the party, while his private views indicate that he wanted to keep the United States politically and economically subordinate to Britain.

Assuming that close Anglo-American ties were part of the natural order, and side-stepping arguments that his policies would turn the United States into a British satellite, Cobbett focused his attention on the designs of France in America. He had plenty of material to go on. France had supported the Republican attempt to block Jay's Treaty in the House of Representatives, and tried to sway the presidential election of 1796 against John Adams, whose policies France regarded as being dangerously pro-British. When these efforts failed, France took a harder line against the United States, breaking off full diplomatic relations and moving vigorously against American vessels trading with Britain. To the north, France supported Ira Allen's plans to revolutionize Lower Canada and link it with Vermont in a new Republic of United Columbia which would at once dismember Britain's North American empire and increase French influence on the continent. In the west, French agents in the guise of botanists or strolling musicians sounded out separatist sentiment in the Ohio and Mississippi regions. And France began to consider taking over Louisiana from Spain as a means of putting more pressure on the United States.[86]

But, as Paine pointed out when he first learned that John Jay was negotiating with Britain, an aggressive French foreign policy would only play into the hands of the "British party in America."[87] No one illustrated the accuracy of that observation more than Cobbett. Reviving century-old American fears of French "encirclement," he in-

85 Cobbett quoted the phrase frequently, echoing Paine's comment that "an army of principles will penetrate where an army of soldiers cannot." See, for example, *PW*, 10: 267.

86 Van Alstyne, *Rising American Empire*, pp. 74–76; J. Miller, *Federalist Era*, pp. 132–39; Palmer, *Age of the Democratic Revolution*, 2: 516–43; Wade, "Quebec and the French Revolution of 1789," pp. 345–68; T. S. Webster, "A New Yorker in the Era of the French Revolution," pp. 251–72; Ojala, "Ira Allen and the French Directory," pp. 436–48. The intercepted dispatches sent from French Minister Joseph Fauchet to his government in 1795 clearly demonstrated Fauchet's belief that French control of Louisiana would give France sufficient leverage to influence the United States. See Whitaker, *Mississippi Question*, pp. 101–29, but especially p. 119.

87 Paine, *Observations on Jay's Treaty*, 2: 569–70.

sisted that the "French Regicides" were practicing the same policy as their monarchical predecessors: to "cut off all communication between this country and Great Britain, as the only effectual means of rendering us totally dependent on themselves."[88] He argued that while French revolutionary ideology was subverting the country from within, French attacks on American commerce and French plans to control the west were designed to reduce the United States to a puppet state similar to those being established in Holland, Switzerland, and Northern Italy. Page after page of the *Porcupine's Gazette* was filled with reports of "French piracy on the American commerce"; in much the same way that Aufrer's *Cannibal's Progress* described French atrocities on land, Cobbett reported acts of French cruelty and aggression at sea. He printed stories that the French were building up a secret army in Georgia to strengthen their position in the south, and publicized French intrigues in the west.[89] "The French are getting round us on every side," he told his readers.[90]

His greatest fear was that France would take over Louisiana, block American access to the Mississippi and New Orleans, and persuade westerners to break away from the United States. In this scenario, France's hold on the back countries together with French sympathies in the southern states would drive the middle and northern states to Britain for protection. "And thus," he wrote, "the basis of an empire will once more be cut out into colonies and provinces." What really bothered him, however, was not so much the disintegration of the American empire as the possible weakening of Britain's position in its struggle with French revolutionary imperialism.[91]

Although he prudently kept quiet about it at the time, Cobbett's real purpose was to replace the threat of French encirclement with the reality of British encirclement. He therefore privately welcomed the efforts of men like Senator William Blount and the Loyalist William Bowles to increase Britain's influence in America. In 1796 and

88 *PC*, January 1797, p. 18; Cobbett, *The Scare-Crow*, p. 12; *PG*, 8 September 1797; *PC*, November 1796, pp. 53–54, 66–67.

89 Typical examples of Cobbett's accounts of "French piracy" can be found in *PG*, 15 March 1797, 16 March 1797, 10 June 1797 and *PW*, 8: 321–480. On French intrigues in the south and west, see *PG*, 13 March 1797, 30 March 1797, 6 April 1797, 8 September 1797.

90 *PW*, 6: 60.

91 *PC*, November 1796, pp. 74–76; Cobbett to Windham, 23 November 1802, in *Life and Letters*, ed. Melville, 1: 172.

1797, Blount tried to enlist British aid in his scheme to drive Spain from Louisiana. Blount feared that Spain would cede the colony to France, and that this would reduce the value of his landholdings in the Mississippi west. His property would be worth more, he felt, if Britain controlled Louisiana and allowed American trade to pass through New Orleans. But Britain, having recently signed Jay's Treaty, did not want to jeopardize its relations with the American government by supporting Blount's schemes.

Further south, Bowles built up the Muskogee Indians in Spanish East Florida and attempted to get British assistance in his struggle against Spain and the United States. Writing as Peter Porcupine, Cobbett stressed that Britain's rejection of Blount's schemes demonstrated British goodwill and superior virtue, and said nothing about Bowles's plans. Back in England after 1800, however, Cobbett sang a different tune, strongly criticizing the British government's failure to grasp the opportunity to clear out the Spanish, to prevent the French from getting a foothold on the continent, and to increase Britain's commercial influence and political presence in North America. If Britain could combine her control of the Atlantic with a stronger presence in the west, he reasoned, the United States would be locked securely into the British sphere of influence.[92]

In public, he tried a different method of strengthening Anglo-American relations. Only six months after Jay's Treaty got through the House of Representatives, he began his attempt to mobilize American opinion behind a declaration of war against France. "Though I am certain that the French will not go to war with America," he announced in November 1796, "I am as certain that America must soon go to war with them. Let not the reader start.—He must accustom himself to think and talk on the subject, and the sooner he begins the better."[93] Seeking to establish an identity of interests between the United States and Britain, Cobbett argued that war would solve all America's problems. It would "cut off the cankering, sans-culotte connexion, and leave the country once more sound and *really independent*." It would remove at a stroke the threat of encirclement, dismember-

92 On the Blount conspiracy, see *Congressional Records of 1797* in *PW*, 9: 135–80; on Bowles, see Douglass, "Adventurer Bowles," pp. 3–24. For Cobbett's views, see Cobbett to Windham, 1803, in *Life and Letters*, 2: 181–82, and *The Porcupine*, 21 July 1801.

93 *PC*, November 1796, p. 73.

ment, and eventual return to colonialism, which he maintained was posed by French machinations in Louisiana. And it would enable the United States and Britain to dislodge the French from the West Indies and drive Spain out of the New World. In short, wrote Cobbett, "America and Great Britain might bid defiance to the world. The map of this continent and its islands lies open before them: they might cut and carve for themselves, and sit down in the quiet enjoyment of their conquests."[94]

Aiming for a joint Anglo-American empire in which the United States would follow Britain's lead, Cobbett based his pro-war arguments not only on American interests and fears but also on an emotional appeal to American pride, honour, and independence. Whether denouncing French depredations on American commerce, French intrigues in the west or French diplomatic rebuffs to the United States, Cobbett always returned to the same theme: no truly independent nation would submit to such humiliating treatment, and war was the only way to preserve American dignity.[95] Refusing to accept or even acknowledge that a full-scale alliance with Britain would compromise American independence, Cobbett increasingly urged the United States to take decisive action against France and warned that Federalist "whinings after *peace* and *reconciliation*, upon *any terms*" only encouraged French contempt for the American nation.

By 1798, when news of the XYZ affair reached the United States at the same time that French privateering against American shipping was reaching new levels, events seemed to be working in his favour.[96]

---

94 *PW*, 8: 64–65; *PG*, 20 May 1797; *PC*, December 1796, p. 46. Cobbett's words are, consciously or unconsciously, an ironic echo of Paine's view in *Common Sense*: "Much hath been said of the united strength of Britain and the colonies, that in conjunction they might bid defiance to the world. But this is mere presumption. . . . Besides, what have we to do with setting the world at defiance? Our plan is commerce, and that, well attended to, will secure us the peace and friendship of all Europe" (Paine, *Common Sense* 1: 20).

95 *PG*, 16 March 1797, 28 April 1797, 16 May 1797, 10 June 1797, 15 July 1797; *PW*, 6: 29.

96 *PG*, 23 November 1797. The XYZ affair occurred in the winter of 1797–98, when Talleyrand, France's minister of foreign affairs, employed three agents (known in Adams's report to Congress as "X," "Y," and "Z") to inform the American commissioners in Paris that Talleyrand would only open negotiations if he was paid $250,000, if the United States would lend France $12 million, and if Adams would retract the anti-French remarks he had made in his speech to Congress in May 1797. See J. Miller, *Federalist Era*, pp. 210–12.

As a wave of anti-French feeling swept over the country and a "Quasi-War" between the United States and France developed, Cobbett's writings reached their peak of popularity. Congress voted money for the navy, ordered that the size of the army be tripled, suspended the Franco-American alliance of 1778, and passed the Alien and Sedition Acts. Adams made warlike responses to the anti-French addresses pouring into his office. If anything was going to provoke the United States into war, thought Cobbett, this was it.

Yet Congress still would not take the initiative; the general feeling was that the United States would be more united by waiting for France to declare war first. Cobbett most emphatically did not share this feeling. In his view, France would not declare war, in case such an action drove the United States into the arms of Britain. Instead, he argued, the French strategy was to "keep the mind of the [American] people, and of Congress, balancing between peace and war," while attacking American commerce and preparing to bring the United States into its sphere of influence through taking over Louisiana.[97] As it appeared to him that the United States was falling into the French trap, Cobbett became increasingly frustrated, angry, and impatient. When the American people were "boiling with rage" against the French, he wrote, the House of Representatives "sit *debating, hesitating, shilly-shallying, whipping the devil round the post*; and no energetic measure is adopted, no *strong alien bill or sedition law is passed*, nor is any declaration of war made, by which *traitors* can, in the eyes of the law, be found guilty and punished. Dreadful, awful state. If ever people on earth were dancing on the edge of a precipice, we are at this moment."[98] Feeling that the opportunity to destroy Jacobinism by joining the war was slipping away, Cobbett complained that Adams "seems to have lost his spirit precisely at the time when that of the people was roused to its highest pitch." After he learnt that Adams intended to reopen negotiations with France in an effort to end the Quasi-War, Cobbett reacted with disbelief and horror. And he was equally shocked to discover that most Federalists actually supported Adams, a position which, he believed, could only be explained through "their having abandoned every idea of consistency, and every principle of honour and freedom."[99]

97 *PG*, 27 May 1797.
98 *PW*, 8: 248–49.
99 *PW*, 9: 186–87; *PW*, 10: 108; *PW*, 11: 42, 59–77.

Reeling from this turn of events, faced with declining sales of the *Porcupine's Gazette*, and hit by a crippling $5,000 fine for libelling Benjamin Rush, Cobbett became an increasingly isolated and bitter figure. Although he was unsuccessful in his attempt to harness the American empire to Britain in a common struggle against democracy, democrats, Paineite influence, and revolutionary French imperialism, he remained defiant to the end. He shut down the *Porcupine's Gazette* in January 1800, but replaced it for a few months with *The Rush-Light*, which dealt almost exclusively with his libel trial. Cobbett's feelings are summed up in the periodical's full title: "The American Rush-Light; by the help of which, Wayward and Disaffected Britons may see a Complete Specimen of the Baseness, Dishonesty, Ingratitude, and Perfidy of Republicans, and of the Profligacy, Injustice, and Tyranny of Republican Governments."[100] His sense of absolute moral certainty, his sense of independence and integrity in the midst of patronage and corruption, and his heroic self-image all remained unshakeable. Driven to paroxysms of fury over the Rush trial, and disgusted by American reluctance to fight France, he packed up and left for England, the land of "true religion, sound morality, good government and *real* liberty," the land where the king and his government would never flinch in their life-or-death struggle against the menace of France—or so he thought.[101]

Cobbett's American experience was central to his career as a political writer. Not only did he establish himself as one of the most widely read pamphleteers and journalists in the Anglo-American world, he also acquired his characteristic writing style and his distinct political mentality during these years. In the United States, Cobbett developed his tendency to view politics in terms of the ideal and the real; judging American realities according to the ideal standards set by Paine in the *Rights of Man*, Cobbett quickly became disillusioned with democratic republicanism. In the United States, Cobbett defined and articulated his patriotism, and developed his idealization of British constitutional

100 *PW*, 11: 209. One can understand Cobbett's fury; the trial was stacked against him from the beginning. The presiding judge, Edward Shippen, was a friend of Cobbett's old enemy Thomas McKean; McKean had just been elected governor of Pennsylvania. The jury lists were drawn up by Shippen's son-in-law, and Rush's chief counsel was connected to the Shippen-McKean interest. Four days after the verdict, McKean appointed Shippen chief justice of Pennsylvania. See Spater, *William Cobbett*, pp. 103–4. Cobbett remained embittered about the trial for the rest of his life.

101 *PW*, 11: 138–40.

liberty which would be projected back onto a mythical Golden Age when it became clear to him that contemporary British political practice contradicted and violated his image. In the United States, Cobbett displayed a deep and permanent revulsion for abstract concepts of the rights of man; his later British Radicalism was rooted in Old English Liberty rather than abstract "rights." In the United States, Cobbett expressed a hostility which he never lost towards democratic societies; even during the political agitation of 1816–17 in which he played such a conspicuous part, one still finds him fulminating against Radical clubs and putting his faith in the "free, unpacked, unbiassed" force of public opinion.[102] And in the United States, Cobbett became acutely aware of the importance to Britain of the American Empire of Liberty—and although his attitude towards American liberty would change, the belief remained that the American empire must not be allowed to challenge Britain's international supremacy. The Tory outlook that Cobbett formed in America became ingrained, but in England he moved towards a species of political Radicalism as a means to realize his essentially conservative ends. In the process, his views of Tom Paine and the United States underwent a remarkable transformation.

102 *PR*, 1 March 1816.

THE

BEAUTIES OF COBBETT:

IN THREE PARTS.

—••●■••—

PART THE FIRST.

LIFE OF THOMAS PAINE,

AUTHOR OF THE

AGE OF REASON, &c. &c.

~~~~~~~~~~~~~~~~~

BY WILLIAM COBBETT.

There was a widespread attempt to discredit the writings of Cobbett the Radical by juxtaposing them with the earlier opinions of Cobbett the Tory. *The Beauties of Cobbett* (1820) was not really written by Cobbett; rather, the anonymous editor quoted Cobbett's anti-Paine sentiments of 1794–1804 to undermine Cobbett's positive comments about Paine after the Napoleonic Wars.

SKETCHES OF THE
LIFE OF BILLY COBB,
AND THE
DEATH OF TOMMY PAIN.

Cobbett's return to England from the United States in 1819 with Paine's bones exposed him to the ridicule of his enemies. This pamphlet, with Cobbett caught between the Devil and the Democrat, was one of many variations on the theme.

VI

The English Radical:
Cobbett, Paine and the United States

DRAWING on his American experiences, Cobbett began his English career with the express purpose of warning his countrymen against the seductive myth of the United States as a republican Utopia. His new daily newspaper, the *Porcupine*, attempted to check the "poisonous stream of republicanism" flowing from the United States. Precisely because America and Britain had so much in common, Cobbett argued, an "it can't happen here" attitude was impossible to sustain.[1] In taking this position, Cobbett aligned himself with the so-called "Alarmists" in Britain who pressed for vigorous anti-Jacobin policies.

Such pressure had already brought results. The Two Acts of 1795, broadening the definition of high treason and narrowing the right of public assembly, had delivered a severe blow to popular Radicalism. In the climate of repression after the acts, many democrats found it useless or dangerous to carry on the struggle; others, however, went underground and linked up with the secret, republican, and revolutionary United Irish movement. After the Irish Rising of 1798, and amid reports of a continuing Anglo-Irish Jacobin conspiracy connected to France, the government renewed its suspension of habeas corpus, suppressed combinations of workers, and outlawed the democratic societies. The republican threat had been contained, but could not be ignored. In the view of Edmund Burke, shortly before his death in 1797, one-fifth of the "political nation" were "pure Jacobins, utterly incapable of amendment; objects of eternal vigilance, and,

---

1 Cobbett, *Prospectus of a New Daily Paper*, pp. 1–2, 6; *Porcupine*, 3 November 1800, 25 November 1800, 5 February 1801, 7 April 1801, 9 June 1801, 10 June 1801; see also *PR*, 30 June 1802, 10 July 1802.

when they break out, of legal constraint." Cobbett intended to ensure that they would not break out.[2]

The tenor of his views and the general direction of his career seemed clear. The *Porcupine* printed articles under the motto "Fear God: Honour the King," and the weekly *Political Register* which replaced it in 1802 was intended to "contribute to the preserving of those ancient and holy institutions, those unsophisticated morals and natural manners, that well-tempered love of regulated liberty, and that just sense of public honour, on the preservation of which our national happiness and independence so essentially depend."[3] Yet within five years of his return to England, Cobbett had broken completely with the "Pitt system" of government; by 1810, he was in jail for seditious libel; between 1817 and 1819 he was forced into exile in the United States, and until his death in 1835 he fought tooth and nail against the British political establishment. Cobbett's career as an English Radical, with his famous *Rural Rides* as the centre-piece, has been well covered by his historians. But the connections between Cobbett's American and English careers have not been fully recognized. This chapter attempts to explain Cobbett's changing images of Paine and the United States, to explain the process that brought Cobbett to that field in New York in 1819 to disinter the bones and resurrect the memory of Tom Paine.

I

In 1804, needled by criticisms that he was "an *American* and a *traitor*" who had reversed himself by turning against Pitt and his policies, Cobbett asserted that he had "exhibited a perfect consistency" based upon "the principles of loyalty and patriotism, which I had inculcated and practiced in America."[4] According to these principles, the state and the subject were bound together by mutual responsibilities. "As the state cannot, by its own arbitrary will, withhold that protection which is the birthright of any individual subject," he had written in 1796, "so no subject can, by his arbitrary will, alienate that allegiance which is the right of the state." The central concern of the king, wrote Cobbett in America, was "the advancement and the preservation of

2 Thompson, *Making of the English Working Class*, pp. 111–203; Goodwin, *Friends of Liberty*, pp. 359–499; Wells, *Insurrection*. Burke is quoted in *Friends of Liberty*, p. 470.
3 *PR*, 16 January 1802.
4 *PR*, 29 September 1804.

the power and glory of the nation, and *the happiness of his subjects in general.*" Special interest groups such as merchants might press for war or peace according to the prospect of profits, he continued, but a firm government would act in the national interest, refusing to be "influenced by their clamours."[5]

But during his first years back in England, it gradually dawned on him that practice deviated sharply from principles; he increasingly came to believe that the state could and did withdraw its protection, that the government was unable to secure the happiness and prosperity of the people, and that special interests not only influenced but actually controlled the government. Under these circumstances, Cobbett insisted that Pitt was guilty of apostasy and that the entire system of British politics contradicted the spirit and traditions it pretended to uphold.[6] A familiar pattern was repeating itself; the ideal which Cobbett had articulated in the United States clashed with the reality he experienced in Britain.

The first major indication that reality diverged from the ideal came shortly after Cobbett's return to England, when in 1801 and 1802 Henry Addington's ministry negotiated peace with France.[7] For Cobbett, who had argued in the United States that Britain was engaged in a Holy War to purge the world of French republicanism, such negotiations bordered on treason. Attacking the government from the right, just as he had attacked the Adams administration in America for refusing to declare war on France, Cobbett denounced the peace in the strongest possible terms. Not only was it morally repugnant to deal with a regicide republic, he argued, the peace proposals allowed Napoleon to consolidate his position in Europe, the Mediterranean, and the Atlantic, thus making Britain more vulnerable when hostilities resumed. Instead of patriotic steadfastness against France, Cobbett

---

5 *PC*, November 1796, p. 32; *PW*, 8: 136.

6 This view was forcefully expressed in *PR*, 20 April 1805, when Cobbett declared war on the "Pitt system," and was confirmed in 1806 when the "Ministry of All the Talents" did not produce any radical changes in the system. Cobbett's break with William Windham, who joined the ministry in 1806, symbolized his estrangement from "official" politics. See Spater, *William Cobbett*, pp. 137–56.

7 Negotiations had already begun in 1800 when Pitt was in power. Addington took over after Pitt's resignation in March 1801, and stayed in power until Pitt resumed office in May 1804. Pitt's refusal in 1801 and 1802 to condemn the peace did nothing to improve Cobbett's opinion of his former hero.

saw an intolerable weakness and timidity; the government, in his view, was betraying everything Britain stood for.[8]

Cobbett's opposition to the peace quickly brought home another reality: the physical danger of proclaiming unpopular opinions. Not surprisingly, he refused to illuminate his house to celebrate either the ratification of the peace preliminaries in October 1801 or the final signing of the Treaty of Amiens in March 1802; as with his shop in Philadelphia, Cobbett would once again defy the "mob." But in London, the "mob" carried the day. On both occasions his windows were smashed, and in October he had been forced to light up to protect his family. Cobbett's shock is not hard to imagine. In Philadelphia, after he was threatened for opening his shop, he had confidently asserted that in Britain a person's "house is not threatened with destruction, because his window exhibits what is indicative of the prowess of his nation, and of the disgrace of their enemies; at any rate, he is not threatened with murder, for having stepped forth in defence of the laws and the government of the country." Now, in 1801 and 1802, he had not only seen some of his property destroyed because of his loyalty and patriotism, but also heard that Addington's supporters regarded the whole affair as an "excellent joke." Caught between "the commencement of the reign of the mob" and the "grovelling statesmen" who engineered a dishonourable peace, Cobbett's idealized image of British politics was beginning to fracture.[9]

At this stage, Cobbett was only partly disillusioned; after all, other leading politicians such as William Windham and William Grenville were equally opposed to the peace. But the more direct experience Cobbett had of British politics and society, the more disenchanted he became. The man who in the United States had praised the impartiality of English justice, and had argued that there was more freedom of the press in England than America, now learnt about the practices of "special juries," by which the government could rig juries to receive favourable verdicts. He himself ran up against the system when he was assessed £500 damages for printing articles criticizing the administration of government in Ireland.[10] And the man who in the United

8 Cobbett's criticisms of the peace were expressed in his *Letters to . . . Hawkesbury.*

9 *Porcupine*, 12 October 1801; *PR*, 6 February 1802, 1 May 1802; Cobbett, *The Scare-Crow*, p. 20.

10 Cobbett, *Observations*, p. 7, and *Democratic Judge*; Spater, *William Cobbett*, pp. 125–26, 128–31.

States had spent his time "defending the cause of monarchy" while "assailing men guilty of corruption" became increasingly aware of the network of corruption and patronage at every level of government in Britain.[11] Before long, the *Political Register* was full of jeremiads against the all-pervasive "degeneracy" which he believed characterized British society.

The concept of degeneracy implies a fall from grace, the betrayal of an ideal. "This degeneracy," he wrote, "extends to all ranks and degrees. There is scarcely a man to be found, who does not treat with contempt those notions of national honour, of patriotism, and of loyalty, which were so dear in the estimation of his ancestors."[12] In presenting himself as a lone crusader against a degenerate society, Cobbett was identifying with his idealized ancestors, men who would never have accepted, let alone welcomed, such a national humiliation as the Treaty of Amiens. It was the England of his imagination, and not the England of Addington's pusillanimity, Wilberforce's shallow humanitarianism, new-fangled Methodists, and weak-minded tea drinkers, which Cobbett had defended against American Republicans and which he would continue to defend against its enemies at home.

Searching for explanations, Cobbett initially attributed this perceived decline in national character to both the "democratic poison" afflicting the country, and the growing power and influence of the "moneyed interests" in Britain. But as the popular radical movement was being contained, he increasingly felt that the greatest threat to his ideal came from above, from the internal power of high finance rather than the international power of democratic principles.[13] Drawing on Country Party traditions of men like Bolingbroke, Swift, and Pope, Cobbett became convinced that commercial values and the conjunction between financial interests and political power in Britain were undermining the true spirit and character of the nation. Like Country Party writers a century earlier, Cobbett believed that the "ancient country gentry" were the backbone of the country, and looked to a

11 *PR*, 19 October 1805. His first experience of corruption after he returned to England came when Francis Freeling, secretary of the Post Office, obstructed deliveries of the *Porcupine* because Cobbett would not agree to an under-the-table deal with him. See *Porcupine*, 15 June 1801, and *PR*, 27 October 1802.

12 *PR*, 3 April 1802.

13 *PR*, 3 April 1802, 10 April 1802, 1 September 1804, 8 September 1804, 6 October 1804.

past where honour, virtue, and personal connections meant more than profit, self-interest, and the cash nexus.

Like these writers, he found the root of the problem in the growth of paper money, the stock market, banks, and the soaring national debt. Cobbett maintained that the taxes needed to support the debt impoverished the traditional gentry while enriching a parasitic new "race of merchants and manufacturers, and bankers and loan-jobbers and contractors," many of whom were "Jews and foreigners." This was vintage Bolingbroke. Similarly, Cobbett echoed Bolingbroke and men like John Brown when he argued that patriotic pride was being replaced by an atmosphere of "luxury and effeminacy," narrow ambition, and a possibly fatal moral decay. He also shared Country Party political notions that a corrupt bargain had been forged between the government and the creditor élite. The "moneyed men" were so powerful that they in effect controlled government policy, contended Cobbett; the government looked after its creditors, and the creditors supplied the government with new sources of wealth which was then used to bribe members of Parliament into supporting the government. In the grip of self-interested fundholders who put the short-term value of their stocks above the "*permanent security*" of the nation and who thus supported the Treaty of Amiens, Britain in Cobbett's view was grovelling at the feet of France, and the people were in danger of becoming "little better than slaves" to the prime minister.[14]

This diagnosis of the British disease remained a central and permanent feature of Cobbett's political thought; everything else was subordinated to the overriding purpose of destroying the financial system and the evils which he believed flowed from it. But while Country Party writings appeared to explain what had gone wrong with his country and reinforced his social nostalgia, Cobbett found them deficient in two major respects. First, they did not tell him enough about the underlying mechanics of the financial system. And second, they did not offer an adequate remedy for the ills they described; the notion of the Patriot King had too much of the *deus ex*

14 On the financial revolution, see Dickson, *Financial Revolution in England*. On Country Party arguments, see Kramnick, *Bolingbroke and His Circle*; Bolingbroke, *Works*, 2: 443, 451, 458; Swift, *Prose Works*, 2: 124; Brown, *Estimate of the Manners and Principles of the Times*, pp. 29, 44–45, 55, 153. For Cobbett's position, see *PR*, 10 April 1802, 26 June 1802, 17 July 1802, 9 July 1803, 21 September 1804, 27 October 1804.

machina about it. In both these areas, Cobbett found himself travelling in new and unexpected directions; in both these areas, he found the answers in the writings of a man he had once admired and more recently condemned. Much to his own surprise, Cobbett was moving back to Tom Paine.

The first crack in Cobbett's monolithic hostility to Paine occurred in 1803, when he became convinced that the key to understanding the nature, development, and ultimate destruction of the financial system lay in Paine's *Decline and Fall of the English System of Finance* (1796). In this work, Paine claimed to have unlocked the inner law that governed the growth of the debt and the depreciation of paper money. Examining the history of the debt since the Glorious Revolution, he argued that with each outbreak of war, the debt increased exponentially "in the series of one-half upon each preceding number," or a sequence of eight, twelve, eighteen and so on. "I have not *made* the ratio any more than Newton made the ratio of gravitation," wrote Paine. "I have only discovered it, and explained the mode of applying it." The logic behind the law was straightforward. Interest payments on accumulated loans increased the quantity of paper money, thus producing depreciation and higher prices. When the government borrowed money for the next war, it had to raise a larger loan to balance the rise of prices; the interest on the new loan further increased the quantity and hastened the depreciation of banknotes, in a continuing upward spiral.[15]

As paper money depreciated, Paine continued, gold and silver initially depreciated with it. In the long run, however, paper money would fall below the value of specie, and at this point the system would begin its death throes. When people realized that gold was worth more than paper, they would try to exchange their banknotes for gold, only to find that the bank could not meet their demands. According to his calculations, there were in 1796 at least £60 million of banknotes in circulation, but no more than £2 million in hard currency at the bank. As he put it, "*public credit is suspicion asleep*"; when suspicion awoke, the system would be convulsed in a crisis of confidence. The first sign of collapse, he wrote, would be a stoppage of cash payments at the bank. From this analysis and from his estimation of the increase in the debt, he concluded that the system had "advanced into the last twenty years of its existence" and that it would not outlast the life of

---

15 Paine, *Decline and Fall of the English System of Finance*, 2: 651–74, esp. 655, 657.

Pitt, "supposing him to live the usual age of a man." Out of financial collapse would come political revolution, he argued; this is what had happened in France in 1789 and was destined to occur in Britain. And Paine's predictions appeared to be confirmed only a year after he had made them, when the Bank of England in 1797 suspended cash payments in an attempt to stave off financial collapse.[16]

The effect of these arguments on Cobbett was electrifying; he quickly adopted the *Decline and Fall* as a kind of financial bible which explained the present and foretold the future. After reading the book, Cobbett recalled, he saw "the whole matter in its true light." "I felt cheered by the *certainty* that I should live to see the day when that scheme of matchless turpitude [the financial system] would become the subject of universal reprobation," he commented on another occasion. "I soon arrived at a conviction of this truth; that, the nation must destroy that monster the Debt; or that the monster must destroy this form of Government." After his awakening, Cobbett maintained, "a new era commenced in the political education of the people of England." "At . . . [Paine's] expiring flambeau I lighted my taper," he wrote in 1819; "and from the year 1803 to the present hour I have been warning the Parliament and the Government against the consequences of this fatal system, which has at last produced in this once happy country, misery such as never was witnessed before in the world. . . ."[17]

It was not quite so simple. While it is true that Paine's financial arguments played a central role in Cobbett's break with the "Pitt system," Cobbett's later comments must be qualified in at least three ways. First, Cobbett had actually read Paine's *Decline and Fall* seven years earlier than he claimed. In Philadelphia in 1796, Cobbett had dismissed it as a malicious piece of work whose predictions would all prove false. "It is extremely favourable for British banknotes," he commented at that time, "that he who doubts of their solidity will not believe in the Bible." Even after the suspension of cash payments in 1797, Cobbett continued to support the government position that the country could absorb the amount of paper money in circulation. In-

---

16 Ibid., 2: 652, 659–60, 662–64. For the development of Paine's views on paper money and the national debt see Paine, *American Crisis III*, 1: 98–99; *American Crisis V*, 1: 110; *American Crisis VII*, 1: 149; *Dissertations on Government*, 2: 405–9; *Prospects on the Rubicon*, 2: 636–46; *Rights of Man, Part 1*, 1: 332–37; *Rights of Man, Part 2*, 1: 444–45.
17 *PR*, 6 July 1811, 21 December 1822, 18 December 1819.

deed, he accepted this view right up to late 1801, when he was still condemning the financial writings of the "arch rebel" Paine.[18] It was not until his idealized image of Britain began to shatter, and not until he turned to Country Party writings, which located Britain's malaise in the financial system, that he rediscovered the *Decline and Fall*. At that point, Paine's financial writings struck him with all the force of a revelation, and Cobbett erased his earlier attitude to the book from his memory.

Second, although Cobbett's writings on financial matters in 1803 and 1804 show unmistakable signs of Paine's influence, he made no acknowledgment of that influence. His writings from the summer of 1803 began to assume that bankruptcy was inevitable, and by the end of the year he was repeating Paine's argument that when paper money depreciated below the value of gold and silver, the "total extinction" of the system was imminent.[19] Yet Cobbett had nothing positive to say about Paine in these years, and continued his attacks on the "wretched traitor and apostate."[20] Although in agreement with the general arguments of the *Decline and Fall*, he could not accept Paine's conclusion that the system's collapse would bring down the monarchy and aristocracy and pave the way for republican revolution. On the contrary, Cobbett hoped that the fall of the system would purify the country and preserve the traditional form of government. Not surprisingly, he remained hostile to Paine's position; rather than "lighting his taper" at Paine's "expiring flambeau," Cobbett reshaped Paine's financial writings to suit his own purposes.

This brings us to the third qualification of Cobbett's later comments. Far from being "cheered" by the *Decline and Fall*, his attitude in 1803 and 1804 was largely one of fear and anxiety. How could one be sure that financial collapse would not in fact produce all the "horrors of revolution" in Britain? War with France had resumed in 1803, an invasion appeared highly likely, and the country was, in Cobbett's view, on the brink of bankruptcy. It seemed that Paine's political predictions might actually be realized; at any rate, it was imperative to prevent the impending financial crisis from "subverting the throne

18 Cobbett, *Antidote*, p. 48; *PG*, 4 March 1797; *Porcupine*, 6 February 1801, 18 September 1801.

19 *PR*, 18 June 1803, 25 June 1803, 16 July 1803, 30 July 1803, 3 December 1803. See also *PR*, 21 April 1804, 5 May 1804.

20 *PR*, 8 January 1803. See also *Porcupine*, 14 September 1801; *PR*, 11 December 1802, 17 September 1803.

and bringing our liberties beneath its ruins." But Cobbett was uncertain whether such an outcome could be avoided. He insisted that Britain's strength lay in men and arms rather than trade and money, and he pressed for a large, well-equipped, voluntary standing army. Yet the government refused to listen to him, and he was plagued with doubt and despair. "Am I asked for my remedy?" he wrote in 1804. "I know of none. Am I then asked why I do not hold my tongue? Because it is my duty, and every man's duty, to endeavour to prepare the country for the trial that awaits it."[21]

As the invasion scare passed, Cobbett's search for remedies continued. On a personal level, he attempted to bring Old England back to life in his farm at Botley, with hunting, coursing, and "manly sports," and paternal relations with his workers. In the *Political Register* he penned a series of articles entitled "Perish Commerce," in which he advocated a self-sufficient economy based on agriculture and ancillary small-scale manufacturing; the idea was to transform England along the lines of Botley. He continued to hammer away at the financial system, arguing that the only way to prevent bankruptcy was to tax heavily the interest on the debt.[22] And before long, his disgust for the interlocking financial and political élite that had taken over his country impelled him not only to declare war against the "Pitt system," or the "Thing" as he sometimes called it, but also to consider *"real reform"* as a means to restore traditional liberties. For this reason, Cobbett supported Francis Burdett in his Reform election campaigns at Middlesex and Westminster, and helped Lord Cochrane's anti-corruption election drive at Honiton. Approaching parliamentary reform with many misgivings and much caution, Cobbett pinned his hopes on "the people who are in the middling walks of life, who have property to preserve and who have judgment to direct their actions."[23] With a wider, middle-class franchise and a sustained effort to root out parliamentary corruption, the way would be open to purge the country of paper money, the debt, and excessive taxation. Then and only then, he believed, would it be possible to restore England to its true character.

Cobbett still rejected universal suffrage or any other *"wild theories*

---

21 *PR*, 5 May 1804, 9 March 1805. See also *PR*, 18 June 1803, 25 June 1803, 16 July 1803, 30 July 1803, 21 April 1804, 2 March 1805.

22 *PR*, 23 February 1805.

23 *PR*, 27 April 1805, 15 March 1806, 15 April 1809.

of liberty," and insisted that his fundamental position remained unchanged. "All I wish and all I strive for," he wrote in 1809, "is *The Constitution of England*, undefiled by corruption."[24] Yet Cobbett's alignment with the Reform movement produced new political perceptions. By 1809 and 1810 he was denouncing the government for branding reformers as Jacobin conspirators. He even maintained that the fund-holders and borough-mongers had invented the whole concept of English Jacobinism to stay in power by deluding the people, and counted himself among those who had been duped by the strategy.[25]

At the same time, Cobbett began to adopt his own version of Paine's dialectic of political change. Instead of a linear argument based on parliamentary reform, Cobbett envisaged a process of interaction between financial crisis and reform. Without reform, he reasoned, the financial system would destroy itself; as the failure of the system shook society to the core, the pressures for reform would become irresistible; reform would then sweep away the last vestiges of a corrupt system and re-establish Old English Liberty. Paine had argued that bankruptcy would culminate in parliamentary revolution; Cobbett now believed that it would result in parliamentary reform. The distance between the two men, while still considerable, was narrowing.

Believing that the Jacobin menace had been exaggerated and manipulated by an unscrupulous government, and sharing Paine's financial views, Cobbett gradually dropped his earlier criticisms of Paine. Significantly, though, it was not until Cobbett found himself in Newgate Prison, serving a two-year sentence for seditious libel, that he began to speak positively about his old enemy.[26] Prison embittered Cobbett and intensified his hostility to the ruling class. His tone became harsher and more abrasive, and his children recalled that Newgate brought out a sterner, more serious side of his character.[27] Under these circumstances, Cobbett shook off his earlier reservations and finally acknowledged Paine's influence on his financial writings. "But, let me not be guilty of robbery, and especially of the *Dead*, and more especially of one whose writings . . . I formerly condemned," wrote Cob-

---

24 *PR*, 15 April 1809, 27 May 1809.

25 *PR*, 22 April 1809, 10 February 1810.

26 Cobbett was prosecuted for remarks he made in 1809 condemning the flogging of five militiamen who had been charged with mutiny. See Spater, *William Cobbett*, pp. 233–38.

27 Spater, *William Cobbett*, pp. 325–26.

bett in 1811. "I allude to the writings of PAINE, the abused, the reprobated, the anathematized TOM PAINE."[28]

In complete contrast to his earlier writings, Cobbett now described Paine as having "infinitely greater depth of thought and general powers of mind" than Pitt and Addington put together, and as possessing abilities "scarcely ever surpassed in any age or country."[29] In a series of articles written from Newgate and eventually reprinted as *Paper against Gold*, he repeated Paine's view that public credit was "SUSPICION ASLEEP," and reiterated Paine's argument that paper money must eventually sink in value beneath gold and silver. Applying Paine's analysis to the early nineteenth century, Cobbett maintained that going back on gold was impossible, since the bank simply did not have enough gold to match the value of paper currency. Nor could he accept the alternative of reducing paper money to 1796 levels. Such a policy, he argued, would cripple the country by attempting to pay back in full debts contracted in depreciated money. Viewing financial matters through a Paineite lense, Cobbett could only see different routes to the system's destruction.[30]

Not only did the imprisoned Cobbett openly embrace Paine's financial writings; he also came to identify himself with Paine as a fellow victim of the "system." Just as the government had refused to follow Paine's advice in the *Rights of Man* to tax the interest on the national debt, argued Cobbett, it was now ignoring the truths contained in *Paper against Gold*.[31] And just as the government had tried to reduce

---

28 *PR*, 6 July 1811. Some contemporaries had already realized that Cobbett was in fact repeating Paine's financial arguments. Thomas Hardy wrote to Cobbett in 1810, praising Cobbett's writings on the debt, but gently chastizing him for claiming to be *"the first public writer in England* who warned the people against the consequences of this species of currency and generally against the whole of the paper system." This distinction, Hardy continued, really belonged to Paine, not Cobbett. BL, Add. Ms. 27818, f. 225, Hardy to Cobbett, 26 July 1810.

29 *PR*, 6 July 1811, 10 October 1810. It is interesting to note that in 1810, Cobbett wrote that Paine's abilities equalled those of Burke. Before this time, of course, Cobbett had praised Burke while condemning Paine; after it, he increasingly praised Paine while condemning Burke.

30 *PR*, 1 September 1810, 6 July 1811. He was still repeating these arguments in old age; see, for example, *PR*, 1 September 1832.

31 *PR*, 23 March 1811, 6 July 1811; compare *PR*, 23 February 1805. On the one hand Cobbett argued that a tax on the interest could have saved the system; on the other he argued that the collapse of the system was inevitable. He did not appear aware of the contradiction in his position.

the influence of Paine's "powerful pen" by issuing the Royal Proclamation, burning him in effigy, and trying him for seditious libel, it
was now trying to break Cobbett by putting him in jail, fining him
£1000, and holding the threat over him of further punishment if he
failed to keep the peace.[32]

Although he continued to dissociate himself from Paine's republican and deist views, Cobbett became less critical of Paine's writings in
general.[33] When he mentioned the *Age of Reason*, Cobbett now stressed
the importance of freedom of speech and the need for dispassionate
debate about the book instead of shouting it down as he had previously
done.[34] And by 1815, Cobbett was praising not only Paine's financial
writings, but also Paine's attack on governmental corruption. "PAINE
observed very truly," he wrote, "that a *rich government* made a *poor
people*. In America, the people are rich and the government poor; and
that, apparently, is the state of things which that queer sort of a nation
prefers."[35] Clearly, Cobbett's view of the United States as well as of
Paine had changed remarkably between 1800 and 1815.

II

During his first years back in England, Cobbett's attitude to the United
States remained relatively straightforward; he continued to attack
American "liberty," and urged vigorous measures to prevent the
emergence of a powerful American empire. Jefferson's election victory of 1800 confirmed and strengthened Cobbett's negative image
of the United States. The Republicans, he argued, motivated by "ambition, revenge and self-interest," would squeeze the Federalists out
of influential positions and pursue a pro-French foreign policy. Although the Senate might check the excesses of that "malignant philosopher" Jefferson and his crew of "atheists and anarchists," although

32 *PR*, 5 June 1811.

33 *PR*, 19 September 1810, 7 November 1810.

34 *PR*, 13 June 1812, 25 September 1813. The occasion of Cobbett's comments in
1812 was the prosecution of D. I. Eaton for publishing the third part of the *Age of
Reason*. It is not clear when—or if—Cobbett actually read the *Age of Reason*. He ridiculed
it frequently in America, but wrote in 1812 that he had only just read the work and
had been surprised at its "*sober, argumentative*" tone. In 1820, however, he wrote that
he had never read the book until December 1819, and defended Paine against the
charge of being a "*blasphemer*" (*PR*, 27 January 1820).

35 *PR*, 11 February 1815.

the Federalists would provide vigorous opposition and although the increasing sales of Burke's writings demonstrated that there was "yet a sound part in America," the overall picture did not strike Cobbett as encouraging. The Federalists were on the defensive, and the dominant republican ideology was threatening to Britain.[36]

Equally dangerous, in Cobbett's view, was the continuing prospect of the United States becoming locked into the French sphere of influence. His fears increased when France acquired Louisiana from Spain and prepared to move into its new territory. Once securely lodged in Louisiana, Cobbett maintained, France would offer the United States free navigation of the Mississippi in return for commercial discrimination against Britain, and would gradually increase the pressure until Anglo-American commerce dwindled to a halt. This, he insisted, must not be allowed to happen. Arguing that the country which dominated the New World would eventually tower over the Old, Cobbett urged that Britain resume hostilities with France immediately, and march into Louisiana before the French were able to establish themselves there. But Britain had to move quickly, since, as he put it, "the fate of Louisiana will decide the fate of Great Britain"; indeed, he even argued that British control of Louisiana was infinitely more important than British control of Malta. If Britain possessed Louisiana, everything would be possible; if France was given free rein, the consequences would "shake the British empire to its base." It was, he wrote, quite simply a matter of "life or death."[37]

As it turned out, Cobbett's worries were misplaced; Napoleon sold Louisiana to the United States in the spring of 1803. On hearing this news, Cobbett was relieved but hardly overjoyed. Things could have been much worse, he believed, but Britain had nevertheless missed a glorious opportunity to strengthen its position in the New World. And France had not only made money on the deal, but also maintained good relations with the United States, thus establishing "an immoveable foundation for the influence of her partizans in that country."[38]

36 *Porcupine*, 5 November 1800, 14 April 1801; *PR, Supplement to Volume 1*, 1: 1167; *PR*, 11 December 1802, 12 February 1803, 4 February 1804.

37 *PR, Supplement to Volume 1*, 1: 1166; *PR*, 30 January 1802, 6 March 1802, 10 July 1802, 17 July 1802, 19 February 1803, 5 March 1803, 19 March 1803, 2 April 1803; Cobbett to Windham, 27 March 1803 and n.d., in *Life and Letters*, 1: 172, 180–82.

38 *PR*, 28 May 1803, 4 June 1803. The reasons for Napoleon's decision to sell Louisiana are considered in Smelser, *Democratic Republic*, pp. 93–95.

Yet the "life or death" continental threat had passed, and after the resumption of war between Britain and France in May 1803, Cobbett turned his attention to a different area of conflict: the Atlantic Ocean, where rival British and French imperialisms attempted to control the rising maritime power of the United States.

This conflict in the Atlantic put the United States in an extremely difficult position. Napoleon's Berlin Decree of 1806 announced the blockade of the British Isles, and stated that goods from Britain, together with the ships that carried them, were liable to seizure. Britain replied with a series of orders in council in 1807, which among other things banned American trade with French-controlled ports unless those ships first called at British ports, paid duties, and obtained permits. Against this, Napoleon's Milan Decree of December 1807 declared that any ships which submitted to British demands would no longer be regarded as neutral. In theory, Britain and France were equally aggressive towards American neutrality, but in practice, especially after Trafalgar, the United States felt the grip of British power much more tightly. To assert its rights as a neutral carrier, the United States adopted in 1806 a Non-Importation Act, which was not actually implemented until December 1807, and also in December 1807 passed an Embargo Act which prohibited American shipments to all foreign ports. By early 1809, however, it was clear that the embargo could not be rigorously enforced. It was replaced in March 1809 by the Non-Intercourse Act, which preserved the fiction of banning trade with Britain and France while creating enough loopholes to make the British feel that the United States had in fact been forced to surrender.[39]

Throughout these disputes, Cobbett consistently took a hard line against American claims for neutral rights; in this respect, there was no difference between the Cobbett of 1794–1800 and the Cobbett of 1803–9. He maintained that American neutrality was a cover behind which the United States was building up its merchant marine to challenge Britain's traditional dominance in transatlantic commerce, and complained that the American flag was sheltering not only "the floating property of France" but also "not less than 25 or 30 thousand British seamen."[40] Insisting that naval superiority was fundamental to

39 Burt, *United States*, pp. 210–55; Smelser, *Democratic Republic*, pp. 138–80. See also Perkins, *Causes of the War of 1812*. For an excellent analysis of the strategy of non-importation and embargo, see Nelson, "Hamilton and Gallatin," pp. 295–301, 352–55.
40 *PR*, 11 June 1803. See also *PR*, 19 November 1803 and 18 February 1804.

British security and independence, Cobbett pushed for vigorous search and seizure measures against American ships. He fully supported the orders in council of 1807, approved of Britain's attempts to impress its subjects serving in the American fleet, and applauded the Royal Navy's use of force in the *Chesapeake* affair.[41] Brushing aside with contempt American economic sanctions against Britain, he argued that an Anglo-American economic war would cripple the United States but hardly be noticed at home. He dismissed the Non-Importation Act as a "bug-bear fit only to frighten children," believed that the embargo would be widely evaded by American merchants, and maintained that the United States was too weak and divided to sustain a full-scale war against Britain. Not surprisingly, he was triumphant when he learned in the spring of 1809 that the United States had watered down its embargo. Believing that his hawkish arguments had been completely vindicated, Cobbett boasted that the result demonstrated the benefits to Britain when the government was wise enough to follow his advice.[42]

The sheer intensity of Cobbett's anti-Americanism at this time is particularly striking. Consider his views in 1806 on the Non-Importation Act: "For my part," he wrote, "I feel great satisfaction that it would be highly injurious to the American States; I rejoice that it would prove the cause of great misery and ruin amongst their inhabitants; I feel great consolation that it would, in all human probability, cause the complete overthrow of their Federal Government. . . ."[43] As the Anglo-American conflict rekindled the fire of his earlier anti-republican writings, Cobbett characterized the United States as "the most unprincipled country in the world," with its endemic

41 *PR*, 20 December 1806, 15 August 1807, 3 October 1807, 2 January 1808, 9 January 1808. For a comparison between these views and Cobbett's arguments during the 1790s, see Cobbett, "A Letter to the Infamous Tom Paine," in *PC*, December 1796, p. 4. The *Chesapeake* incident occurred in June 1807, when H.M.S. Leopard opened fire on the American frigate *Chesapeake* to search for deserters.

42 *PR*, 3 January 1807, 24 January 1807, 1 August 1807, 22 August 1807, 2 January 1808, 8 April 1809.

43 *PR*, 20 December 1806. While such sentiments recurred in his writings between 1805 and 1809, it is worth noting that on other occasions he remembered the Federalists and was less comprehensive in his denunciations. In *PR*, 2 January 1808, for example, he wrote that he did not wish to see the "many valuable people" in the United States "harassed and torn to pieces," but nevertheless insisted that if Americans continued to pursue unfriendly policies, "war let them have, and let it be war once for all." See also *PR*, 22 August 1807.

corruption, its lack of respect for law and order, and its high divorce rate. The United States had no sense of tradition or history to guide it, he argued; rejecting the past, its people lived permanently in the present with no purpose or direction and no moral principles to regulate their behaviour.[44]

Beneath such arguments lay a strong sense of affronted nationalism. The United States, in his view, was aggressively challenging Britain and must be beaten down.[45] But there was also a deep-seated desire to get revenge for his personal treatment in the United States:

The Americans, under pretences the most false, by means the most base that ever were employed, by the violent mockery of judicial proceedings, by openly-avowed and boasted-of perjury, robbed me of the earnings of my life up to that time, left me to begin anew with a family dependent solely upon my exertions, and have since cruelly persecuted several of my friends. For the sake of these friends more than for my own sake I hate the unprincipled nation. This hatred will never cease, until they do me justice, and, therefore, it will end but with my life.[46]

He would, in short, make the Americans pay for the way they had treated him during the Benjamin Rush libel trial. Cobbett equated American attacks on himself and his friends with American attacks on his country, and set out to defend both his own honour and that of Britain against such hostility.

It is also significant that Cobbett remained bitterly opposed to American ideology and interests after he moved towards reform in Britain. George Spater's comment that by mid-1806 Cobbett had "definitely made a break with the past" does not apply to Cobbett's American writings.[47] For Cobbett, the whole point of reform was to protect true British liberty, national honour, and imperial power against their internal enemies; similarly, he would not allow British liberty, honour, and power to succumb to the external threat of the United States. Indeed, his fear that the American empire might weaken Britain's international position impelled him towards an unholy alliance with the government. Just as he attacked the government's domestic poli-

44 *PR*, 22 August 1807, 2 April 1808.
45 BL, Add. Ms. 22906, f. 310, Cobbett to John Wright, 15 August 1807; *PR*, 19 December 1807.
46 *PR*, 26 March 1808.
47 Spater, *William Cobbett*, p. 156.

cies for subverting Old England from within, he supported the government's American policy for strengthening Old England from without. During the American embargo, one finds him praising the ministers in general and foreign minister George Canning in particular for their "firmness" against American "aggression."[48]

Many of his fellow reformers, already surprised by Cobbett's conversion to Radicalism, reacted with incredulity. Writing to Paine in 1807 about the current state of British politics, Thomas Hardy noted the existence of a weekly paper

published by that camelion Wm. Cobbett who is incessant in his scurrility of the Americans. That fellow had the impudence to turn democrat about three or four years ago. Since his conversion he was the only political writer that was at all noticed—but since he has begun to show his cloven foot again he is despised by many of his greatest admirers and friends. He does not appear to be that steady friend to the happiness of mankind which we was wishing to give him credit for. He seems to be destitute of good principle.[49]

Cobbett was unmoved. He had not become a reformer to relinquish his nationalism; indeed, in many respects, he had become a reformer because of his nationalism. Among the threats to his country, he believed, were the government's suppression of liberty at home, and the challenge of an increasingly assertive American empire. If the government took strong measures to deal with the United States, Cobbett would support those measures without softening his attack on its other policies.

This, at any rate, was his position in 1808. But then something unusual happened. After writing at length on Anglo-American relations, Cobbett suddenly dropped the subject; between April 1808 and December 1810 there was a strange, almost unbroken silence on the conflict in the Atlantic. During that time, he mentioned the dispute only twice: once in April 1809 to rejoice that the United States was losing the economic war, and again in January 1810 to announce that he was sick to death of the whole affair.[50] By the time he returned to the issue in December 1810, the conditions of the conflict had changed.

48 *PR*, 26 March 1808.

49 PP, Add. Ms. 27817, f. 72, Hardy to Paine, 15 October 1807. Hardy also included Cobbett's purchase of "an Estate" at Botley with the profits of the *PR* as further proof of Cobbett's self-interest and lack of principle.

50 *PR*, 8 April 1809, 13 January 1810.

In May 1810, the United States had declared that it would trade with both Britain and France, but stated that, if either country repealed its restrictions, then Americans would stop trading with the other country until it followed suit. In response, Napoleon made it seem that he had already revoked the Berlin and Milan decrees; when President Madison learned of this in November 1810, he gave Britain three months to repeal its orders in council or face renewed non-intercourse. Britain refused to change its policy.[51]

At this point, Cobbett re-entered the controversy. Without warning, he stood his earlier position on its head and began to rewrite Anglo-American relations with the British government cast as the principal villain. Arguing that the government was behaving in an arbitrary, high-handed manner, he accused the Royal Navy of intercepting American ships, seizing neutral American property and impressing native American sailors. In the revised version, the United States was the victim and the British government was the aggressor.[52] Moreover, Cobbett now argued that an Anglo-American economic war would hurt Britain much more than the United States. By 1811, he contended that the "astonishing" rise of American manufactures, stimulated in part by earlier disruptions in commerce, had given the United States a substantial degree of economic independence. Most American politicians welcomed and encouraged this development, he added, since they wanted to wean their country away from the British world of corruption and financial oligarchy. Although he retracted his former "errors" about the rise of American manufactures, Cobbett kept quiet about his earlier support for British policies which were intended to throttle those manufactures and keep the United States in a state of economic subordination. Nor did he mention his previous position that America was too weak and divided to sustain economic sanctions or full-scale war against Britain. Such a notion, he asserted in 1811, was "no more than a continuation of the series of deceptions practiced upon this nation for the last twenty years with such complete and such fatal success." Yet Cobbett himself had played a major role in fostering those "deceptions" only three years earlier.[53]

51 The words "made it seem" are crucial; there is ample evidence to show that Napoleon revoked the decrees in theory while retaining them in practice. This helps to explain why Britain refused to repeal its orders in council. See Smelser, *Democratic Republic*, pp. 197–98.

52 *PR*, 1 February 1811, 31 August 1811, 7 September 1811, 26 September 1812.

53 *PR*, 14 September 1811. See also *PR*, 6 March 1811, 17 April 1811, 18 January

In part, Cobbett's American conversion was the product of changing international conditions; this, at least, was his own explanation. Before 1810, he argued, he had supported the government's position that the orders in council were necessary defensive measures against Napoleon's economic warfare. But now that France had revoked the Berlin and Milan decrees, wrote Cobbett, Britain's failure to repeal the orders demonstrated the hollowness and hypocrisy of the government's earlier arguments. He would no longer support a government which disguised aggressive intentions behind the language of self-defence.[54] It must be remembered that Cobbett was in prison when he reinterpreted Anglo-American relations; at Newgate, he came to believe that the government was acting as despotically abroad as it was at home, and began to draw parallels between the government's behaviour towards the Americans and its treatment of William Cobbett. In his approach to the United States, no less than in his changing attitude to Paine, prison radicalized Cobbett.[55]

There was also a deeper logic behind Cobbett's new outlook. As he attacked the "system" in Britain, he gradually began to alter his perceptions of the United States. In 1805, he had urged the British government to adopt American methods of redeeming the national debt, and had apologized to the American public for his earlier attitude to Pitt's enemies.[56] But as late as May 1810, only weeks before his imprisonment, Cobbett still rejected the American political system as an example to his own country. "I disliked, and I still dislike, the governments . . . of the American States," he wrote.[57]

In Newgate, things began to change. During his attacks on the financial system he increasingly praised the United States for its lack of paper money and its fiscal responsibility.[58] Serving his sentence for seditious libel, he supported New York's libel laws in which truth was the central defence against conviction.[59] Denouncing placemen, si-

---

1812, 26 August 1815. For Cobbett's earlier comments about Britain's need to strangle American manufactures, see *The Rush-Light*, 30 August 1800.

54 *PR*, 15 December 1810, 6 March 1811.
55 *PR*, 26 September 1812.
56 *PR*, 9 March 1805, 19 October 1805.
57 *PR*, 26 May 1810.
58 *PR*, 15 September 1810, 29 September 1810, 13 April 1811, 17 April 1811.
59 *PR*, 15 September 1810. It comes as a shock to the system to read Cobbett praise freedom of the press in America. He wrote that other states had adopted the same

necures, tithes, and taxation in Britain, Cobbett came to see the United States as a country free from such encumbrances. "Yet is America now exceedingly well governed," he wrote in 1812; "the people are *happy* and *free*; there are about *eight million* of them, and there are *no paupers*; in that country poor men do not, to be sure, crawl almost upon their bellies before the rich. . . . Here, then, we have a proof, an experimental proof, of the practicability of conducting a government without giving placemen seats in the Legislature."[60] The contrast with his earlier writings could not have been sharper. Cobbett now believed that the United States could provide British reformers with a powerful weapon against the "Pitt system."

With this conviction, the "real" reason for Britain's aggressive American policy became clear to him. It was not a matter of keeping down a rival imperial power; rather, the government wanted to destroy the American source of inspiration for the British reform movement. The government, he asserted, "would, if they could, kill them [Americans] to the last man, in revenge for their having established a free government, where there are neither sinecures, jobs, or selling of seats."[61] For this reason, Cobbett supported the United States in the War of 1812. He saw the war essentially as a struggle between Liberty and Tyranny, and not as a conflict of empire. During the war, his images of Britain and the United States began to polarize; many British politicians, he wrote, were "animated solely by their hatred of whatever gives liberty to man," while the United States was "an asylum for the oppressed; a dwelling for real liberty." Indeed, Cobbett's view of the United States became increasingly Paineite in tone; he praised the American republic for its cheap government, described its militia as "a nation of freemen in arms," wrote approvingly about American egalitarianism, and even maintained that in America "bribery and corruption are unknown," a statement which is rather hard to swallow in the light of his earlier writings.[62] By 1814, Cobbett sounded very like those American Republicans he had previously reviled.

In the course of these arguments, Cobbett inverted his earlier image

---

principle, only noting in passing that this law had been "in many cases, most shamefully stretched."

60 *PR*, 15 August 1812. See also *PR*, 6 March 1811, 7 September 1811, 13 June 1812.

61 *PR*, 8 August 1812.

62 *PR*, 2 January 1813, 23 April 1814, 11 June 1814, 10 December 1814. See also Spater, *William Cobbett*, pp. 337–40.

of internal American politics. Just as he had previously attacked the Republicans as a pro-French fifth column, he now warned Americans that the pro-British Federalists were the real enemy within. The Federalists, in this view, were not only secret aristocrats who hankered after honours and titles in an hierarchical society; they also encouraged British aggression by making the United States appear more divided than it really was. In a complete *volte face*, Cobbett criticized Adams for bowing to Federalist pressure in 1798 and passing the Alien and Sedition Acts, argued that the *"slow poison"* of Federalist ambition was threatening American liberty, and took comfort in the belief that most Americans were "Republicans *at heart*."[63] Behind this position lay the conviction that an American victory, by strengthening liberty in the United States, would boost the reform movement in Britain. And the cause of reform in Britain, it must be emphasized, was at the core of Cobbett's outlook.

When peace came with the United States in 1814, Cobbett was euphoric. He believed that the United States had won the war, and became sufficiently carried away to call the result "an event of infinitely greater importance to the world than any that has taken place since the discovery of the Art of Printing." A republic whose chief characteristics were cheap government, low taxes, freedom of thought, and social egalitarianism had, according to Cobbett, humbled the corrupt and arrogant British politicians who attempted to crush the American example of freedom, and who realized that, "while this spectacle was in the world, they were never safe."[64] He also rejoiced that the war had utterly discredited the American Federalists and ensured that "the triumph of republican principles is now complete in America."[65]

Having beaten its enemies at home and abroad, he argued, the United States would become stronger and stronger, with a growing population steeped in liberty and with "the creation of a great maritime force." He actually maintained that in the long run the fall of Napoleon was of marginal significance compared to the rise of the American navy, which he felt was probably "destined to make a much greater revolution, as far, at least, as England is concerned."[66] A free and powerful American nation, in Cobbett's opinion, would inspire

63 *PR*, 23 April 1814, 26 November 1814, 10 December 1814.
64 *PR*, 7 January 1815, 14 January 1815.
65 *PR*, 11 February 1815. See also *PR*, 3 June 1815, 15 July 1815.
66 *PR*, 14 January 1815, 5 August 1815.

reformers in Britain and hasten the overthrow of the detested "system." The United States, he wrote at the end of 1815, "is the only country in the world in the fate of which one can feel much interest. If political good is to come at last, it must come through that channel."[67]

And yet, beneath the surface, deep tensions remained in Cobbett's attitude to the United States, for along with the hope of American liberty lay the fear of American imperial power. This fear explains his negative writings about the United States well after his conversion to Radicalism, and it continued to linger at the back of his mind, ready to erupt when conditions were suitable. "That we ought to prefer the safety and honour of England to all other things is certain," he wrote in 1811; "and, if the American government aimed any blow at them, it would become our duty to destroy that government if we could. But . . . , I suspect, that there are some persons in this country, who hate the American government because it suffers America to be the habitation of freedom."[68] During the 1810s, the importance to British Radicalism of protecting and preserving the American example of freedom outweighed the anxiety that the United States might challenge Britain's safety and honour.

American liberty, for Cobbett, was a means to the end of strengthening British reform, and British reform was itself a means to restore Britain's former greatness. While praising the United States as an example, he rejected it as a "model." The true model for British liberty, he reminded his readers, lay in the ancient constitution, and not across the Atlantic.[69] And the means were difficult to reconcile with the ends. The way to strengthen Britain's national and international position was to support American liberty, but the price of supporting American liberty was to welcome an American "victory" in the War of 1812 which weakened Britain's international position, at least in the short run. This cut strongly against Cobbett's grain. "I, who had always felt anxious for the freedom of America; I whose predictions have been so completely fulfilled in the result of this contest," he wrote after reading American reports of the peace; "even I cannot keep down all feeling of mortification at these demonstrations of triumph, related in the American prints now before me. Even in me, the Englishman so far gets the better of all other feelings and

67 *PR*, 9 December 1815.
68 *PR*, 14 September 1811.
69 *PR*, 19 November 1814, 17 June 1815.

consideration."[70] Moreover, there remained the nagging possibility that America's rising navy might ultimately threaten the safety and security of Britain.[71] In the immediate aftermath of war in Europe and the Atlantic, however, such misgivings were very much in the background. And during the post-war Radical agitation of 1816–19, they were almost completely suppressed.

III

The post-war depression released reform energies which had been driven underground during the late 1790s. With wide-scale riots against the Corn Laws, the resurgence of Luddism, the proliferation of popular Radical Hampden Clubs, the Spa Fields riot of December 1816, and the attack on the Prince Regent's coach at the opening of Parliament the following month, the movement for reform reached a new pitch of intensity.[72] In the course of these events, Cobbett emerged as the most popular journalist in the country; if 1792 was Paine's "*annus mirabilis*," 1816 was Cobbett's.[73] Moving towards universal suffrage, Cobbett after much hesitation lowered the price of his *Register* from 1s. ¹/₂d. to 2d., addressed himself directly to "journeymen and labourers," and became the chief spokesperson for discontented working people.[74] From appealing to the aristocracy, the gentry, the people in "the middling walks of life," and even the Prince Regent (a most unlikely Patriot King) to implement reform, Cobbett now tried to bring all the "productive classes" into the struggle against the parasitic moneyed men and borough-mongers.

70 *PR*, 13 June 1815.

71 *PR*, 1 January 1814.

72 On the post-war popular Radical agitation, see Perkin, *Origins of Modern English Society*, pp. 208–17; Royle and Walvin, *English Radicals and Reformers*, pp. 108–23; Thomis and Holt, *Threats of Revolution*, pp. 29–61; Thompson, *Making of the English Working Class*, pp. 660–780; White, *Waterloo to Peterloo*.

73 Thompson applied the phrase to Paine in *Making of the English Working Class*, p. 121. Both Paine and Cobbett reached the peak of their popularity in England in their late middle age. Paine was fifty-five in 1792; Cobbett was fifty-three in 1816.

74 Cobbett's "Address to the Journeymen and Labourers" first appeared in *PR*, 2 November 1816. On 19 October 1816, Cobbett argued that *"every man who pays a tax of any sort into the hands of a taxgatherer, should vote for members of the Commons House."* A month later he explicitly announced his conversion to universal suffrage, influenced by the veteran reformer Major John Cartwright and, possibly, the young Samuel Bamford. See *PR*, 23 November 1816 and Bamford, *Passages in the Life of a Radical*, 2: 21.

In response to those people who remembered his earlier views and accused him of inconsistency, he simply stated that he had been "in *error*" as a Tory. "To the utmost of my power," he wrote, "I have not only made full compensation for the harm done by those errors, but have further done to my country whatever degree of good has been within my reach." Cobbett the Radical was viewing his Tory period in exactly the same way that Cobbett the Tory had treated his earlier republicanism.[75] Having discovered the "truth," he injected into the ideology of protest his new attitudes towards Tom Paine and republican America.

Cobbett's explanation of the "ruin and desolation and misery" which he saw around him was firmly grounded on Paineite principles. Pointing out that the *Decline and Fall* had already accurately predicted the suspension of cash payments, Cobbett in 1816 noted with relish Paine's prophecy that "the system would come to an end in *about twenty years*! He wrote in 1796! Let corruption think of this and tremble."[76] Behind the depression, he maintained, lay the dying convulsions of the financial system, which was about to expire at Paine's appointed time:

And what disturbs the country? Why, the miseries of the people. And what makes the people miserable? Why, the great weight of taxes and the fluctuations in the Currency. And what makes the great weight of taxes and the fluctuations in the Currency? Why, the Debt and the Paper-money. And what makes the Debt and the Paper-money? Why, the *Funding System*. Thus it is to this system, that we owe . . . every evil that oppresses us; the whole of that combination of evils, which now astounds even me who have been anticipating those evils for many years.[77]

As Paine had written, and as Cobbett had come to believe, the collapse of the system would bring down the entire edifice of political corruption, while the distress caused by last-ditch efforts to pay interest on the debt would increase the pressure for parliamentary reform. But Cobbett still insisted that reform must restore traditional liberties, not replace them with republicanism. "We have great constitutional laws and principles, to which we are immovably attached. We want *great alteration*, but we want *nothing new*. Alteration, modification to suit the times and circumstances, but, the great principles

75 *PR*, 26 October 1816. Compare Cobbett, *Prospectus*, p. 7 and *PG*, 26 September 1797, 4 October 1797.

76 *PR*, 17 August 1816; see also *PR*, 16 November 1816.

77 *PR*, 8 February 1817.

ought to be and must be, the same, or else confusion will follow." And those "great principles" were essentially the same as those which he had defended as a Tory in the United States. "Our excellent *form* of government; our excellent *ancient laws*; our excellent modes of carrying on the business of a nation," he wrote in 1816, "leave us *nothing new* to wish for." The same words could easily have been written by Cobbett back in 1794.[78]

Nevertheless, Cobbett's emphasis on wide-ranging democratic reform as a means to this end resonated with the broad Paineite culture of popular Radicalism; moreover, it is entirely conceivable that his readers were more impressed by his means than his ends. In his support for annual parliaments, the secret ballot, equal electoral districts, payment of members of parliament, and universal suffrage, Cobbett consciously placed himself within the Paineite tradition. And to those anti-democrats who dismissed the people as "the Rabble, the Mob, the Swinish Multitude," to those who sneered at Tom Paine for being a mere "*staymaker*," Cobbett replied that the labouring classes were at least as intelligent as their rulers and that the career of Paine was in itself sufficient proof of the genius which lay within the "lower orders."[79] Arguing for an equality of respect, Cobbett adopted and adapted Paine's financial and political arguments in much the same way that Richard Carlile transmitted Paine's deist arguments to the post-war generation. In both cases, Paine's supporters selected and reinterpreted aspects of his democratic writings to produce new syntheses which Paine himself had not anticipated.[80]

While Cobbett's financial and political views drew on Paineite ideology, his generally positive image of the United States fed into pro-American traditions in the British democratic movement. The notion that the United States was a "beacon of freedom"—a notion which, as has been seen, was popularized in the *Rights of Man*—permeated the language of radical reform up to and beyond the Chartist era.[81] Stressing the importance of America to the cause of reform at home, Cobbett in early 1816 established the short-lived *American Political Register*, operating out of New York, to open up transatlantic channels

78 *PR*, 12 October 1816, 2 November 1816, 19 October 1816. See also *PR*, 27 April 1816, 12 July 1817.
79 *PR*, 2 November 1816, 23 November 1816.
80 On Richard Carlile's use of Paine's thought, see Royle, *Infidel Tradition*, pp. 16–37.
81 See Lillibridge, *Beacon of Freedom*.

of radical discourse.[82] Convinced that the national debt, corruption, and taxation were at the root of Britain's "wretchedness," and insisting that the United States was not afflicted with these ills, Cobbett was impelled by the logic of his position to show that America was more prosperous than his own country.

It has been a constant theme with the writers on the side of corruption to exhibit *America* as being in a state of distress. . . . If these tools of corruption could have succeeded in making the nation believe that the people *in America* were suffering in the same degree with themselves, the conclusion would be, that heavy taxation, great standing armies, sinecures, pensions, grants, etc. did not tend to produce this national misery; or, at least, that great national misery might exist where these things did not exist, it being well known, that they do not exist in America. It was, therefore, of importance, that this assertion respecting the state of America, should be met by such a contradiction as the truth would warrant. . . . [83]

As had happened during the debate over the *Rights of Man* in 1791–92, America in 1816–17 became an ideological battleground, with Cobbett claiming that the United States was the land of liberty and prosperity, and his opponents attacking him for propagating "transatlantic falshoods."[84] In making such comparisons, Cobbett had to swallow a lot of national pride; the difference between the two countries, he commented, was "painful for us to contemplate, because it is so humiliating to England."[85] Such humiliation only underlined the condition to which the "system" had reduced England and gave heightened urgency to the question of reform.

Although the example of the United States was clearly important to Cobbett, it did not play the same kind of central role in his thought that it had done in Paine's writings. For Paine, republican democracy as practiced in the United States was the key to the future, while for Cobbett the central task was to return to the past. At times, however, Cobbett fused the myth of America with the myth of the past, char-

82 *PR*, 27 January 1816; see also *PR*, 9 December 1815. One reason for the venture was to circumvent libel laws in England. Cobbett argued that material which the government considered seditious could be published in the *American PR* and then transmitted back to England.

83 *PR*, 10 August 1816.

84 *PR*, 13 January 1816, 4 May 1816, 2 November 1816, 1 February 1817; *Detector* 4: 11.

85 *PR*, 10 August 1816.

acterizing American society as "the state of England four hundred years ago . . . with the *polish* of modern times added." Most immigrants to the New World, his argument ran, had transmitted the values of Old England across the Atlantic before the "bishop-begotten and hell-born system of Funding" had stripped the country of "every vestige of what was her ancient character."[86] If Paine had seen the future, Cobbett had seen the past in America—and for both men, it worked. But in the last analysis, the example of the United States, like the writings of Paine, remained a means to an end; ultimately, Cobbett argued, England must rediscover its own history and draw on its own resources to re-establish its traditional liberty.[87]

Given Cobbett's political outlook, the force with which he expressed his opinions, and his prominent position in the post-war Radical agitation, he became an obvious target of governmental repression. Lord Sidmouth's "Gagging Acts" and the suspension of habeas corpus in 1817 were directed largely against Cobbett's writings, just as the Royal Proclamation of 1792 and the earlier suspension of habeas corpus in 1794 had been intended to counter Paineite influence.[88] Faced with these threats, and unwilling to spend more time in prison, Cobbett chose exile over martyrdom. In March 1817, at the height of his popularity, he sought refuge in the United States, just like those "Emigrated Patriots" whom he had previously condemned. He did not, this time, involve himself in domestic American politics, preferring to concentrate on the struggle for reform back in Britain. And from across the Atlantic, he continued to use America and Paine as sources of inspiration for British reformers.

Identifying himself with Paine as a fellow fighter against and victim of the British government, Cobbett began to make amends for his earlier Toryism. To assuage his guilt, the man who had written a libellous biographical sketch of Paine in 1796 now resolved "to write an Account of the Life, Labours and Death of that famous Englishman THOMAS PAINE; and, perhaps, to collect and republish the whole of his writings in a *Cheap form.* . . . "[89] The man who had regarded Paine as the personification of evil now eulogized the staymaker who had

86 Cobbett, *Year's Residence*, p. 198; *PR*, 12 July 1817.

87 *PR*, 27 April 1816, 4 October 1817.

88 On the government's repressive legislation of 1817, see Aspinall, *Politics and the Press*, pp. 42–54.

89 *PR*, 24 January 1818. Nothing ever came of these plans. See also *PR*, 15 June 1816, 25 January 1817, 4 October 1817, 4 September 1819.

shaken corruption to its foundation. And the man who had gloated over the fate of Paine's carcass now gathered up Paine's bones to revitalize reform in Britain.[90]

IV

Returning to England in 1819 with those bones, Cobbett failed to recapture the influential position he had enjoyed before his exile, and was unable to regenerate British Radicalism. The government's Six Acts of 1819 had effectively put the lid on discontent, and forced him to raise the price of the *Register* to 6d.[91] Yet while the *Register* struggled during the 1820s, Cobbett continued to make his presence felt through immensely popular books like *Cottage Economy* (1821), the *History of the Protestant Reformation* (1824), and, of course, *Rural Rides* (1830).[92] Between 1830 and 1832, as pressure again built up for parliamentary reform, Cobbett became one of the most articulate supporters of the Reform Bill; after it was passed, he was elected as a member of Parliament for Oldham.

Although the Whigs argued that the Reform Bill would take the steam out of Radical agitation, Cobbett hoped that the Bill would pave the way for further change; his criticism of the "system" therefore remained as strident as ever. In the House of Commons he appeared as an eccentric intruder in a semi-exclusive club; Cobbett was always more at home as a political writer than as a member of Parliament. The last years of his life were spent fighting the New Poor Law and continuing his attack on the public finance system. His struggle against the New Poor Law ended in failure; his repeated predictions of financial collapse failed to materialize. Yet Cobbett steadfastly refused to admit defeat or that he might be mistaken in his financial views. When his critique of public finance was challenged, he merely restated his earlier arguments, assumed that bankruptcy was imminent, and took refuge in his own ego—a large enough home. He fought corruption right up to the end: "NOW, I AM DETERMINED TO STAND THIS

90 *PR*, 1 May 1819, 4 September 1819, 13 November 1819.

91 The Newspaper Stamp Duties Act (1819) was designed to prevent the spread of cheap Radical newspapers. For the struggle against this measure, see Wickwar, *Struggle for the Freedom of the Press*, and Wiener, *War of the Unstamped*.

92 Pearl, *William Cobbett*, pp. 119–21, 132–37, and 160–62, provides estimates of the sales of these books. The *History of the Protestant Reformation* sold a staggering 700,000 copies.

NO LONGER," he proclaimed with his usual defiance only four weeks before he died.[93] Even now, reading the *Register*, one gets a sense of surprise when his death was announced. The man seemed unstoppable.

By the time of his journey to Paine's grave, Cobbett's conversion was complete; the years between 1819 and 1835 represent the elaboration of a radical position whose main outlines had already been established. From the perspective of his attitude to the United States and to Paine, there was no fundamental break with his immediate post-war position, although there were shifts of emphasis as the conditions for reform changed. Between 1816 and 1819, Cobbett had stressed the importance of the United States as an inspiration and example for British reformers, but stifled his fears about the rise of American imperial power. Yet, as the British government contained the Radical movement, and as the prospects of reform receded during the 1820s, the tension in Cobbett's thought between American liberty and American empire became more acute. In effect, Cobbett saw two Americas: the America which could boost the reform movement in Britain, and the America which threatened to turn Britain into a satellite of the United States. Depending on which image was uppermost in his mind, Cobbett's attitude to the United States oscillated between qualified approval and straightforward fear.

The image of America as the land of liberty remained broadly similar to the position he had taken between 1811 and 1819, and became particularly pronounced during the Reform Bill agitation of 1830–32. Arguing that "the example of the republican government in America is inexpressibly captivating," Cobbett repeated his earlier views that the United States benefitted from cheap, efficient, and representative government, low taxes, frequent elections, and the use of pledges to bind representatives to the voters' wishes.[94]

At the same time, however, Cobbett began to distinguish between the conditions of liberty in different American states. "There are *twenty republics* in America," he wrote in 1824. "Some of them where freedom and virtue reign; and some where the worst of slavery exists, and the blackest villany lords it over the people."[95] Connecticut was presented as a classic example of the former kind, while the "corrupt and ty-

93 *PR*, 23 May 1835.
94 *PR*, 23 July 1831. See also *PR*, 23 May 1829, 11 September 1830, 6 August 1831, 31 December 1831, 7 July 1832.
95 *PR*, 31 January 1824.

rannical" government of Pennsylvania exemplified the latter.[96] Clearly, Cobbett had neither forgotten nor forgiven his treatment by Pennsylvania; there is no doubt that his unsuccessful attempt in 1818 to recover losses incurred during the Benjamin Rush libel case some twenty years earlier reopened old wounds and revived old animosities.[97] But by the 1820s and early 1830s, Cobbett regarded Pennsylvania as the exception rather than the rule. It was an exception, nevertheless, which should remind Englishmen that the *"mere name"* of republicanism did not in itself produce liberty.[98]

Towards the end of his life, Cobbett also put new emphasis on the struggle in America against paper money and the Bank of the United States. After reading William Gouge's influential history of the American financial system, Cobbett was "filled with astonishment" about the strength of the moneyed interests in the United States. He had, after all, previously argued that America had no equivalent to the financial corruption which was degrading Britain. Armed with this book, Cobbett strongly supported Andrew Jackson's battle against "the monster of paper money" and the new *"aristocracy of money"* which it supposedly produced.[99] With characteristic enthusiasm, he wrote an adulatory biography of Jackson, and began to argue that the existence of the financial system in Britain hinged on the fate of Jackson's policies in America. If the United States replaced paper money with gold and silver, argued Cobbett, Anglo-American trade would draw so much hard currency out of Britain that Britain's own paper money system would quickly collapse, resulting in a "real radical revolution" which would restore the ancient constitution.[100]

As long as this generally positive image of the United States prevailed, Cobbett felt that anything which strengthened the American republic would also strengthen the cause of liberty. Thus in 1820 he

96 For Cobbett's comments about Connecticut, see *PR*, 31 May 1823, 29 December 1832; for his remarks about Pennsylvania, see *PR*, 24 January 1824, 31 January 1824, 22 January 1825, 2 November 1833.

97 His attempts to recover this money are described in M. Clark, "Peter Porcupine in America," pp. 119–23, and Spater, *William Cobbett*, pp. 373–75.

98 *PR*, 2 November 1833.

99 *PR*, 20 July 1833, 16 November 1833; Gouge, *Short History of Paper Money and Banking*.

100 Cobbett, *Life of Andrew Jackson*; *PR*, 1 March 1834. This theme persisted in his writings during the spring and summer of 1834.

welcomed the American acquisition of the Spanish Floridas, commenting that such territorial expansion meant "an extension of that *room* which Mr. PAINE said they [the United States] would make for honest men to live in."[101] If the power of the United States could stimulate radical change at home, he later wrote, reformers "ought to wish for that greatness not only to continue, but to increase."[102] Yet Cobbett's "if" is critically important. Conflicting with his benign image of the United States was Cobbett's other America, the dangerous rival imperial power. If American "greatness" became a threat rather than an example to Britain, then his countrymen must not let their admiration of American liberty prevent them from supporting measures to contain American power—even if those measures were undertaken by what he saw as an oppressive British government.

Cobbett believed that British and American interests collided in two main areas: the struggle for hegemony in South America, and the question of naval supremacy, especially in the Atlantic. While Cobbett supported Spanish American liberation movements, he wanted to ensure that they came under the British rather than the American sphere of influence. When in 1817 the United States adopted a policy of neutrality in South America, Cobbett urged the British government to seize the opportunity and recognize the new republics, thus preempting any attempts by the United States to become the preponderant power in the region.[103] Cobbett later argued that the Monroe Doctrine contradicted British interests, since for Britain to keep out of Spanish American affairs would be to leave emerging nations like Mexico in the American camp by default. "The thing to do," he insisted, "is, at once to declare Mexico independent, and to send out a good stout fleet with twenty thousand men to establish that independence." In this way, he contended, Britain could turn Mexico into a loyal ally and "put an everlasting bridle into the mouth of the United States."[104] To take this position, Cobbett wrote, was simply to follow Britain's best interests. "I love my country too well, and hate the example of the Boroughmongers too much," he explained back in 1817, "to suffer me to do any thing to injure the former in order to

101 *PR*, 15 January 1820; Paine, *American Crisis IV*, 1: 105.
102 *PR*, 18 April 1835; see also *PR*, 23 May 1829.
103 *PR*, 27 December 1817.
104 *PR*, 3 January 1824; see also *PR*, 8 January 1825.

gratify any angry feeling against the latter, however just that feeling may be." He would not, in short, emasculate the country to get revenge on its leaders.[105]

The rise of the American navy was an even greater challenge to Britain, argued Cobbett, since it directly threatened Britain's traditional control of the seas. Maintaining that American foreign policy was motivated by the interests of empire rather than the cause of liberty, Cobbett believed that the United States intended to break Britain's economic and naval dominance of the Atlantic and replace Britain as the world's leading nation.[106] Although he had supported the rise of American naval power during the War of 1812 as a necessary defence measure against British aggression, and had even hoped that the American navy would carry liberty to Britain's shores, by the mid 1820s he felt that this navy had moved from the defensive to the offensive and must be restrained. It was thus essential that Britain should "*stop the growth of the Navy of the United States.*"

In contrast to the Cobbett who saw America as the land of liberty, the Cobbett who saw America as a rising imperial power could write:

I will not profess to be animated with any very anxious desire to promote the well-being of America as a state. . . . I must naturally wish, that England should always preserve the mastership of the seas; and it is my bounden duty to give effect to that wish by every means in my power . . . to keep the rivalship of America in check, and to prevent her from ever possessing the means of lessening the power, or of doing injury in any possible way to my own country.[107]

It was true, he commented in 1832, that America had afforded him an asylum from oppression between 1817 and 1819. But he had paid back the debt, he argued with splendid eccentricity, by introducing British fodder crops into American agriculture. Having repaid political liberty with "Swedish turnips, mangel-wurzel, and cabbages," Cobbett felt that the slate was clean. "I . . . owe them nothing," he wrote: "and, when our country shall have got a good and cheap government, we can, with clear consciences, recommend the paring of their nails. . . . I always said, that I should never die in peace without making them

105 *PR*, 27 December 1817.
106 *PR*, 17 January 1824, 25 September 1824, 26 January 1833.
107 *PR*, 17 January 1824, 2 November 1833.

again bow to England; and that bow to her again they *should*, whenever we shook off the power of the hellish boroughmongers. . . . "[108]

Such sentiments reflect the deep ambivalence running through Cobbett's writings on America. On the one hand, he felt that the cause of the United States was the cause of liberty, and on the other he was afraid that American imperial ambitions would subvert the traditional strength, security, and honour of Britain which reform was intended to establish in the first place. Cobbett was caught between supporting the United States as a means to reform and fearing the United States as a threat to the ends of reform, between siding with American liberty against the British government and urging the British government to challenge and check the American empire. He was acutely aware of this tension in his thought, admitting that he had been torn between love of his country and the conviction that had the United States lost the War of 1812 "it would have been better to be a dog than an Englishman." "This is a very cruel dilemma to be reduced to," he continued, "but, reduced to it I am, and so is every Englishman, who is not content to be a slave himself, and to leave his children slaves behind him."[109] It was a dilemma which Cobbett was unable to resolve.

His attitude to Paine avoided such ambivalence, if only because Cobbett remodelled Paine after his own image. The Tom Paine who wrote the *Age of Reason* or who supported the Bank of North America was erased from Cobbett's mind.[110] Instead, Cobbett chose to revere the "injured, insulted, scorned, and despised EXCISEMAN" who symbolized the worth and intelligence of the common people and who avenged the "borough thing" through establishing almost single-handedly the independence of America. "It appears to me very clear," Cobbett wrote, "that some beastly insults, offered to Mr. Paine, while he was in the Excise in England, was the real cause of the Revolution in America." Elsewhere, he argued that no matter who had actually written the document, Paine was the "real" author of the Declaration of Independence. Cobbett had, of course, argued as much during his Tory period; as a Radical, he simply reversed the image and turned the negative into a positive. "It was a very happy circumstance that

108 *PR*, 2 June 1832.
109 *PR*, 3 September 1825.
110 In *PR*, 15 January 1820, Cobbett commented that "it is the *politics*, and not the *religion* of PAINE, that make his works an object of terror with the borough folks." After these remarks, Cobbett simply chose to ignore for the rest of his life Paine's religious writings.

the borough thing drove PAINE to America," he maintained, seeing the United States through the lense of liberty rather than empire; "for, if America had been subdued at that time, what hope would there have been for Englishmen?"[111]

In addition, Cobbett continued to repeat Paine's predictions about the collapse of the financial system. Like a prophet who continually proclaimed the imminent day of judgment, but who kept revising his timetable, Cobbett believed that the time was "fast approaching, when the Pitt-system will receive its doom." In 1816, as has been seen, he had reminded his readers of Paine's comments in 1796 that the system was probably in the last twenty years of its existence. When 1816 passed without financial collapse, Cobbett seized on Paine's remark that the system would not outlast the life of Pitt, and noted that Pitt, had he lived, would reach his three score and ten years in 1829. "Do you *laugh*, then," Cobbett asked his opponents in 1826, "at this prophesy of PAINE?"[112] And when 1829 passed without incident, he still kept the faith and insisted in 1831 that he had "all along said that these evils would come by slow degrees; that the nation would *not fall down in a fit*, but would sink gradually, like an ill-kept and finally starved animal; and that, at last, an explosion, in some shape or another, would come."[113]

Although he saw the Reform Bill of 1832 as a step in the right direction rather than the long-awaited explosion, he did maintain that the Bill was the direct result of the system's gradual disintegration. The resumption of cash payments in 1819, he argued, involved paying back in deflated currency debts incurred during a period of inflation; the burden of taxes to meet these payments had thus become insupportable; the people had been reduced to misery, and the misery had produced the "fires" which goaded the government into conceding a measure of reform.[114] To Cobbett, the logic seemed obvious. It was only a matter of time, he believed, before Paine's prophecy would be realized; the financial apocalypse was always just around the next corner.

The year before he died, Cobbett wrote a letter "To the People of the United States of America" in which he pulled together his per-

111 *PR*, 11 December 1819, 15 January 1820, 21 December 1822, 11 July 1829.
112 *PR*, 17 August 1816, 16 December 1826; Paine, *Decline and Fall*, 2: 652.
113 *PR*, 27 August 1831.
114 *PR*, 24 August 1833.

ceptions of Paine, American liberty, and the British financial system. In Cobbett's view, Paine's writings had provided the intellectual foundations of American independence, and the American example of cheap and representative government had inspired the reform movement throughout the Old World. Under the presidency of Andrew Jackson, Cobbett continued, the United States was carrying the struggle for liberty still further. The American campaign against paper money and the bank not only offered an important lesson to Britain, but also promised to trigger a transatlantic financial revolution which would bring the system in Britain to its knees.[115] The circle was complete: Paine had liberated America, and America heralded the financial liberation of Britain, thus fulfilling Paine's original predictions. Once again, Cobbett eagerly anticipated the day of reckoning for the moneyed interests. Once again, he was wrong. The United States failed to regenerate the Old World, just as Paine's bones, which were eventually lost, had failed to produce "radical reform" in Britain.[116] When Cobbett died, the England that actually existed was more distant than ever from the England of his imagination. And the marble of Pitt's monument had still—has still—not been converted into a monument to the memory of Paine.

115 *PR*, 1 February 1834.
116 No one knows the whereabouts of Paine's bones. After Cobbett died, his estate was declared bankrupt and his effects were put up to auction. The auctioneer refused to sell the bones, and what happened to them then is anybody's guess. According to one tradition, they were passed on to a day labourer and then to a furniture maker from Surrey; according to another, they were buried on family property by one of Cobbett's descendants.

Epilogue

BOTH Tom Paine and William Cobbett, founding fathers of British popular Radicalism, developed their ideology in an Anglo-American context during the Atlantic Revolution. They responded to the American Empire of Liberty in separate and distinct ways, although they eventually came to share many ideas about political liberty in the United States and its relevance to Britain. For Paine, the American experience was central. He became aware of Real Whig and republican ideas early in life, participated in the radical transformation of those ideas in America, and transmitted democratic republican ideology back to Britain. The United States, in Paine's view, supplied a model of the benefits of government based on the rights of man, where hereditary rule had been rejected and the "productive classes" had come into their own.

In Cobbett's case, the pattern was different. An idealistic Paineite and admirer of American liberty in his youth, Cobbett became disillusioned with democratic republicanism shortly after moving to the United States in 1792. By the time he returned home in 1800, Cobbett had become a John Bull High Tory who idealized England and who believed that American ideology and imperialist ambitions seriously threatened his country. Yet in much the same way that the United States had failed to live up to Cobbett's Utopian expectations, his image of English liberty and justice began to crack under the pressure of reality. With much difficulty, and using Paine's financial writings as a lever, Cobbett lurched uneasily towards a populist brand of socially conservative political Radicalism. Although he remained deeply suspicious of American imperialism, he increasingly believed that many aspects of the American political system could inspire the reform movement in Britain.

As he developed this view, Cobbett's comments about the United States became increasingly "Paineite" in tone and content. Nevertheless, there were still real differences between the two men. While Paine hoped that the symbolic power of the United States would impel British Radicals towards democratic republicanism, Cobbett used the American example to further the cause of parliamentary reform and lead Britain out of the modern world towards the ancient constitution, traditional liberties, and national glory. And in contrast to Paine's democratic internationalism, Cobbett remained a patriotic Englishman, continually worrying that American imperial power could contradict the ends that he wanted the example of American liberty to serve in Britain.

Despite these differences, Paine and Cobbett had much in common. In a sense, their complementarity stemmed from the complementarity of the traditions on which they drew. Paine transformed eighteenth-century Real Whig thought into a new form of democratic republicanism; Cobbett developed eighteenth-century Country Party ideology into a new form of Tory-Radicalism. Although the original traditions started from opposite ends of the political spectrum, they converged at a number of key points. Real Whig and Country Party writers alike denounced corruption, patronage, and the insidious influence of high finance in eighteenth-century politics. Because Real Whigs and the Country Party Opposition attacked the same targets, and because the new order appeared to threaten the "natural magistracy" as much as the "people," there was an odd compatibility between eighteenth-century Radicals and Tories; the essentially conservative outlook of the Country Party contained radical tendencies within itself.[1]

If we cast the net forward to the late eighteenth and early nineteenth centuries, we find that even as Paine and Cobbett transformed their respective traditions they inherited the common ground which those traditions had occupied. While Paine approached politics from the democratic "left" and Cobbett embraced an agrarian conservatism, both men eventually became united in their struggle against the oli-

1 On radical tendencies within Country Party ideology, see Kramnick, *Bolingbroke and His Circle*, pp. 169–81; on the "ambivalence of the Augustan Commonwealthmen," see pp. 236–60.

garchical political establishment in Britain. Like their Real Whig and Country Party predecessors, both men attacked placemen, sinecures, the debt, taxation, and the whole web of manipulative politics which enveloped the country. It is significant, moreover, that the bridge between the Radical Paine and the Tory Cobbett was effected through Paine's critique of the English financial system, since that critique itself had its roots in common Real Whig and Country Party attitudes to the financial revolution. Having identified the problems facing his country, Cobbett pushed the radical elements within Country Party thought to their democratic extreme, sounding in the process re-markably—and in some respects, deceptively—like Paine.

By transforming earlier traditions, both Paine and Cobbett at-tempted to realize different visions of an alternative society. Paine wanted to establish a democracy of small-scale property owners and producers, in which free competition underpinned by a social welfare scheme would benefit men of talent but prevent excessive inequality. This was not, Paine insisted, a Utopian dream. In the United States, he argued, the "productive classes" had already shaken off the op-pressive weight of monarchy, aristocracy, and established religion; the point now was to establish in Britain the conditions of liberty which existed in America. In contrast, Cobbett wanted to recreate Old Eng-land. Beneath his toughest, most pragmatic political writings, behind his changing, contradictory, and incoherent political outlook, lay a strikingly consistent purpose: to re-establish a paternalistic, hierar-chical, agrarian society in which well-fed, well-clad, honest industrious labourers respected and were respected by a virtuous, patriotic, and God-fearing landed gentry. Everything—including his image of America—was subordinated to that aim.

Yet there was an inescapable paradox in their position. Products of the Age of Revolution, the process of revolutionary change which brought Paine and Cobbett to prominence also made their visions increasingly anachronistic and unattainable. The Industrial Revolu-tion, with its class conflict, unprecedented economic growth, and mas-sive capital accumulation, left them gasping on the pre-industrial shore. Paine belonged to eighteenth-century Philadelphia, not nineteenth-century Manchester. He assumed an identity of interests among the "productive classes" against the aristocracy, and did not think in terms of "middle class" and "working class." On both sides of the Atlantic, he attempted to unite labourers, artisans, manufacturers, merchants, and professional men behind the rights of man. But on both sides of the Atlantic, industrial change was increasingly dividing society along class lines.

In the United States, the labour conspiracy trials of 1806 and 1809 against combinations of journeymen-shoemakers signalled the emergence of a distinct working-class consciousness which implicitly challenged Paineite notions of republican harmony. As Richard Twomey has shown, American Jacobins displayed a uniform and deep hostility to such trade unions, which they saw as a threat to the common good.[2] In England, many Paineites of the 1790s wound up as successful businessmen in the early nineteenth century. At a meeting in 1822 to celebrate the twenty-eighth anniversary of Thomas Hardy's acquittal on charges of high treason, Francis Place noted that many of the central figures in the London Corresponding Society had risen from shopmen to journeymen to become "all in business all flourishing men, some of them were rich."[3] But many more artisan supporters of Paine, reeling from the impact of technological innovation, unskilled labour, and increased concentration of ownership, were driven down into the working class rather than up into the middle class. Under the pressure of class conflict, Paine's Anglo-American social ideal could not be sustained.

More obviously, the Industrial Revolution also made Cobbett's return to the past utterly impossible to achieve. Applying pre-industrial solutions to industrial problems, and only dimly aware of the factory system, Cobbett focused all his attention on the unholy trinity of the national debt, paper money, and taxation. Class conflict, in his view, was a kind of false consciousness which diverted attention away from the real struggle against the "Pitt system." Cobbett believed that employers and labourers had the same interests, and insisted that "when journeymen find their wages reduced, they should take time *to reflect on the real cause*, before they fly upon their employers, who are, in many cases, in as great, or greater, distress than themselves."[4] For Cobbett, class conflict was essentially a symptom of the financial system; once that system was overthrown, employers could afford to pay decent wages, and all classes would share in the general prosperity. The irony, as Marx pointed out, was that Cobbett, through trying to establish an alliance of all the "productive classes" against the "system"

2 Twomey, "Jacobins and Jeffersonians," pp. 171–213.
3 PP, Add. Ms. 27808, ff. 60–61.
4 *PR*, 2 November 1816.

of fund-holders and borough-mongers, actually lent support to the very middle class that was undermining Cobbett's own ideal of traditional English liberties.[5]

The process of industrialism not only subverted Paine's and Cobbett's social visions, but also worked against their strategies for change. Both men eventually pinned their faith on the conjunction of "objective" and "subjective" forces; the advent of inevitable financial collapse together with the pressure of massive popular democratic sentiment would, they believed, produce revolution or radical reform. Yet this approach had serious difficulties at each major point. Paine's and Cobbett's financial predictions suffered from internal problems of logic and external industrial developments. The arguments of Paine's *Decline and Fall* were overly mechanistic, transforming insights about the inflationary consequences of war into an iron law of impending bankruptcy. Similarly, Cobbett viewed paper money simply as an unmitigated evil once it exceeded the quantity of gold and silver it promised to pay; he refused to recognize any connection between the financial revolution and Britain's economic growth. But beyond this, the enormous increase in wealth produced during the Industrial Revolution pulled the government through the financial crisis of 1796 and 1797, and enabled the "system" to stay alive long after Paine's predicted date of expiry. Under these circumstances, the "objective" conditions for political change could not be met.

In the absence of financial collapse, the weakness of the "subjective" component in their strategies became apparent. For both men, public opinion guided by truth and reason would overawe an increasingly crisis-stricken government. Cobbett put so much faith in "*Petition and Remonstrance*" that he explicitly rejected "all sorts of *combinations, associations, and correspondencies* of *societies*" which attempted to give the reform movement organizational and institutional expression. And although Paine supported democratic clubs and regarded petitions as a humiliating waste of time, he could also argue in the *Rights of Man* that "Reason, like time, will make its own way."[6] Yet even in the context of national bankruptcy, the force of argument backed by the sheer weight of numbers would not have been sufficient to make the government back down; in what became a common Radical weakness, the strength of the state was underestimated. In his darker moments,

5 Marx and Engels, *Collected Works*, 10: 301; 13: 188–89; Marx, *Capital*, p. 829.
6 *PR*, 1 March 1817; Paine, *Rights of Man, Part 1*, 1: 355.

Cobbett conceded as much, adding gloomily that without reform "the people would become the most beggarly and slavish of mankind, and nothing would be left of England but the mere name."[7] Massive popular sentiment, truth, and reason would not in themselves dislodge powerful vested interests backed up with significant powers of coercion.

Furthermore, even had these difficulties been overcome and either republican democracy or fundamental parliamentary reform been established, it is far from certain that such political changes would have produced the social order Paine and Cobbett envisaged. With their absolute faith in democratic reform as a panacea for Britain's problems, Paine and Cobbett did not pay enough attention to the relationship between political power and socio-economic developments. In their view, political democracy could control social and economic change; it did not occur to them that social and economic changes might strongly influence the nature of political democracy, that representative government could coexist with glaring inequalities of property or that political emancipation was partial emancipation.[8]

We cannot know how Paine would have reacted to the United States over two hundred years after *Common Sense*; it can be said, however, that the modern capitalist industrial order contradicted the kind of small-scale property-owning, harmonious, roughly egalitarian society which Paine had associated with republican democracy. And just as the financial system did not destroy the British government, democracy in Britain did not destroy the financial system; Cobbett's Utopia remained unfulfilled.

All this helps to explain the failure of their visions; it does not imply that their views are "irrelevant" or that their arguments should be consigned to the pre-industrial scrap heap. Yet the question of "relevance" is a complex and contradictory one. Paine and Cobbett were men whose ideas were grounded in eighteenth-century Anglo-American Radicalism; once their ideas were torn out of this context and transposed onto the nineteenth- and twentieth-century world, ambiguities were bound to appear and tensions were bound to be magnified. The ambiguities and tensions are apparent in the shifting images of Paine and Cobbett in America and Britain. For a century and a half, they had almost no image at all in the United States; they became

7 Cobbett, *Mr. Cobbett's Taking Leave of His Countrymen*, pp. 19–23.

8 For Marx's critique of the rights of man and thus by implication Paineite democracy, see "On the Jewish Question," pp. 101–8.

famous in the land that neglected them, and neglected in the land that made them famous. It is true that a minority of "freethinking" deists, reinforced by Radical British immigrants, honoured Paine's memory in the nineteenth century, but it was not until the mid-twentieth century that Paine was rehabilitated into the American mainstream.

This was the Paine of the *American Crisis* papers, the Paine whose "tyranny, like hell, is not easily conquered" became the motto of General Patton's army. But it was also the Paine of the American Progressives, the Paine called into life by Howard Fast's novel: a down-and-out corset maker who came to the New World from the gutters of England, who was dirty, drunk, insecure, abrasive, and self-pitying, but who knew in his heart how working people thought and felt, and who stood up for the common man against the rich, the powerful, and the corrupt.[9] After World War II, both the American left and the right claimed Paine as one of their own. Many modern American radicals admired his democracy, his faith in the common people, and his humanitarianism. On the other hand, right wing Republicans such as presidents Ford and Reagan approvingly quoted Paine as an apostle of *laissez-faire* individualism and as a spokesperson for America's mission to free the world by making it more American.

Cobbett, in contrast, could not be pressed into such service; indeed, he has been almost completely ignored in the United States. Cobbett's opinions were too closely linked with another country and another political system to be "serviceable" to most Americans; moreover, those intellectuals who compared America's position in the Cold War with Britain's position in the 1790s were attracted to the more sophisticated thought of Burke rather than the polemics of Cobbett.

In Britain, Paine and Cobbett left a deeper and different mark. At much the same time that modern American Republicans were moving towards aspects of Paine's thought, Conservative councillors in his native Thetford were outraged by a Labour Party proposal to erect a statue of Paine and one resigned in protest. In Britain, it was the politically blasphemous Paine who was remembered; this was the Paine who attacked and ridiculed the monarchy and the aristocracy, the Paine who poured scorn on revealed religion, the Paine whose social program appeared as a precursor of the welfare state. A powerful presence through the Chartist movement, Paine's political and religious writings became an important strand of the labour movement,

9 Fast, *Citizen Tom Paine.*

where they became entwined with Owenism and the emerging socialism of men like Bronterre O'Brien and William Thompson. It all depended on what elements of Paine's thought were selected and how they were transformed to meet changing conditions; at any rate, the Paine whom the Labour councillors revered at Thetford was very different from the Paine whose faith in the free market and whose hostility to government and taxation appealed so much to contemporary American conservatives.

As for Cobbett, the tensions within his thought are reflected in current images. He has attracted more attention and approval from the left than from the right, but his writings flow into both radical and Tory traditions; one can focus on his critique of corruption, his sympathy with ordinary people and his attack on the political and financial élite, or one can embrace his anti-Jacobin writings and his consistent social conservatism. On the one hand, Raymond Williams has written a penetrating essay on the contemporary relevance of Cobbett's thought to the British left. On the other, Cobbett has been treated with sympathy and admiration by Daniel Green, a conservative former agricultural correspondent with the *Daily Telegraph*. And in another development, Cobbett's agrarian writings have been picked up by the "back-to-the-land" movement, which itself contains both radical and conservative tendencies. Clearly, Paine's and Cobbett's work has been used to realize new visions which often contradict one another and which are far removed from each man's original intentions.

This continuing process of renewal and reinterpretation not only testifies to the persistence of Paine's and Cobbett's influence, but also has its own strengths and weaknesses. To the extent that their thought has been ransacked to find support for *a priori* political positions, their work has been seriously distorted. But we can also draw on the insights and limitations of their ideas, methods, and goals within their specific historical context to shed light on present dilemmas, such as the problems facing those who believe that our present conditions are unjust and irrational and who seek to realize their own radical alternative visions. To do this, however, it is essential to recognize the wide gulf that separates us from them.

Paine thought that he was on the threshold of a new era, and in a very real sense he was. But it was not the kind of future he had anticipated. When he wrote of progress, commercial growth, social welfare, and democracy, Paine was trying to refashion pre-industrial society along American lines; he was not heralding an Industrial Revolution which eventually shattered his social vision. Nor could Cobbett turn the clock back, despite a stridency which became more pronounced as his agrarian ideal became less likely. Both men developed their ideas in an eighteenth-century world of Anglo-American Radical discourse which preceded the emergence of modern industrial class-based society. Paine and Cobbett were not the first men of a new world; they were the last men of a dying one.

Bibliography

WORKS BY PAINE AND COBBETT

Paine

The Complete Writings of Thomas Paine. Edited by Philip S. Foner. 2 vols. New York: The Citadel Press, 1945.

The Writings of Thomas Paine. Edited by Moncure D. Conway. 4 vols. 1902–8. Reprint (4 vols. in 2). New York: Burt Franklin, 1969.

Rotherham Public Library, Yorkshire, England. Letter to Thomas Walker, 16 January 1789.

Cobbett

Advice to Young Men and (Incidentally) to Young Women in the Middle and Higher Ranks of Life. London: Cobbett, 1830.

An Antidote for Tom Paine's Theological and Political Poison. Philadelphia: Cobbett, 1796.

The Autobiography of William Cobbett. Edited by William Reitzel. 1937. Reprint. London: Faber and Faber, 1967.

A Bone to Gnaw for the Democrats; or Observations on a Pamphlet entitled "The Political Progress of Britain." Philadelphia: Bradford, 1795.

A Bone to Gnaw, for the Democrats, Part II, containing, 1st Observations on a Patriotic Pamphlet Entitled Proceedings of the United Irishmen, 2dly Democratic Principles Exemplified by Example, 3dly Democratic Memoires; or An Account of Some Recent Feats Performed by the Frenchified Citizens of the United States of America. Philadelphia: Bradford, 1795.

Mr. Cobbett's Taking Leave of His Countrymen. [London ?]: Molineux, 1817.

Cobbett's Two-Penny Trash; or, Politics for the Poor. 2 vols. London: Cobbett, 1831–32.

Cobbett's Weekly Political Register. 88 vols. 1802–35.

Cottage Economy: Containing Information Relating to the Brewing of Beer, Making of Bread, Keeping of Cows, Pigs, Bees, Ewes, Goats, Poultry and Rabbits, and Relative to Other Matters Deemed Useful in the Conducting of the Affairs of a Labourer's Family. London: Clement, 1822.

The Democratic Judge: or the Equal Liberty of the Press, as Exhibited, Explained and Exposed, in the Prosecution of William Cobbett, for a Pretended Libel against the King of Spain and His Ambassador, before Thomas M'Kean, Chief Justice of the State of Pennsylvania. Philadelphia: Cobbett, 1798.

Detection of a Conspiracy, Formed by the United Irishmen, with the Evident Intention of Aiding the Tyrants of France in Subverting the Government of the United States of America. Philadelphia: Cobbett, 1798.

A Grammar of the English Language, in a Series of Letters. Intended for the Use of Schools and Young Persons in General; but, More Especially for the Use of Soldiers, Sailors, Apprentices, and Plough-Boys. New York: Cobbett, 1818.

The Gros Mousqueton Diplomatique; or Diplomatic Blunderbuss, Containing Citizen Adet's Notes to the Secretary of State, As Also His Cockade Proclamation, with a Preface by Peter Porcupine. Philadelphia: Cobbett, 1796.

History of the American Jacobins, Commonly Denominated Democrats. Philadelphia: Cobbett, 1796.

A History of the Protestant "Reformation," in England and Ireland; Showing How That Event Has Impoverished and Degraded the Main Body of the People in Those Countries. London: Clement, 1824–26.

A Kick for a Bite; or, Review upon Review; with a Critical Essay on the Works of Mrs S. Rowson; in a Letter to the Editor or Editors, of the American Monthly Review. Philadelphia: Bradford, 1795.

Letters from William Cobbett to Edward Thornton Written in the Years 1797 to 1800. Edited by G. D. H. Cole. London: Oxford University Press, 1937.

Letters to the Right Honourable Lord Hawkesbury, and to the Right Honourable Henry Addington, on the Peace with Buonaparte. London: Cobbett, 1802.

The Life and Adventures of Peter Porcupine, with a Full and Fair Account of All His Authoring Transactions; Being a Sure and Infallible Guide for All Enterprising Young Men Who Wish to Make a Fortune by Writing Pamphlets. Philadelphia: Cobbett, 1796.

The Life and Letters of William Cobbett in England and America. 2 vols. Edited by L. Melville [L. S. Benjamin]. London: Bodley Head, 1913.

Life of Andrew Jackson, President of the United States of America. London: Cobbett, 1834.

A Little Plain English, Addressed to the People of the United States; on the Treaty, Negotiated with His Brittanic Majesty, and on the Conduct of the President Relative Thereto; in Answer to "The Letters of Franklin." Philadelphia: Bradford, 1795.

A New-Year's Gift to the Democrats; or Observations on a Pamphlet, Entitled "A Vindication of Mr. Randolph's Resignation." Philadelphia: Bradford, 1796.

Observations on the Emigration of Dr. Joseph Priestley and on the Several Addresses Delivered to Him on His Arrival at New York. Philadelphia: Bradford, 1794.

Paper against Gold and Glory against Prosperity. Or, An Account of the Rise, Progress, Extent and Present State of the Funds, and of the Paper-Money of Great Britain. London: J. M'Creery, 1815.

The Political Censor, or Monthly Review of the Most Interesting Political Occurrences, Relative to the United States of America. 1796–97.

The Porcupine. 1800–1801.

Porcupine's Gazette. 1797–1800.

Porcupine's Works, Containing Various Writings and Selections, Exhibiting a Faithful Picture of the United States of America. 12 vols. London: Cobbett and Morgan, 1801.

A Prospect from the Congress Gallery, during the Session, Begun December 7, 1795. Philadelphia: Bradford, 1796.

Prospectus of a New Daily Paper, to Be Entitled The Porcupine. London: Gosnell, 1800.

Rural Rides in the Counties of Surrey, Kent, Sussex, Hampshire, Wiltshire, Gloucestershire, Herefordshire, Worcestershire, Somersetshire, Oxfordshire, Berkshire, Essex, Suffolk, Norfolk, and Hertfordshire: With Economical and Political Observations Relative to Matters Applicable to, and Illustrated by, the State of Those Counties Respectively. London: Cobbett, 1830. Reprint. Harmondsworth: Penguin Books, 1967.

The Rush-Light. New York, 1800. Republished in London as *The American Rush-Light; By the Help of which Wayward and Disaffected Britons May See a Complete Specimen of the Baseness, Dishonesty, Ingratitude, and Perfidy, of Republicans and of the Profligacy, Injustice, and Tyranny, of Republican Governments.* 1800.

The Scare-Crow; Being an Infamous Letter, Sent to Mr. John Oldden, Threatening Destruction to His House, and Violence to the Person of His Tenant, William Cobbett, with Remarks on the Same by Peter Porcupine. Philadelphia: Cobbett, 1796.

The Soldier's Friend; or, Considerations on the Late Pretended Augmentation of the Subsistence of the Private Soldiers. London: J. Ridgway, 1792.

A Year's Residence in the United States of America. New York: 1818–19.

MANUSCRIPT SOURCES

British Library, London. Additional Manuscripts. Place Papers.

27808: Notes on the London Corresponding Society.

27809: Place collections on political societies, 1792–1832.

27811: Letter book of the London Corresponding Society, 27 October 1791–23 March 1793.

27812: Minutes and letter book of the London Corresponding Society, 2 April 1792–2 January 1794.

27814: Thomas Hardy, "A Sketch, of the History of the London Corresponding Society."
27815: Correspondence of the London Corresponding Society, 2 July 1795–30 November 1797.
27818: Draft letters of Thomas Hardy.
Public Record Office, London. Home Office Papers.
HO 42 (domestic): 19–23 (1791–92).
East Sussex Record Office, Lewes.
Lewes Non-Conformist registers, 1768–74.
St. Michael's parish vestry minute book, 1770–73.
Records of the Westgate Unitarian Chapel, Lewes, 1768–74.

PRINTED SOURCES

Abingdon, Willoughby Bertie, Earl of. *Thoughts on the Letter of Edmund Burke.* Oxford: W. Jackson, 1777.
Adams, John. *Diary and Autobiography of John Adams.* Edited by L. H. Butterfield, L. C. Faber, and W. D. Garrett. 4 vols. Series 1 of *The Adams Papers.* Cambridge, Mass.: The Belknap Press of Harvard University Press, 1961.
— "Thoughts on Government." In *The Life and Works of John Adams*, edited by C. F. Adams, vol. 4. Boston: Little and Brown, 1851.
Adams, John [Quincy]. *An Answer to Pain's Rights of Man.* Dublin: Wogan et al., 1793.
Adams, W. Paul. "Republicanism in Political Rhetoric before 1776." *Political Science Quarterly* 85, no. 3 (1970): 397–421.
Adams Family Correspondence. Edited by L. H. Butterfield, W. D. Garrett, and M. Sprague. 2 vols. Series 2 of *The Adams Papers.* Cambridge, Mass.: The Belknap Press of Harvard University Press, 1963.
An Address to the Inhabitants of Great Britain and Ireland; in Reply to the Principles of the Author of the Rights of Man. London: J. Matthews, 1793.
Aldridge, Alfred. "The Influence of New York Newspapers on Paine's *Common Sense.*" *New York Historical Society Quarterly* 60 (1976): 53–60.
— "The Influence of Thomas Paine in the United States, England, France, Germany, and South America." In *Comparative Literature* 24: 369–83, edited by Werner Friederich. Chapel Hill: University of North Carolina Press, 1959.
— *Man of Reason.* New York: J. B. Lippincott, 1959.
— "Some Writings of Thomas Paine in Pennsylvania Newspapers." *American Historical Review* 56 (1951): 832–38.
— "Thomas Paine and the New York *Public Advertiser.*" *New York Historical Society Quarterly* 37 (1953): 361–82.
— "Thomas Paine in Latin America." *Early American Literature* 3 (winter 1968–69): 139–47.

— *Thomas Paine's American Ideology*. Newark: University of Delaware Press, 1984.

— "Why Did Thomas Paine Write on the Bank?" *Proceedings of the American Philosophical Society* 93 (1949): 309–15.

An Answer to the Second Part of Rights of Man. London: F. and C. Rivington, 1792.

Appleby, Joyce. "The Social Origins of American Revolutionary Ideology." *Journal of American History* 64 (1978): 935–58.

Aspinall, A. *Politics and the Press, c.1780–1850*. London: Home and Van Thal, 1949.

Aufrer, A. *The Cannibal's Progress; or, The Dreadful Horrors of French Invasion*. [Transl. by Cobbett]. Philadelphia: Cobbett, 1798.

Bailyn, Bernard. "Common Sense." In *Fundamental Testaments of the American Revolution*. Washington: Library of Congress, 1973.

— *The Ideological Origins of the American Revolution*. Cambridge, Mass.: Harvard University Press, 1967.

Baldwin, Ebenezer. *The Duty of Rejoicing under Calamities and Afflictions*. New York: Hugh Gaine, 1776.

Bamford, Samuel. *Passages in the Life of a Radical and Early Days*, edited by H. Dunckley. 2 vols. London: T. Fisher Unwin, 1893.

Barlow, Joel. *Advice to the Privileged Orders in the Several States of Europe, Resulting from the Necessity and Propriety of a General Revolution in the Principle of Government*. London, 1792. Reprint. Ithaca: Cornell University Press, 1956.

— *Life and Letters*. Edited by C. B. Todd. New York: Putnam's Press, 1886.

Barry, Alyce. "Thomas Paine, Privateersman." *Pennsylvania Magazine of History and Biography* 101 (1977): 451–61.

The Beauties of Cobbett. London: H. Stamman, 1820.

Bell, David. *Early Loyalist Saint John: The Origin of New Brunswick Politics, 1783–1786*. Fredericton: New Ireland Press, 1983.

Bemis, Samuel F. *Jay's Treaty, a Study in Commerce and Diplomacy*. New York: Macmillan, 1924.

— *Pinckney's Treaty*. New Haven: Yale University Press, 1960.

Betka, James. "The Ideology and Rhetoric of Thomas Paine: Political Justification through Metaphor." Ph.D. dissertation, Rutgers University, 1975.

Bjork, Gordon C. "The Weaning of the American Economy: Independence, Market Changes, and Economic Development." *Journal of Economic History* 24 (1964): 541–60.

Black, Eugene. *The Association: British Extraparliamentary Political Organization, 1769–1793*. Cambridge, Mass.: Harvard University Press, 1963.

Bolingbroke, Henry St. John, Viscount. *The Works of Lord Bolingbroke*. 4 vols. Philadelphia: Carey and Hart, 1841.

Bonwick, Colin. *English Radicals and the American Revolution*. Chapel Hill: University of North Carolina Press, 1977.

The Book of Wonders. London: H. Stamman, 1820.

Boothby, Brooke. *Observations on the Appeal from the New to the Old Whigs, and on Mr. Paine's Rights of Man.* London: J. Stockdale, 1792.

Boulton, James. *The Language of Politics in the Age of Wilkes and Burke.* Toronto: University of Toronto Press, 1963.

Bowles, John. *A Protest against T. Paine's "Rights of Man": Addressed to the Members of a Book Society.* London: T. Longman, 1792.

Boyd, Julian P. *Number 7. Alexander Hamilton's Secret Attempts to Control American Foreign Policy.* Princeton: Princeton University Press, 1964.

Bradford, Samuel. *The Imposter Detected; or, A Review of Some of the Writings of "Peter Porcupine."* Philadelphia: T. Bradford, 1796.

Bressler, Leo. "Peter Porcupine and the Bones of Thomas Paine." *Pennsylvania Magazine of History and Biography* 82 (1958): 176–85.

A British Freeholder's Address to His Countrymen, on Thomas Paine's Rights of Man. London: B. White, 1791.

"A Briton." *Letter to William Cobbett.* Birmingham: Knott, 1819.

Brown, John. *An Estimate of the Manners and Principles of the Times.* London: Davis, 1757.

Brown, Wallace. "William Cobbett in the Maritimes." *Dalhousie Review* 56 (1976): 448–61.

Browne, Ray. *The Burke-Paine Controversy: Texts and Criticisms.* New York: Harcourt, Brace and World, 1963.

Buel, Richard, Jr. *Securing the Revolution: Ideology in American Politics, 1789–1815.* Ithaca: Cornell University Press, 1972.

Buff; or, A Dissertation on Nakedness: A Parody on Paine's Rights of Man. London: J. Matthews, 1792.

Burgh, James. *The Art of Speaking.* 1762. Reprint. Philadelphia: Aitken, 1775.

– *Political Disquisitions.* 3 vols. London, 1774–75.

Burke, Edmund. *A Letter from Edmund Burke, Esq.; One of the Representatives in Parliament for the City of Bristol, to John Farr and John Harris, Esqs. Sheriffs of that City, on the Affairs of America.* London: Dodsley, 1777.

– *A Philosophical Enquiry into the Origin of Our Ideas of the Sublime and Beautiful.* London: Dodsley, 1757.

– *Reflections on the Revolution in France and on the Proceedings in Certain Societies in London Relative to that Event.* 1790. Reprint. Harmondsworth: Penguin Books, 1968.

Burt, A. L. *The United States, Great Britain and British North America.* New Haven: Yale University Press, 1940.

Callender, James Thomson. *The Political Progress of Britain.* Philadelphia: Callender, 1795.

The Cameleon; or, The Cobbett of 1802, Contrasted with the Cobbett of 1807. London: Jordan and Maxwell, 1807.

Carey, Matthew. *Information to Europeans Who are Disposed to Migrate to the United States.* Philadelphia: Carey and Stewart, 1790.

— *The Porcupiniad*. Philadelphia: Carey, 1799.

Carpenter, T. *A Report of an Action for a Libel, Brought by Dr. Benjamin Rush, against William Cobbett*. Philadelphia: W. W. Woodward, 1800.

Cartwright, John. *American Independence the Interest and Glory of Great Britain*. London: Wilkie, 1774.

— *Give us our Rights! or, A Letter to the Present Electors of Middlesex and the Metropolis*. London: Stockdale, 1782.

— *A Letter to the Earl of Abingdon*. London: J. Almon, 1778.

— *The Memorial of Common Sense, upon the Present Crisis between Great-Britain and America*. London: J. Almon, 1778.

— *The People's Barrier against Undue Influence: or, The Commons' House of Parliament According to the Constitution*. London: J. Almon, 1780.

— *Reasons for Reformation*. London: Bone and Hone, 1809.

— *Take Your Choice!* London: J. Almon, 1776.

Chalmers, George [Oldys]. *The Life of Thomas Pain*. London: Stockdale, 1791; 7th ed., 1793.

Chalmers, James. *Plain Truth*. Philadelphia: R. Bell, 1776.

Cheetham, James. *The Life of Thomas Paine*. New York: Southwick and Pelrue, 1809.

Christie, Ian. *Wilkes, Wyvill and Reform*. London: Macmillan, 1962.

The Civil and Ecclesiastical Systems of England Defended and Fortified. London, 1791.

Clark, Harry. *Thomas Paine: Representative Selections*. Rev. ed. New York: Hill and Wang, 1961.

— "Thomas Paine's Theories of Rhetoric." *Wisconsin Academy of Sciences, Arts, and Letters* 28 (1933): 307–39.

— "Toward a Reinterpretation of Thomas Paine." *American Literature* 5 (1933): 133–45.

Clark, Mary. "Peter Porcupine in America: The Career of William Cobbett, 1792–1800." Ph.D. dissertation, University of Pennsylvania, 1939.

"Cobbett Against Cobbett" in *The Times*, 14 November 1816.

Cobbett's Penny Trash. London, 1817.

Cole, G. D. H. *The Life of William Cobbett*. 3d ed. London: Home and Van Thal, 1947.

Committee of Secrecy of the House of Commons Respecting Seditious Practices (May 1794). House of Commons, Sessional Papers of the Eighteenth Century, vol. 93.

Condon, Ann. *The Envy of the American States: The Loyalist Dream for New Brunswick*. Fredericton: New Ireland Press, 1984.

Cone, Carl. *The English Jacobins*. New York: Charles Scribner's Sons, 1968.

Connell, J. M. *An Account of Thomas Paine's Residence in Lewes*. London: Eyre and Spottiswoode, 1924.

— *Lewes: Its Religious History*. Lewes and London: Baxter, 1931.

— *The Story of an Old Meeting House*. London: Longmans, 1916.

Considerations on Mr. Paine's Pamphlet on the Rights of Man. Edinburgh: W. Creech, 1791.

Conway, Moncure D. *The Life of Thomas Paine.* 1892. Reprint. London: R. Watts, 1909.

Cooper, Samuel. *The First Principles of Civil and Ecclesiastical Government, Delineated (in Two Parts) in Letters to Dr. Priestley, Occasioned by His to Mr. Burke.* Yarmouth: Downes and March, 1791.

Cooper, Thomas. *Some Information Respecting America.* London: J. Johnson, 1794.

Copeland, Thomas W. *Our Eminent Friend Edmund Burke.* New Haven: Yale University Press, 1949.

The Correspondence of the London Corresponding Society. London, [1795].

Crane, Verner. "The Club of Honest Whigs: Friends of Science and Liberty." *William and Mary Quarterly* 3d ser. 23 (1966): 210–33.

Cursory Remarks on Paine's Rights of Man. London: Parsons, 1792.

[Dallas, Alexander J.]. *Letters of Franklin on the Conduct of the Executive.* Philadelphia, 1795.

Davis, Ralph. *The Rise of the Atlantic Economies.* London: Weidenfeld and Nicolson, 1973.

A Defence of the Constitution of England against the Libels That Have Been Lately Published on It; Particularly in Paine's Pamphlet on the Rights of Man. London: R. Baldwin, 1791.

Defence of the Rights of Man; Being a Discussion of the Conclusions Drawn from those Rights by Mr. Paine. London: T. Evans, 1791.

The Detector. 4 vols. London: Thomas, 1817.

Dickson, Peter. *The Financial Revolution in England: A Study in the Development of Public Credit, 1688–1756.* London: St. Martin's Press, 1967.

Dictionary of National Biography. Volumes consulted: 2, 6, 12, 17. Edited by Leslie Stephen and Sidney Lee. London: Smith, Elder and Co., 1908.

Dorfman, Joseph. "The Economic Philosophy of Thomas Paine." *Political Science Quarterly* 53 (1938): 372–86.

Douglass, Elisha P. "The Adventurer Bowles." *William and Mary Quarterly* 3d ser. 6 (1949): 3–23.

Duché, Jacob. *The Duty of Standing Fast in Our Spiritual and Temporal Liberties.* Philadelphia: Humphreys, 1775.

Duff, Gerald. "William Cobbett's Agrarian Vision of National Reform." Ph.D. dissertation, University of Illinois, 1966.

Duncan, William. *The Elements of Logick.* London: Dodsley, 1748.

Dundas, David. *Principles of Military Movements, Chiefly Applied to Infantry.* London: Cadell, 1788.

Durey, M. "Transatlantic Patriotism." In *Artisans, Peasants and Proletarians, 1760–1860: Essays Presented to Gwyn A. Williams*, edited by Clive Emsley and James Walvin, 7–31, London: Croom Helm, 1985.

Eaton, Daniel Isaac. *The Proceedings, on the Trial of Daniel Isaac Eaton.* London: Eaton, 1793.

— *Revolutions without Bloodshed; or, Reformation Preferable to Revolt.* London: Eaton, 1791.

Edwards, Samuel. *Rebel! A Biography of Tom Paine.* New York: Praeger Publishers, 1974.

Elements of Reform; or, an Account of the Motives and Intentions of the Advocates for Parliamentary Reformation. London: J. Gold, 1809.

Elliot, Charles Herrington. *The Republican Refuted; in a Series of Biographical, Critical and Political Strictures on Thomas Paine's Rights of Man.* London: W. Richardson, 1791.

Emsley, Clive. "Political Disaffection and the British Army in 1792." *Bulletin of the Institute of Historical Research* 48, no. 118 (1975): 230–45.

An Explanation of the Word Equality. n.p., n.d.

"A Farmer." *A Plain and Earnest Address to Britons, Especially Farmers.* Durham: L. Pennington, 1792.

Fast, Howard. *Citizen Tom Paine.* New York: Duell, Sloan and Pearce, 1943.

Fennessy, R. R. *Burke, Paine and the Rights of Man.* The Hague: Martinus Nijhoff, 1963.

Ferguson, James. *Lectures on Select Subjects.* Edited by D. Brewster. 3 vols. Philadelphia: Carey, 1814.

— *The Young Gentleman and Lady's Astronomy.* London, 1768.

Ferns, Henry. *Britain and Argentina in the Nineteenth Century.* Oxford: The Clarendon Press, 1960.

Foner, Eric. *Tom Paine and Revolutionary America.* New York: Oxford University Press, 1976.

— "Tom Paine's Republic: Radical Ideology and Social Change." In *The American Revolution,* edited by Alfred Young. Dekalb: Northern Illinois University Press, 1976.

Franklin, Benjamin. *The Autobiography and Other Writings.* Edited by Jesse Lemisch. New York: Signet, 1961.

— *The Papers of Benjamin Franklin.* Edited by Leonard Labaree. 22 vols. New Haven: Yale University Press, 1959.

Gaines, Pierce W. "William Cobbett's Account Book." *Proceedings of the American Antiquarian Society* 78 (1968): 299–312.

Gibbs, F. W. "Itinerant Lecturers in Natural Philosophy." *Ambix* 8 (1960): 111–17.

Gilbert, Felix. "The English Background of American Isolationism in the Eighteenth Century." *William and Mary Quarterly* 3d ser. 1 (1944): 138–60.

Gimbel, Richard. "Thomas Paine Fights for Freedom in Three Worlds: The New, The Old, The Next." *Proceedings of the American Antiquarian Society* 70 (1961): 397–492.

Ginsberg, Elaine. "The Rhetoric of Revolution: An Analysis of Thomas Paine's *Common Sense.*" Ph.D. dissertation, University of Oklahoma, 1971.

Ginter, D. E. "The Loyalist Association Movement of 1792–93 and British Public Opinion." *Historical Journal* 9 (1966): 179–90.

Goldsmith, Oliver. *Collected Works of Oliver Goldsmith.* Edited by Arthur Friedman. 5 vols. Oxford: The Clarendon Press, 1966.

Goodwin, Albert. *The Friends of Liberty: The English Democratic Movement in the Age of the French Revolution.* London: Hutchinson, 1979.

Gottschalk, L. *Lafayette between the American and French Revolution, 1783–1789.* Chicago: University of Chicago Press, 1950.

Gouge, William. *A Short History of Paper Money and Banking in the United States.* Philadelphia: Ustick, 1833.

Green, Daniel. *Great Cobbett: The Noblest Agitator.* Oxford: Oxford University Press, 1985.

Guthrie, Warren Alan. "The Development of Rhetorical Theory in America, 1635–1800." Ph.D. dissertation, Northwestern University, 1940.

Hall, John. "The Grounds and Reasons of Monarchy Considered." In *The Oceana and Other Works of James Harrington.* London, 1771.

Hampson, Norman. *The First European Revolution.* London: Thames and Hudson, 1969.

Hans, Nicholas. *New Trends in Education in the Eighteenth Century.* Rev. ed. London: Routledge and Kegan Paul, 1966.

The Happy Reign of George the Last. An Address to the Little Tradesmen, and the Labouring Poor of England. London: R. Lee, n.d.

Hardy, Thomas. *Memoir of Thomas Hardy.* London: Ridgway, 1832.

Hardy, Thomas, D. D. *The Patriot. Addressed to the People on the Present State of Affairs in Britain and in France, with Observations on Republican Government, and Discussions of the Principles Advanced in the Writings of Thomas Paine.* Edinburgh, 1793.

Harvey, Samuel Clay, and Oliver MacAllester. *The Popular Budget, by an Experienced Practitioner in Political Anatomy; Inscribed to Lord B. Lord N. Lord S. and the rest of the Junto.* London, 1772.

Hawke, David. *Paine.* New York: Harper and Row, 1974.

Hawtrey, Charles. *Various Opinions of the Philosophical Reformers Considered; Particularly Pain's Rights of Man.* London: Stockdale, 1792.

Hay, Carla. "The Making of a Radical: The Case of James Burgh." *Journal of British Studies* 18 (1979): 90–117.

Hazlitt, William. "Character of Cobbett." In *The Complete Works of William Hazlitt,* edited by P. P. Howe, 8: 50–59. London: J. M. Dent and Sons, 1930.

Henretta, James A. *The Evolution of American Society, 1700–1815.* Lexington: Heath, 1973.

Hervey, F. *A New Friend on an Old Subject.* London: J. F. and C. Rivington, 1791.

Hey, Richard. *Happiness and Rights. A Dissertation upon Several Subjects Relative to the Rights of Man and his Happiness.* York: W. Blanchard, 1792.

Hill, Christopher. *Puritanism and Revolution: Studies in the Interpretation of the English Revolution of the 17th Century.* London: Secker and Warburg, 1958.
– "Republicanism after the Restoration." *New Left Review* 3 (1960): 46–51.
– *The World Turned Upside Down.* London: Temple Smith, 1972.
Hobsbawm, Eric. *The Age of Revolution: Europe 1789–1848.* 2d ed. London: Weidenfeld and Nicolson, 1969.
– *Industry and Empire: An Economic History of Britain since 1750.* London: Weidenfeld and Nicolson, 1968.
– *Labouring Men.* 2d ed. London: Weidenfeld and Nicolson, 1971.
"An Honest Man." *A Letter to the Right Honourable William Pitt, on his Apostasy from the Cause of Parliamentary Reform.* London: T. Gillet, 1792.
Howe, John R., Jr. "Republican Thought and the Political Violence of the 1790s." *American Quarterly* 19 (1967): 147–65.
Howell, Wilbur. "The Declaration of Independence and Eighteenth-Century Logic." *William and Mary Quarterly* 3d ser. 18 (1961): 463–84.
– *Eighteenth-Century British Logic and Rhetoric.* Princeton: Princeton University Press, 1971.
– Review of *The Language of Politics in the Age of Wilkes and Burke*, by James T. Boulton. *William and Mary Quarterly* 3d ser. 22 (1965): 520–23.
An Humble Address to the Most High, Most Mighty, and Most Puissant, The Sovereign People. London: I. Colles, 1793.
Hunt, Isaac. *Rights of Englishmen. An Antidote to the Poison Now Vending by the Transatlantic Republican Thomas Paine.* London: J. Bew, 1791.
Inglis, Charles. *The True Interest of America Impartially Stated, in Certain Strictures on a Pamphlet Intitled Common Sense.* Philadelphia: Humphreys, 1776.
Jefferson, Thomas. *The Papers of Thomas Jefferson.* Edited by J. P. Boyd. 19 vols. Princeton: Princeton University Press, 1950–74.
Jepson, G. *Letters to Thomas Payne, in Answer to His Late Publication on the Rights of Man.* London: J. Pridden, 1792.
Jones, Howard Mumford. "American Prose Style: 1700–1770." *Huntingdon Library Bulletin* 6, no. 3 (1934): 115–51.
Jones, John. *The Reason of Man: With Strictures on Paine's Rights of Man, and Some Other of His Writings.* Canterbury: Simmons, Kirkby and Jones, 1793.
– *The Reason of Man: Part Second, Containing Strictures on Rights of Man.* Canterbury: Simmons, Kirkby and Jones, 1793.
Jones, Richard F. "Science and English Prose Style in the Third Quarter of the Seventeenth Century." *Publications of the Modern Language Association* 45 (1930): 977–1009.
Jordan, Winthrop. "Familial Politics: Thomas Paine and the Killing of the King, 1776." *Journal of American History* 60 (1973): 294–308.
Jorgenson, Chester. "Sidelights on Benjamin Franklin's Principles of Rhetoric." *Revue Anglo-Americaine* 11 (1933–34): 208–22.
Junius [pseud.]. *The Letters of Junius.* New York: H. Durell, 1821.

Kerber, Linda. *Federalists in Dissent: Imagery and Ideology in Jeffersonian America.* Ithaca: Cornell University Press, 1970.

King, Arnold. "Thomas Paine in America, 1774–1787." Ph.D. dissertation, University of Chicago, 1951.

King, John. *Mr. King's Speech, at Egham, with Thomas Paine's Letter to Him on It, and Mr. King's Reply.* Egham: C. Boult, 1793.

Knudson, Jerry. "The Rage Around Tom Paine: Newspaper Reaction to His Homecoming in 1802." *New York Historical Society Quarterly* 53 (1969): 34–63.

Koch, Adrienne. *Jefferson and Madison: The Great Collaboration.* New York: Knopf, 1950.

Kramnick, I. *Bolingbroke and His Circle: The Politics of Nostalgia in the Age of Walpole.* Cambridge, Mass.: Harvard University Press, 1968.

– "Tom Paine: Radical Democrat." *democracy* 1 (1981): 127–38.

Lafayette, Marie-Joseph-Paul Du Motier, Marquis de. *The Letters of Lafayette to Washington, 1777–1799.* Edited by L. Gottschalk. *Memoirs of the American Philosophical Society,* vol. 115 (1976). Philadelphia: American Philosophical Society, 1976.

A Letter from a Magistrate to Mr. William Rose, of Whitehall, on Mr. Paine's Rights of Man. London: J. Debrett, 1791.

Letters to a Friend, on the Test Laws, Containing Reasons for Not Repealing Them. London: Egerton, 1791.

Letters to Thomas Paine; In Answer to His Late Publication on the Rights of Man. London: W. Miller, 1791.

Lewelyn, William. *An Appeal to Men against Paine's Rights of Man.* 2 vols. Leominster: F. Harris, 1793.

Liddle, William. " 'A Patriot King, or None': Lord Bolingbroke and the American Renunciation of George III." *Journal of American History* 65 (1979): 951–70.

Lillibridge, G. D. *Beacon of Freedom: The Impact of American Democracy upon Great Britain, 1830–1870.* Philadelphia: University of Pennsylvania Press, 1955.

Link, Eugene. *Democratic-Republican Societies, 1790–1800.* 1942. Reprint. New York: Octagon Books, 1966.

List, Karen. "The Role of William Cobbett in Philadelphia's Party Press, 1794–1799." Ph.D. dissertation, University of Wisconsin – Madison, 1980.

Livermore, Shaw. *The Twilight of Federalism: The Disintegration of the Federalist Party, 1815–1830.* Princeton: Princeton University Press, 1962.

Lynch, John. *The Spanish American Revolutions, 1808–1826.* New York: Norton, 1973.

Macleod, N. *Letters to the People of North Britain.* London: J. Ridgway, 1793.

Maier, Pauline. "The Beginnings of American Republicanism, 1765–1776." In *The Development of a Revolutionary Mentality,* 99–117. Washington: Library of Congress, 1972.

– *From Resistance to Revolution.* New York: Vintage Books, 1974.

Malcolmson, Robert W. "Custom, Customary Rights and Popular Culture in Eighteenth-Century England." Paper presented at Queen's University, Kingston, Canada, November 1982.

Malone, Dumas. *The Public Life of Thomas Cooper, 1783–1839.* Columbia: University of South Carolina Press, 1961.

Martin, Benjamin. *Institutions of Language; Containing a Physico-Grammatical Essay on the Propriety and Rationale of the English Tongue.* London: S. Birt et al., 1748. Facsimile Reprint. Menston, Yorkshire: The Scolar Press, 1970.

– *Philosophia Britannica: or, A New and Comprehensive System of the Newtonian Philosophy. In a Course of Twelve Lectures.* 2 vols. London: J. Hodges et al., 1752.

– *The Philosophical Grammar; Being a View of the Present State of Experimented Physiology, or Natural Philosophy.* 1735. 2d ed. London: J. Noon, 1738.

Marx, Karl. *Capital: A Critique of Political Economy.* Chicago: Kerr and Company, 1909–10.

– "On the Jewish Question." In *Karl Marx: Early Texts,* edited by David McLellan. Oxford: Blackwell, 1971.

– and F. Engels. *Collected Works.* 17 vols. New York: International Publishers, 1975–1981.

Mercer, Caroline G. "The Rhetorical Method of Thomas Paine." Ph.D. dissertation, University of Chicago, 1948.

Metzgar, Joseph. "Thomas Paine: A Study in Social and Intellectual History." Ph.D. dissertation, University of New Mexico, 1965.

Millburn, John. "Benjamin Martin and the Royal Society." *Notes and Records of the Royal Society of London* 28 (1973): 15–23.

– *Benjamin Martin, Author, Instrument-Maker, and "Country Showman."* Leyden: Noordhoff International Publishing, 1976.

Miller, John. *Alexander Hamilton: Portrait in Paradox.* 2d ed. New York: Harper and Row, 1964.

– *The Federalist Era, 1789–1801.* London: Hamish Hamilton, 1960.

Miller, Perry. *The New England Mind: The Seventeenth Century.* 1939. Rev. ed. Cambridge, Mass.: Harvard University Press, 1963.

Milton, John. *A Defence of the People of England.* In *Complete Prose Works of John Milton,* edited by D. Wolfe, vol. 4. New Haven: Yale University Press, 1966.

– *The Tenure of Kings and Magistrates.* In *Complete Prose Works of John Milton,* edited by D. Wolfe, vol. 3. New Haven: Yale University Press, 1966.

Mitchell, A. "The Association Movement of 1792–3." *Historical Journal* 4 (1961): 56–77.

Nash, Gary. "The Transformation of Urban Politics, 1700–1765." *Journal of American History* 60 (1973): 605–32.

– *The Urban Crucible: Social Change, Political Consciousness and the Origins of the American Revolution.* Cambridge, Mass.: Harvard University Press, 1979.

Neatby, Hilda. *Quebec: The Revolutionary Age, 1760–1791.* Toronto: McClelland and Stewart, 1966.

Nelson, John R., Jr. "Alexander Hamilton and American Manufacturing: A Reexamination." *Journal of American History* 65 (1979): 971–95.

— "Hamilton and Gallatin: Political Economy and Policy-Making in the New Nation, 1789–1812." Ph.D. dissertation, Northern Illinois University, 1979.

Neville, Sylas. *The Diary of Sylas Neville, 1767–1788.* Edited by B. Cozens-Hardy. London: Oxford University Press, 1950.

North, Douglass C. *Growth and Welfare in the American Past: A New Economic History.* Englewood Cliffs, N. J.: Prentice-Hall, 1966.

Ojala, Jeanne A. "Ira Allen and the French Directory, 1796: Plans for the Creation of the Republic of United Columbia." *William and Mary Quarterly* 3d ser. 36 (1979): 436–48.

Ontario, Department of Archives. *Sixteenth Report of the Department of Archives for the Province of Ontario, 1920.* Edited by Alexander Fraser. Toronto: Clarkson W. James, 1921.

Osborne, John. *William Cobbett: His Thought and His Times.* New Brunswick, N. J.: Rutgers University Press, 1966.

Paley, William. *Reasons for Contentment: Addressed to the Labouring Part of the British Public.* London: R. Faulder, 1793.

Palmer, R. R. *The Age of the Democratic Revolution: A Political History of Europe and America, 1760–1800.* 2 vols. Princeton: Princeton University Press, 1959–64.

Parssinen, T. M. "The Revolutionary Party in London, 1816–20." *Bulletin of the Institute of Historical Research* 45, no. 112 (1972): 266–82.

Pearl, M. L. *William Cobbett: A Bibliographical Account of His Life and Times.* London: Oxford University Press, 1953.

Penniman, Howard. "Thomas Paine—Democrat." *American Political Science Review* 37 (1947): 244–62.

Pennsylvania Journal. Consulted for 1775–76.

Pennsylvania Ledger. Consulted for 1775–76.

Pennsylvania Magazine. 1775.

Perkin, Harold. *The Origins of Modern English Society, 1780–1880.* London: Routledge and Kegan Paul, 1969.

Perkins, Bradford, ed. *The Causes of the War of 1812: National Honor or National Interest?* New York: Holt, Rinehart and Winston, 1962.

Perrin, Porter Gale. "The Teaching of Rhetoric in the American Colleges Before 1750." Ph.D. dissertation, University of Chicago, 1936.

Persons, Stow. "The Cyclical Theory of History in Eighteenth-Century America." *American Quarterly* 6 (1954): 147–63.

Pigott, Charles. *A Political Dictionary: Explaining the True Meaning of Words.* London: D. I. Eaton, 1795.

Pindar, Peter [John Wolcot]. *Odes to Mr. Paine.* London: J. Evans, 1791.

"A Plain Man." *Ten Minutes Reflections on the Late Events in France.* London, 1792.

Playfair, William. *Inevitable Consequences of a Reform in Parliament*. London: John Stockdale, 1792.

Plumb, J. H. *In the Light of History*. Boston: Houghton Mifflin, 1973.

— "The Public, Literature and the Arts in the 18th Century." In *The Triumph of Culture: 18th Century Perspectives*, edited by P. Fritz and D. Williams, 27–48. Toronto: A. M. Hakkert, 1972.

Pocock, J. G. A. "Virtue and Commerce in the Eighteenth Century." *Journal of Interdisciplinary History* 3 (1972): 119–34.

The Political Death of Mr. William Cobbett. Edinburgh: Blackwood, 1820.

Potter, Janice. *The Liberty We Seek: Loyalist Ideology in Colonial New York and Massachusetts*. Cambridge, Mass.: Harvard University Press, 1983.

Powell, William. "The Diary of Joseph Gales, 1794–1795." *North Carolina Historical Review* 26 (1949): 335–47.

Price, Richard. *A Discourse on the Love of Our Country*. London: Cadell, 1789.

— *Observations on the Nature of Civil Liberty, the Principles of Government, and the Justice and Policy of the War with America*. London: Cadell, 1776.

Priestley, Joseph. *An Answer to Mr. Paine's Age of Reason, being a Continuation of Letters to the Philosophers and Politicians of France, on the Subject of Religion; and of the Letters to a Philosophical Unbeliever*. London: Johnson, 1796.

— *Essay on the First Principles of Government*. In *Priestley's Writings on Philosophy, Science and Politics*, edited by J. A. Passmore. New York: Collier Books, 1965.

— *Letters to the Rt. Hon. Edmund Burke Occasioned by His Reflections on the Revolution in France*. Birmingham, 1791.

"Rationalis." "Appendix to *Plain Truth*" in James Chalmers, *Plain Truth*. Philadelphia: R. Bell, 1776.

Raynal, Abbé Guillaume-Thomas-François. *The Revolution of America*. London: Lockyer Davis, 1781.

Richardson, Lyon. *A History of Early American Magazines*. New York: Thomas Nelson and Sons, 1931.

Rickman, Thomas. *The Life of Thomas Paine*. London: Rickman, 1819.

Rights of Citizens; Being an Inquiry into Some of the Consequences of Social Union, and an Examination of Mr. Paine's Principles Touching Government. London: J. Debrett, 1791.

The Rights of Nobles. Consisting of Extracts from Pigott's Political Dictionary. London: R. Lee, n.d.

Riland, John. *The Rights of God, Occasioned by Mr. Paine's "Rights of Man," and His Other Publications*. Birmingham: E. Jones, 1792.

The Rival Imposters; or, Two Political Epistles to Two Political Cheats. The First Addressed to G. L. Wardle, Esq. M.P. and the second to William Cobbett. London: Gillet, 1809.

Robbins, Caroline. *The Eighteenth-Century Commonwealthman*. Cambridge, Mass.: Harvard University Press, 1961.

— "The Lifelong Education of Paine, Thomas (1737–1809)—Some Reflections upon His Acquaintance among Books." *Proceedings of the American Philosophical Society* 127, no. 3 (1983): 135–42.

A Rod in Brine, or a Tickler for Tom Paine, in Answer to His First Pamphlet, Entitled The Rights of Man. Canterbury: Simmons, Kirkby and Jones, 1792.

Rose, Richard. "The Priestley Riots of 1791." *Past and Present* 18 (1960): 68–88.

Royle, Edward. *The Infidel Tradition from Paine to Bradlaugh.* London: Macmillan, 1976.

– *Radical Politics, 1790–1900: Religion and Unbelief.* London: Longman, 1971.

Royle, Edward, and James Walvin. *English Radicals and Reformers, 1760–1848.* Lexington: University Press of Kentucky, 1982.

Rudé, George. *Hanoverian London, 1714–1808.* London: Secker and Warburg, 1971.

– *Revolutionary Europe, 1783–1815.* London: Collins, 1964.

– *Wilkes and Liberty.* Oxford: The Clarendon Press, 1962.

Rush, Benjamin. *The Autobiography of Benjamin Rush.* Edited by G. W. Corner. Westport, Conn.: Greenwood Press, 1970.

– *Letters of Benjamin Rush.* Edited by L. H. Butterfield. 2 vols. Princeton: Princeton University Press, 1951.

Ryerson, Richard A. "Political Mobilization and the American Revolution: The Resistance Movement in Philadelphia, 1765–1776," *William and Mary Quarterly* 3d ser. 31 (1974): 565–88.

– *"The Revolution Is Now Begun": The Radical Committees of Philadelphia, 1765–1776.* Philadelphia: University of Pennsylvania Press, 1978.

Sambrook, James. *William Cobbett.* London and Boston: Routledge and Kegan Paul, 1973.

Scott, George Lewis, ed. *A Supplement to Mr. Chambers's Cyclopaedia: or, Universal Dictionary of Arts and Sciences.* 2 vols. London: W. Innys et al., 1753.

Sheps, Arthur. "The American Revolution and the Transformation of English Republicanism." *Historical Reflections* 2 (1975): 3–28.

– "English Radicalism and Revolutionary America." Ph.D. dissertation, University of Toronto, 1973.

– "Ideological Immigrants in Revolutionary America." In *City and Society in the 18th Century*, edited by P. Fritz and D. Williams, 231–46. Toronto: A. M. Hakkert, 1973.

Sherwin, W. T. *Memoirs of the Life of Thomas Paine.* London: R. Carlile, 1819.

Sketches of the Life of Billy Cobb, and the Death of Tommy Pain. London: Dean and Munday, 1819.

Smelser, Marshall. *The Democratic Republic, 1801–1815.* New York: Harper and Row, 1968.

Smith, Frank. "The Authorship of 'An Occasional Letter on the Female Sex.' " *American Literature* 2 (1930): 277–80.

– "New Light on Thomas Paine's First Year in America, 1775." *American Literature* 1 (1930): 347–71.

Smith, Robert F., Jr. "Thomas Paine and the American Political Tradition." Ph.D. dissertation, University of Notre Dame, 1977.

Smith, Verena, ed. *The Town Book of Lewes, 1702–1837.* Sussex Record Society, vol. 69. Lewes: Barbican House, 1972.

Spater, George. "The Quest for William Cobbett: A Revisionist View of an English Radical." *Times Higher Educational Supplement*, 18 September 1981, 12–13.

– *William Cobbett: The Poor Man's Friend.* 2 vols. Cambridge: Cambridge University Press, 1982.

Sprat, Thomas. *The History of the Royal Society of London.* London, 1667. Facsimile reprint. St. Louis: Washington University Studies, 1959.

Sussex Weekly Advertiser, or Lewes Journal. Lewes. Consulted for 1769–93.

Swift, Jonathan. *The Prose Works of Jonathan Swift.* 14 vols. Oxford: Blackwell, 1939–68.

Thelwall, John. *Sober Reflections on the Seditious and Inflammatory Letter of The Right Hon. Edmund Burke to a Noble Lord.* London: H. D. Symonds, 1796.

Thistlethwaite, Frank *The Anglo-American Connection in the Early Nineteenth Century.* Philadelphia: University of Pennsylvania Press, 1959.

Thomis, Malcolm, and Peter Holt. *Threats of Revolution in Britain, 1789–1848.* Hamden, Conn.: Archon Books, 1977.

Thompson, Dorothy. *The Early Chartists.* London: Macmillan, 1971.

Thompson, E. P. *The Making of the English Working Class.* 1963. Reprint. Harmondsworth: Penguin Books, 1970.

Thornton, William. *Cadmus: or, A Treatise on the Elements of Written Language.* Philadelphia: Aitken, 1793.

Thoughts on Libels; and an Impartial Inquiry into the Present State of the British Army: with a Few Words, in Answer to Cobbett's Critique on the Book. London: Egerton, 1809.

The Trial of Thomas Muir. London: J. Ridgway, 1794.

The Trial of Thomas Paine. London: W. Richardson, 1792.

The Trial of William Winterbotham, Assistant Preacher at How's Lane Meeting, Plymouth. London: J. Ridgway, 1794.

Twomey, Richard. "Jacobins and Jeffersonians: Anglo-American Radicalism in the United States, 1790–1820." Ph.D. dissertation, Northern Illinois University, 1974.

Van Alstyne, Richard. *Empire and Independence.* New York: Wiley and Sons, 1965.

– *The Rising American Empire.* Oxford: Basil Blackwell, 1960.

Wade, Mason. "Quebec and the French Revolution of 1789: The Missions of Henry Mezière." *Canadian Historical Review* 31 (1950): 345–68.

Walvin, James. "English Democratic Societies and Popular Radicalism, 1791–1800." Ph.D. dissertation, University of York, 1969.

Webster, Noah. *Dissertations on the English Language: with Notes, Historical and Critical.* Boston: I. Thomas, 1789.

Webster, T. S. "A New Yorker in the Era of the French Revolution: Stephen Thorn, Conspirator for a Canadian Revolution." *New York Historical Society Quarterly* 53 (1969): 251–72.

Wecter, Dixon. "Thomas Paine and the Franklins." *American Literature* 12 (1941): 306–17.

Wells, Roger. "The Grain Crises in England, 1794–96; 1799–1801." Ph.D. dissertation, University of York, 1978.

– *Insurrection: The British Experience, 1795–1803.* Gloucester: Sutton Publications, 1983.

Werkmeister, L. *A Newspaper History of England, 1792–1793.* Lincoln, Neb.: University of Nebraska Press, 1967.

Whitaker, Arthur. *The Mississippi Question, 1795–1803: A Study in Trade, Politics, and Diplomacy.* Gloucester, Mass.: P. Smith, 1934.

White, Reginald. *From Waterloo to Peterloo.* London: Heinemann, 1957.

Wickwar, W. H. *The Struggle for the Freedom of the Press, 1819–1832.* London: Allen and Unwin, 1928.

Wiener, Joel. *The War of the Unstamped: The Movement to Repeal the British Newspaper Tax, 1830–1876.* Ithaca: Cornell University Press, 1969.

Williams, David. "John Evans' Strange Journey." *American Historical Review* 54 (1949): 277–95.

– "John Evans' Strange Journey, Part II. Following the Trail." *American Historical Review* 54 (1949): 508–29.

Williams, Gwyn A. *Artisans and Sans-Culottes.* London: Edward Arnold, 1968.

– "The Atlantic Revolution." Paper presented at the University of York, 1974.

– *The Search for Beulah Land: The Welsh and the Atlantic Revolution.* New York: Holmes and Meier, 1980.

– "Tom Paine." *New Society,* 6 August 1970, 236–38.

Williams, Raymond. *Cobbett.* New York: Oxford University Press, 1983.

Williams, William A. *The Contours of American History.* 1961. Reprint. Chicago: Quadrangle, 1966.

Williamson, Audrey. *Thomas Paine: His Life, Work and Times.* London: Allen and Unwin, 1973.

Wills, Gary. *Inventing America: Jefferson's Declaration of Independence.* New York: Doubleday, 1978.

– Review of *Tom Paine and Revolutionary America,* by Eric Foner. *New York Times Book Review,* 7 March 1976, 21–23.

Wilson, Jerome. "Thomas Paine in the Twentieth Century: His Reputation in America, 1900–1970, and an Annotated Bibliography, 1900–1970." Ph.D. dissertation, Auburn University, 1972.

Wilson, Jerome, and William Ricketson. *Thomas Paine.* Boston: Twayne, 1978.

Winslow, Cal. "Sussex Smugglers." In *Albion's Fatal Tree: Crime and Society in Eighteenth-Century England,* edited by Douglas Hay, et al, 119–66. New York: Pantheon, 1975.

Winterbotham, William. *An Historical, Geographical, Commercial, and Philosoph-ical View of the American United States, and of the European Settlements in America and the West-Indies.* 4 vols. London: J. Ridgway, 1795.

Wise, Sydney. "Sermon Literature and Canadian Intellectual History." United Church of Canada Committee on Archives, *Bulletin* 18 (1965): 3–18.

Witherspoon, John. *Lectures on Eloquence.* In *The Works of John Witherspoon,* vol. 7. Edinburgh: Ogle *et al,* 1805.

Wollstonecraft, Mary. *A Vindication of the Rights of Men, in a Letter to the Right Honourable Edmund Burke; Occasioned by His Reflections on the Revolution in France.* London: Johnson, 1790.

Wood, Gordon. *The Creation of the American Republic, 1776–1787.* Chapel Hill: University of North Carolina Press, 1969.

Wright, Esmond. *Fabric of Freedom, 1763–1800.* New York: Hill and Wang, 1961.

Wright, Esther. *The Loyalists of New Brunswick.* Fredericton, 1955.

Index